40TH ANNIVERSARY / 65TH ISSUE

GARGOYLE

Editor/Publisher:	Richard Peabody
Associate Editor:	Lucinda Ebersole
Design/Copyedit:	Nita Congress
Layout:	Stephen Caporaletti
Webmaster/EMT:	John Morton
Interns:	Jenn Bennett
	Katharine Carlon
	Rebecca Conway
	Victoria Gaffney
	Marisha Jones-Lennon
	Terese Ohnsorg

Gargoyle is on the web at www.gargoylemagazine.com.

Founded 1976
Gargoyle is published annually in the USA by Paycock Press.

Contact us:
GARGOYLE
3819 13th Street North
Arlington, VA 22201
Phone: 703-380-4893
Email: rchrdpeabody9@gmail.com

Our next reading period will begin August 1, 2018, and we accept/reject until we're full. Please use the Submittable tool on our website.

Contributors are paid with one copy of the issue in which their work appears. They can buy unlimited additional copies at 50 percent of cover price. *Gargoyle* reserves electronic archival rights and the right to reprint material in a "Best of" anthology. All other rights revert to individual contributors upon publication. *Gargoyle* is a proud member of the Council of Literary Magazines and Presses and appears in both the *Humanities International Complete* and the *Index of American Periodical Verse*.

Price per single issue varies.

Subscriptions: $30/two issues to individuals; $40/two issues for institutions

ISBN-10: 0-931181-53-4
ISBN-13: 978-0-931181-53-5
ISSN 0162-1149

Maria Nazos's "When the Beloved Asks "What Would You Do If I Woke up One Morning as a Loch Ness Monster?" was originally published in *North American Review* Fall 2016. John O'Dell's "Chekhov at the Moscow Zoo" was originally published in *At Beauty's Pawnshop* (Xlibris 2013). A. D. Winan's "Back from an MRI" was originally published in *Litbreak* in December 2016. Source for Jessy Randall's *Monotone Functions*: L. C. Young, "The Theory of Integration," *Cambridge Tracts in Mathematics and Mathematical Physics* 21, 1964.

Cover: Julia Geiser, *Louise Brooks* 1/14/2013

Gargoyle is distributed by:

· Direct from us through our website
· Amazon.com
· Sundial Books, 4065 Main Street, Chincoteague, VA 23336
· NewPages Magazine Webstore, www.newpageswebstore.com

Copies are also available from Bell and Howell Information and Learning.

Printed by Main Street Rag Publishing, Charlotte, NC.

What an astonishing thing a book is. It's a flat object made from a tree with flexible parts on which are imprinted lots of funny dark squiggles. But one glance at it and you're inside the mind of another person, maybe somebody dead for thousands of years. Across the millennia, an author is speaking clearly and silently inside your head, directly to you. Writing is perhaps the greatest of human inventions, binding together people who never knew each other, citizens of distant epochs. Books break the shackles of time. A book is proof that humans are capable of working magic.

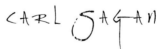

Nick Winewriter

Pete Best

Extra industrial sparkle kudos to Barbara DeCesare, M. Scott Douglass, Blair Ewing, everybody at One More Page Books, James Patterson, everybody at Politics and Prose, and Rose Solari. Plus lilac timely thanks to: Cynthia Atkins, Allison Barlow, Linda Blaskey, Jody Bolz, Shirley Brewer, Doritt Carroll, Susann Cokal, Teri Cross-Davis, Rocky Delaplaine, Julia Geiser, Eric D. Goodman, Barbara Grosh, Margaret Grosh, Joanna Howard, George Kalamaras, Gerry LaFemina, Jenna Le, Gregory Luce, Meghan McNamara (Stillhouse Press), Devon Miller-Duggan, Gloria Mindock, Amanda Newell, Susan Okie, Jonathan Kevin Rice, Ruth E. Thaler-Carter, Eleanor Tipton, Randi Ward, Gregory Osina Weatherford, Pamela Murray Winters, and Katherine E. Young.

IN MEMORIAM

Ken Adam
Chantal Akerman
Ian Allen
Muhammad Ali
Signe Toly Anderson
George Barris
Yogi Berra
Leon Bibb
Theodore Bikel
Carmen Balcells
Ken Beatrice
Paul Bley
Cilla Black
Grace Lee Boggs
Julian Bond
David Bowie
Svetlana Boym
Gabrielle Burton
Harry Calhoun
Judy Carne
Alan Cheuse
Kevin Corcoran
Catherine Coulson
Yvonne Craig
Madeline DeFrees
E. L. Doctorow
Ann Downer
Tim Drummond
Lori Ellison
Buddy Emmons
Mel Farr
Wilton Felder
Brian Friel
Ernst Fuchs
Wes Funk
Frank Gifford
Michael C. Gross
Eddie Hardin
Lee Harwood
Eddie Hoh
Lena Horne
John Hudson
Kenneth Irby
Carol Brown Janeway
John Jennings
Dean Jones
Don Joyce
Paul Kantner

Carey Lander
Christopher Lee
Harper Lee
Barbara F. Lefcowitz
Guy Ligier
Robert Loggia
Cynthia Macdonald
Moses Malone
Henning Mankell
Michael Mariotte
Gary Marker
Melissa Mathison
Ann McGovern
William McIlvanney
Anne Menebroker
Christopher Middleton
Martin Milner
Scotty Moore
Harry Morgan
Mark Murphy
Prince Rogers Nelson
Andy "Thunderclap"
   Newman
Maureen O'Hara
Milt Pappas
Natasha Parry
Melody Patterson
Edgar Stanley Peabody
John Perreault
Terry Plumeri
Brianna Lea Pruett
Tessa Ransford
Alan Rickman
Frances Kroll Ring
Cynthia Robinson
Wayne Rogers
Billy Joe Royal
Candida Royalle
Oliver Sacks
Morley Safer
Carolyn See
Tim Seles
Richard Selzer
Peter Shaffer
Garry Shandling
Herschel Silverman
Jim Simpson
Ingrid Sischy
P. F. Sloan

William Jay Smith
Gilli Smyth
Frances Sokolov (aka Vi
   Subversa)
Ralph Stanley
Karl Stirner
Pat Summitt
Elizabeth Swados
Dave Swarbrick
Sharon Tandy
Toots Thielemans
Richard Thompson
Robbin Thompson
Alvin Toffler
Michel Tournier
Allen Toussaint
John Trudell
Sara Little Turnbull
Nana Vasconcelos
Rudy Van Gelder
Bill Wade
Ed Walker
Hugh Walthall
Ray Warleigh
Colin Welland
Arnold Wesker
Paul West
Haskell Wexler
Kiernan White
Maurice White
Elie Wiesel
Gene Wilder
C. K. Williams
Elmo Williams
William S. Wilson
Holly Woodlawn
Terry Wogan
Phil Woods
Bernie Worrell
C. D. Wright
Stevie Wright
Glenn Yarbrough
Alan Young
Steve Young
Gail Zappa
Pete Zorn
Vilmos Zsigmond
Joost Zwagerman

CONTENTS

NONFICTION

POETRY

x GARGOYLE

FICTION

ART

David Sheskin

You Are a Person of Interest

Jamie Brown

THE CLUB THAT WANTS TO KEEP JIMMY GATZ OUT

(or, What Baz Luhrman, Robert Markowitz, Jack Clayton, Elliott Nugent, and Herbert Brenon Should Have Thought About Before Directing Their Versions of Fitzgerald's Class-Conscious Tale)

suspect that what has made Fitzgerald's *The Great Gatsby* unfilmable for lo these seven decades is that no filmmaker has yet understood, at an organic, personal level, exactly what it is that makes Jay Gatsby tick. Partly, this is because they are not familiar with the book's author's *own* life, except, perhaps, as a gloss. Folks like Baz Luhrman (himself, as an Australian, even more of an outsider to the American upper class than every previous director), always seem more interested, like characters at one of Gatsby's parties, in the external display of the nouveau riche, which is exactly the problem for Gatsby. In some ways his outsider status makes Luhrman admirably suited to the emotional spine of the novel, but one must suspect that his concern with the trappings of the film, and the fact that, whether he regards himself as Hollywood "royalty" or Hollywood "outsider," his role as Hollywood "auteur" gets in the way of his understanding that spine.

What was primarily Jay Gatsby's attempt to attract the attention of Daisy Buchanan, or that of someone who knew her and might facilitate Gatsby's reconnection with her, seemed to be merely a confirmation of exactly *why* Jay Gatsby would never be, to people like the Buchanans or Sloanes, "people like us." Among "society," nobody except the black sheep of prominent, old-money families behaved as Gatsby did. And Gatsby knew it.

Gatsby, who had struggled so hard and for so long to attain the trappings of genteel wealth and privilege, was willing to give up this much of the pretense to class which he affected in order to make that reconnection. In other words, Gatsby had only set about to become the Gatsby-of-the-parties in order to win Daisy back by giving up any pretense to class beyond his conspicuous consumption—which, ironically, clearly and indelibly marked him as an outsider. *That* was the power Daisy had over him. Just *why* that is an important point is at the crux of the matter.

Gatsby's effort to become a big wheeler-dealer among the families of the north Long Island shore had only one cause, and it was made manifest because Gatsby believed that whatever he wanted he could achieve by hard work. If he just *wanted* something enough, if he worked hard enough to achieve it, he could turn the wheels of fate and shape people's lives so that he would be in the proper position to grab that brass ring the next time it went by.

Jimmy Gatz would never have been acceptable to Tom Buchanan's social class. Let me reiterate: *never*. What Gatz lacked was generations of forebears who had achieved what he himself set about to achieve as Jay Gatsby. Cornelius van der Bilt, for all *his* wealth, was, for nearly his entire life, looked down upon by the very upper class by whom he wanted so desperately to be accepted. The Commodore would have understood Jimmy Gatz perfectly.

The problem, it seems to me, is that Daisy Fay, daughter of landed gentry, remnants of the Southern antebellum aristocracy, married Tom Buchanan, scion of a Northern upper-class family that had achieved its wealth two or more generations before. Both of these individuals under ordinary circumstances would not have given Jimmy Gatz more than a moment's notice. It was as the ambitious, social-climbing Jay Gatsby that he found the eye of the impressionable ingénue, Daisy Fay, and the force of both his dreams and his unbridled affection for her, which initially made her fall for him. That, and he looked good in uniform.

Even so, Lieutenant Jay Gatsby achieved a small measure of glory for himself because he had adopted what he thought of as the upper-class sense of *noblesse oblige*, and because that sense of propriety meant that one kept a cool head in battle for the sake of one's men as much as for one's own survival or reputation. Valor is valor is valor, whatever the initial motivation for it, and even tiny Montenegro recognized that Gatsby had it. Having adopted the cloak of upper-class "respectability," *Major* Gatsby, the honored and much-decorated veteran, would have been struck by how much, even at Oxford, he was viewed as an interloper. It was this continuing sense of being regarded by the upper class *there* as a social climber that undoubtedly led him to abandon his studies at Oxford—along with the news of the marriage of Daisy Fay to Tom Buchanan.

Nick Carraway is the ultimate insider; born into the same extended family as Daisy Fay, he was as much a privileged member of the upper class as Daisy or Tom, albeit his side of the family was perhaps less well-off in the current day of the novel than the Buchanan or Fay families. But this is the important point: Nick was, without ever having to try, a member by birth in the very club that Gatsby so desperately wanted to join. After all, he had what Gatsby wanted, and Nick could hardly have cared, in part because he had been born into it, and had never actually known what Gatsby understood about the class structure in America.

It is interesting that Nick's passive voice speaks of coming East to enter the bond market, as if it were a foregone conclusion that, having determined to come East, after a little study of the books he needed (purchased without apparent thought to the cost), he could immediately step into such a position.

Gatsby, on the other hand, had had to work hard to achieve whatever meager success he had managed, at least prior to his meeting Meyer Wolfsheim, and must have regarded Nick as a sort of lightweight, or of being so privileged that his sincere offer to help Nick with his business was dismissed rather more casually than someone who had risen from the underclasses might have done. From Gatsby's perspective, Nick's casual, perhaps even cavalier, approach to earning money and his long-term financial sense of security speak volumes about the difference between the two men.

Nick is clearly of the class of Tom Buchanan and Daisy. He moves comfortably in the rooms at the Buchanan home, handles social niceties with aplomb, and is as comfortable at dinner as his hosts.

Gatsby, in both Nick's cottage and the Buchanans' home, is, by contrast, awkward and ill at ease. Nervous at reconnecting with Daisy in the first case, and awkward as any man cuckolding his host might be in the second, we must nonetheless begin to suspect that not knowing which fork to use at dinner would frighten Gatsby far more than any threat Tom might make about having him exposed for the gangster he really is. When Tom plays his trump card at the Plaza and says, "You're one of that bunch that hangs around with Meyer Wolfsheim—that much I happen to know. I've made a little investigation into your affairs—and I'll carry it further tomorrow..." it is not the threat of exposure that makes Gatsby uncomfortable, but that Daisy was within earshot, and might begin to think less of him.

Where Gatsby moves comfortably and assuredly is in the speakeasies and gambling dens and "dance-halls" (a euphemism for houses of prostitution) and pseudo-pharmacies set up primarily to sell black-market hooch, rubbing elbows comfortably with politicians and gangsters and public servants—who, like him, have risen to their positions through hard work and, we must naturally assume, the "gonnegtions" each has fostered along the way.

The rich will have their playthings, after all, and we must begin to suspect that despite all of his superficial refinement, Gatsby, *who began life on or below the same social level as George and Myrtle Wilson*, is essentially as much Daisy's indulgence—justified by Tom's philandering—as her husband's, with a dash of romantic nostalgia thrown in for good measure. This is not to suggest that either she or Tom, though careless, is heartless. Tom is clearly moved by Myrtle's death as, we must assume, Daisy is later by Gatsby's, but what's done is done; by the end of the book, both Tom and Daisy are once again on an equal footing with the deaths of their respective paramours.

Tom Buchanan undoubtedly felt that the peace and tranquility of his home and domestic arrangements was being undercut by Gatsby, but there seems to be no point at which he himself ever actually felt threatened by Gatsby's existence.

Gatsby, on the other hand, must have felt like a two-headed beast when Tom and Mr. Sloane and a young woman dropped by his opulent home on horseback. Gatsby so desperately wanted to be the proper host in order to prove that he belonged among their company that he seems overeager to please, despite Tom's palpable condescension. With his other head, Gatsby must have wanted to kill them for shaming him so by their exclusivity, while simultaneously burning with shame at his having wanted to earn their approval and acceptance in the first place.

It is *this* shame, a burning sense of humiliation and rage, that runs to the core of one's being, which the rejection and condescension of Tom Buchanan and his class brings about in any person like Gatsby, victimized first by the circumstances of birth, which lies at the core of the novel. It would be easy enough to film if the director—any director—was less interested in the superficiality of Gatsby's ostentatious lifestyle, which, please note, absolutely *ends* the moment he has won Daisy back.

No more parties, the house is dark on weekends, and the new staff do not talk to anyone. Gatsby attempts to revert to the quiet, respectable upper-class lifestyle to which he had once pretended, which is to say private and reserved, but in this too he fails, for he tries to protect Daisy from any hint of approbation. As a result, he becomes as socially abstemious as he had been socially profligate, raising all sorts of further questions as to his identity and the source of his fortune.

Gatsby hates Tom and all that he stands for, not his wealth or his privilege by themselves, but for his overweening sense of social superiority—the entire class structure which Gatsby must have perceived as the reason for his separation from Daisy in the first place. His involvement in criminal activities—especially so where those activities served to corrupt, destabilize, or ruin members of Tom's social class—must have seemed excusable as an almost revolutionary act. Daisy alone of all her class Gatsby seems to hold faultless, though he seems to come to respect Nick as not being like all the others. But it is Gatsby's double-headed hatred—of the class structure which he cannot abide and of his own desire to become the very thing he despises—that is missing from every film version of the book.

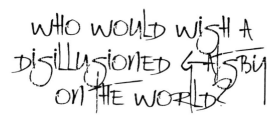

WHO WOULD WISH A DISILLUSIONED GATSBY ON THE WORLD?

Two Notes on Gatsby's Criminal "Gonnegtions"

There are two telling yet heretofore overlooked clues to the depths of Gatsby's involvement in the organized criminal activities of Meyer Wolfsheim which suggest he is no mere front man, and certainly no stranger to the gathering of background information on individuals which he might use for coercion or blackmail.

The first instance is in the apparent "coincidence" of Nick's renting the gatehouse of Gatsby's fabulous estate. The very fact that Gatsby resides where he does is based on the fact of visual proximity to the Buchanan household with its green-lit dock on the far side of the bay. Yet the gatehouse is rented, seemingly at random, to the one man who may effect a reconnection between Daisy and Gatsby, Daisy's second cousin once removed.

The house is dusty when Nick first leases the property; surely no one has lived there since Gatsby himself moved in next door. Is it purely coincidence, as Nick initially thinks, that brings him to rent Gatsby's gatehouse, or was the gatehouse left vacant until Mrs. Buchanan's second cousin once removed inquired about the availability of a small property in the neighborhood? (Nick's coworker, with whom he had originally planned to rent the gatehouse, is mysteriously and serendipitously transferred to Washington at just the right moment as well.)

It seems likely that Gatsby either knew who Nick was in advance of Nick's initial inquiry, or that Gatsby investigated the young Mr. Carraway through his network of informants upon receiving the rental application. Is it not likely that, had it been anyone *but* Nick, Gatsby would have left the gatehouse vacant, as he certainly needed privacy for the illicit activities he undertook on behalf of Mr. Wolfsheim?

Alternatively, we know that Gatsby has connections in the bond market; if, learning of Nick's identity, he had followed Nick every step of the way, he might well have arranged for Nick's coworker's connivance in getting Nick out to Long Island.

Regardless, when Nick remarks to Jordan on the coincidental nature of Gatsby's buying a home across the bay from the Buchanans, he betrays a certain Midwestern naïveté which she quickly dismisses. "But it wasn't a coincidence at all," she says, and the reader ought, by extension, to apply that assessment to Nick's rental arrangement as well.

The second instance occurs the fateful night Daisy and Gatsby drive back to the Buchanans' home, when Daisy strikes and kills Myrtle. Tom and Nick and Jordan arrive at the Buchanan house after Gatsby has dropped Daisy and taken the damaged vehicle back to his place and garaged it. When Nick leaves the Buchanan home to wait for the taxi Tom has had called for, he discovers Gatsby, who has been hiding outside.

"'I'm just going to wait here and see if he tries to bother her about that unpleasantness this afternoon. She's locked herself into her room, and if he tries any brutality she's going to turn the light out and on again,'" Gatsby tells him.

Is it just because Tom might object to Daisy's dalliance with Gatsby or Gatsby's insistence that Daisy is going to leave Tom that make Gatsby worry? Remembering that Tom had earlier threatened to expose Gatsby as a bootlegger, are we to imagine that Gatsby, who is indeed involved in organized crime, is entirely without guile or resources?

As far as Gatsby is supposed to have known, Daisy "merely" struck some innocent pedestrian. Certainly this alone would not have been cause for Tom's potential violence. I would argue that it is likely that Gatsby was not without his own "research" on Tom, and not only knew that Tom was having an affair and cheating on Daisy (this seems to have been common knowledge to the characters who know Tom in the novel, so it would hardly have been a difficult thing for Gatsby to have ascertained, gangster or no), but also may well have known that Myrtle was, in fact, Tom's mistress. Small wonder Gatsby was worried what Tom might do, for any combination of reasons. Gatsby had, we may be quite sure, availed himself of the same network of intelligence gatherers in order to prevent Tom from exposing *him* as Tom threatened to do in the hotel room at the Plaza in New York. In such a case, with Myrtle dead, at least some of his sway over Tom would have been lost.

Ironically, while nearly everyone who has been bullied on the playground as a child has wanted to kill their tormentors, here Gatsby actually had the power and connections to do it. That he chose *not* to is no guarantee that, had he survived, he might not eventually have had Tom eliminated.

While he believed his future with Daisy was assured, Gatsby was guided by his nobler aspirations. It may be a good thing that he died with his dreams intact, for who would wish a disillusioned Gatsby on the world?

Embittered, deserted by the object of his affection, he may well have thrown himself into his criminal activities with abandon, becoming a true don or capo, and forever severing himself from the person whom he had once believed himself capable of becoming.

Andrew Gifford

PRELUDE: AT THE LAKE, 1979

Excerpt from *We All Scream: The Fall of the Gifford's Ice Cream Empire*

We were ice cream people.

We ran a multimillion-dollar empire that had thrived since 1938. For generations of Washingtonians, our name was on the tip of the tongue when they thought of ice cream and candy. Presidents lined up for a scoop next to office workers and laborers. At the scarred wooden tables in the various Gifford's parlors around the D.C. area, lovers held hands and children celebrated their birthdays, year after year. Come opening time, there was almost always a line at the door. On more than one occasion, when a first-shift worker failed to show and the store didn't open on time, small mobs broke in and served themselves. Almost everyone left payment on the counter.

In the Gifford's parlor, watching a waitress balance a tray of sundaes as she approached your table, everything must have seemed perfect. Beautiful, even. Maybe I seemed perfect, too, that boy under his mother's wing as she swanned past the tables toward the back of the store. What a dream to be the prince of ice cream!

Except it wasn't.

In 1979, I was five—too young to understand much about our family business, let alone what was about to happen to it and to us. Today, I'm still not sure I understand.

Gifford's Ice Cream and Candy Company was founded by my grandfather, John Nash Gifford. He died in 1976, leaving the business in turmoil. His wife, my grandmother Mary Frances, lay dying in a hospital bed. My father, Robert Nash Gifford, struggled for control of the empire against both his father's last surviving partner and my maternal grandfather, Allen Currey, who maneuvered to take over in my name. In the chaos, my mother, Barbara, signed on with my dad in an elaborate plan to siphon off profits and plunder the payroll and pension accounts.

As a child, I knew none of this. My paternal grandparents were strangers to me—their history hidden, muddled, erased. From my parents I learned only that I was an accident, easily ignored. What little I thought I knew about my family was a lie, and it would take me over three decades to figure that out. The fact was, long before the public end of Gifford's Ice Cream, my father had decided to kill it.

This is a story about what was lost. It's a story about the dead. It's a story about me. It begins at a lake in western Maryland.

My earliest memory.

THE WATER IN Deep Creek Lake was dark, calm, and chilly, even under the harshest summer sun. My mother called it "mountain water" with a strange, spooky reverence in her voice. Water without a bottom, she said. Deep Creek Lake, though tamed by man, seemed primordial. There were a few manmade beaches, maintained by the Wisp or Alpine Village, the two major resort hotels, but most of the shoreline was comprised of drowned trees, rocks, and sticky black mud.

As we approached in our Caprice station wagon, we passed a turnoff just before the Wisp that led to an abandoned quarry. Three great caves had been blasted through the side of the mountain, and ruined chainlink fences had been thrown up as ineffectual barriers. Around these gaping maws, rusting equipment lay forgotten. Slippery humps of rocks made dangerous trails back into the darkness, each surrounded by oily black water.

Mom was a rockhound. The first thing we did after we checked into our hotel, instead of going to the lake, was cross the road and climb to the quarry site. On our trip in 1979, new fences had been installed to block access to the caves. But Mom had anticipated this and carried along a set of bolt cutters. She made a hole in one of the fences, grabbed my hand, and led me through, producing a cheap flashlight that cast a weak beam as we slowly moved into the caves.

A cold breeze blew from within the heart of the mountain. A barely audible hum, punctuated by sounds of dripping water and skittering rocks, summoned mental visions of ghosts and monsters. Mom stopped to chip rocks out of the walls while I nervously watched the crumbling ceiling. Occasionally she would shout in triumph and bend down to show me the fossils she'd been extracting—strange, ancient creatures trapped in stone. I carefully touched the outlines of their bodies, and Mom told me that, one day, we would become fossils, too.

Eventually, we went far enough for the daylight behind us to grow distant and then vanish, leaving us alone with the flickering beam of Mom's flashlight. In that darkness, she shouted:

"I am here! I have come!"

I feared that this might be a summons and waited nervously for a response. I looked up at her, her face hidden in shadow. She stood unflinching, waiting.

"I have brought Andrew!" she added.

Her hand, hard on my shoulder, kept me pinned at her side. After a few tense, quiet moments, we turned and left. She seemed disappointed. I asked what was wrong as we emerged back into the warm summer day. She shook her head, now sullen and distant, and pushed me along the dirt road. She didn't speak for the rest of the evening.

FIRST THING EVERY morning for the entire vacation—for every vacation at Deep Creek, year after year, rain or shine—my parents would rouse me and we would go out on the lake in a rented boat and motor around without any sort of goal in mind. We spent whole days motoring the lake like this, my father making endless circuits of the erratic shoreline, pausing to float near the most desolate stretches, where the water disappeared behind the gnarled branches of sunken trees.

Between the two of them, they would empty a cooler of beer and bourbon. Mom would take each can out and tap the top with her fingers before cracking it open with a sigh. When the gas got low, Dad would pull into a dock and refuel, and then we'd start off again. As we drifted aimlessly, my father sat in the captain's chair, staring ahead, while my mother turned the number of flattened beer cans into a math quiz.

"How many cans now, Andrew?"

I'd dutifully count them, prouder and prouder of my ability as the number went up throughout the day.

Despite the lazy tours of the lake and the alcohol, neither of them relaxed. They always seemed on edge, living underneath a layer of fear that scared me. If a fellow boater hailed us or asked if we were in trouble, Dad would start the engine and speed away at full throttle as Mom looked back and shouted:

"I think they're following!"

My mother told me that I shouldn't trust anyone. I wasn't to speak to strangers, or leave the hotel room, or get out of the boat. If anyone spoke to me, she said, I must not forget that they were "the enemy." She told me that everyone out there—"a world full of strangers"—wanted to "steal" me. Because we were famous, my father would chime in. Mom would nod and say that they would "brutally rape and torture" me.

I learned three rules:

"Trust no one, speak to no one, and tell no one your name."

These warnings extended beyond our summer vacations at the lake. Every Halloween, at Gene's Costumes in Kensington, Maryland, both Mom and Dad would point to a policeman costume and whisper in my ear:

"Don't trust police officers, because they are probably just evil men in disguise. You can buy a cop's outfit and ID right here. Anyone can. Always remember that."

At Deep Creek Lake, by six each evening, we'd tie up the boat and head back to our rented cottage on the grounds of the Alpine Village. My parents ordered room service, and then they would sit together to drink and argue steadily until I passed out in front of the TV, their harsh, hushed voices my troubled lullaby.

Part of our daily circuits around the lake brought us into the long, thin cove where the dam loomed on the horizon. We usually gave the dam a wide berth, but one day we came very close to it, and Dad cut the engine. For several minutes, the boat drifted slowly closer, and I watched, staring in awe at the large structure in front of us, the tips of trees just visible in the valley beyond. In my child's mind, I pictured the dam from its other side—a colossal wall with all that dark, dark water backed up behind it and our tiny boat floating on top. It made me feel so very small, so very fragile. We were maybe a few hundred yards away from the dam, the current gently pulling us towards it, when Mom leaned down and told me a story.

"There once was a family just like ours," she said. "Mommy, Daddy, and a little boy. They used to always visit this lake, just like we do. Then, one day, something terrible happened..."

She let the tension build, the boat drifting closer to the dam as my father watched me levelly, occasionally sipping from a Dixie cup of bourbon.

"They were lost," Mom continued. "They got sucked under the dam, and nobody knew what happened to them until, weeks later, they found their boat far down the river."

Her arm stretched toward the dam and beyond to the hardscrabble woods of western Maryland, her face serious, her eyes hidden behind aviator sunglasses that reflected the summer sky and the dark water around us.

"All that was left were three skeletons," she said, pointing at her chest, at Dad, and then at me. "Mommy, Daddy and a little boy..."

We drifted closer and closer, and then Mom laughed good-naturedly and went to start the engine. She turned the key, but nothing happened. A look of alarm spread across her face as she tried again, then again. She rushed back to the motor and pulled the emergency ripcord. The engine choked and sputtered but didn't start. Her voice low, shaking, she called my dad over and he tried to start the engine. One, two, three pulls on the chain. The motor coughed but never came to life.

"It won't start! Oh my god!"

Mom turned to me, her face a mask of terror. She clung to my father, who grimly stared at the engine. It was the first time I had seen them frightened, and I started to cry and shake, tearing my eyes off of them to look fearfully at the dam as we drew ever closer.

The warning signals from the dam started to sound—to my child's mind they seemed like great, piercing Klaxons that screamed through the air. I covered my ears. We were close enough to see people watching from the shore and an observation platform, close enough to see the water being sucked towards the dam, to feel the boat pick up speed. I pissed my swim trunks and screamed.

Then Mom started to laugh. She gave my dad a playful punch on the shoulder. Grinning and chuckling under his breath, he took his seat at the wheel and turned the key. The engine started up right away. The boat turned and sped away from the dam. The Klaxons cut off and, with nothing but the roar of the boat's engine and my mom's laughter in my ears, I lapsed into a shuddering silence, sitting in a puddle of my piss, staring back at the dam. I couldn't stop crying. I couldn't feel anything. My mother's laughter faded.

She watched me for a moment, then sneered and said:

"Pull yourself together. Boys don't cry!"

But I couldn't stop crying. I stared at her, gasping, sobbing, shaking. She set her jaw and turned to my father, screaming at him, saying that he had frightened me. She yelled at him all the way back to the hotel docks, then through the lobby, out the back, and all along our short walk to the cottage. Guests and staff stared at us. Mom dragged me by my hand, and I stumbled behind her, still numb. My dad never shouted back—he only nodded meekly and mumbled his familiar refrain, repeating:

"Sorry, Barb, sorry, Barb..."

They fought into the night as I huddled in my bed, unable to sleep, the sound of the dam's sirens echoing in my head. I couldn't stop crying, sucking in dry, heaving breaths, sweating through the sheets and shivering. A hotel worker came by and knocked on the door. I heard him say that Dad had forgotten to tie up the boat and that it had drifted into the lake. Mom yelled and screamed at him, then slammed the front door of the cottage repeatedly—banging it shut, opening it up again, and smashing it closed again, all the while unleashing incoherent animal shrieks.

Finally, there was silence. I heard the door open again, slam shut, and then Mom burst into my room, throwing the door aside with enough force to drive the doorknob into the drywall.

"Your dad's gone," she said in calm, even tones. "He left us because you cried. Because you just had to ruin a perfect vacation."

She ordered me to take down my pajama bottoms and lie on my stomach. Then she turned her diamond rings around so the big, sharp stones were facing inward. She spanked me until blood started to flow freely onto the sheets, each blow punctuating her words:

"Your...father...is...gone...because...of...you..."

Dad had run away. He'd rented a car and was driving home while Mom spanked me until I bled.

MY CHILDHOOD IS defined by moments like those at Deep Creek Lake. It was our summer getaway, but for me, especially after that 1979 trip, it was an annual torture. At the lake, they were free of the family business, not to mention most of the family itself. My parents behaved like animals briefly escaped from their cages, drinking wildly and concocting pranks at my expense or at the expense of neighboring guests and hotel employees.

After that episode in 1979, my parents avoided the dam. I developed a lifelong phobia of water, and on future trips to the lake, I huddled at the bottom of the boat and tried never to look at the water, tried to push the thought of it beneath me from my mind. I spent each outing on the lake in a near-catatonic state, thinking only of that dam.

I still dream of that dam. In my dreams, we get sucked under and I have to fight my way awake through the impenetrable, inescapable blackness of that cold, rushing mountain water.

Alice Hatcher

ROUGH (DRAFT) SEX, OR FIFTY SHADES OF IMPOSSIBLE

Recently, while cleaning out my office, I came across a binder bursting with snatches of purple prose and dozens of crude sketches that could pass for the confused renderings of a sex-obsessed adolescent doodling in algebra class. Some of the sketches featured naked people with grossly exaggerated appendages and limbs locked in preposterous poses. Others depicted contorted stick figures awkwardly conjoined on couches, in the backseats of cars, and in one case, on the edge of a cliff. All featured some overtly sexual act that defied anatomical possibility, gravity, and good sense. There was nothing sexy in any of them. Worse yet, I was the author of every single one. In my defense, I've never claimed talents as a visual artist. I hadn't intended to draw anything pornographic. I'd produced the etchings simply to diagram impenetrable literary passages and flesh out the actions of fumbling characters. I'd illustrated confounding scenes merely to help members of a fiction writers' critique group comprehend each other's work.

The sketches, along with hundreds of loose pages framed in marginalia, represent the only record of my fleeting involvement with my very first critique group. My relationship to the group, dominated by erotica writers, lasted all too briefly. Formed in desperation, it hardly represented a good match. It ended quickly, in anticlimax and an awkward parting of ways. Like many ill-fated relationships, it dissolved before the parties involved could overcome plaguing insecurities or resolve troubling questions—in this case, about the guidelines that should govern craft-oriented critiques of fictional sex. Looking back, I wish my first critique group had been something other than it was—a somewhat random encounter of inexperienced writers blindly groping for insights. Given the nature of its inception, though, it was bound to be disappointing.

I discovered the group through an online social networking site. I'd just quit a teaching job to begin work on a novel about the prison-industrial complex. I'd also just moved into a new town, where I didn't know a single person. With long and lonely evenings to fill and little outlet for my intellectual energies, I started trolling the classifieds, looking for any book club or critique group that would have me. I settled too quickly on an ad posted by "Ladybug," the online name of someone hoping to expand a "literary fiction writers critique group for people serious about craft." The ad, like many others on social networking sites, was full of misleading statements. At its fuzzy heart, its subject was a group of erotica writers, admittedly with "genre-crossing and literary aspirations." I discovered the group's sexual bent when Ladybug emailed me directions to her house and the pieces she and two other members had submitted for the next critique session.

I found it odd that three authors would share their unpublished work with a total stranger. Authors generally vet prospective readers before swapping material, and fools rush in, as the saying goes. That said, some people are just more forward than others. "Nothing ventured, nothing gained," my aunt, a four-time divorcée, is fond of saying. Still, the authors' lack of inhibition raised at least one of my eyebrows, not least because all three pieces contained fairly graphic depictions of what seemed to be sex. It did occur to me that I might be ill suited to a group so dedicated to the erotic arts. But then writers are writers, I assured myself, all bound by a love of words. Besides, I desperately needed human contact.

The next Friday evening, I drove to Ladybug's house, an unassuming ranch on the outskirts of town. In Ladybug's living room, I found several people seated around a narrow coffee table, picking over snacks and quietly talking. These included, in addition to Ladybug, two middle-aged women "dabbling" and "chipping away" at romance novels; Rhonda, a young woman writing about "a workplace affair"; Taylor, a painfully shy transgendered man "working in the genre of interstellar fantasy"; a male psychoanalyst drafting a novel about "murder and sexual intrigue"; and a sullen young man, "a huge fan of Chuck Palahniuk" who'd just obtained an MFA from an online university. I learned most of what I would about the members over the next three months. Initial introductions amounted to little more than mumbled remarks before Ladybug reviewed the ground rules established to ensure productive critique sessions.

Each author would briefly introduce his or her excerpt and discuss the techniques they'd employed to achieve an effect. Each would remain silent during critiques of their work, so they wouldn't derail discussions with knee-jerk rebuttals. Beyond that, I can't remember much. At the time, I wasn't feeling so hot. Perhaps it's more accurate to say I was feeling too hot, cramped and distracted by the perspiration running down my neck and a sense that the air in the room was growing close. Sitting between the psychoanalyst and Taylor, I felt conscious of my body in a way that recalled changing in my high school's gym locker room. I shifted as much as space allowed, unable to find a comfortable position on the couch, a soft sinkhole swallowing all of us. I drew my knees together and my shoulders inward, but nothing eased the pressure of Taylor's elbow poking my ribs or the psychoanalyst's shoulder pushing my arm against my breast. My thighs trembled from prolonged strain, and it grew difficult to balance my binder on my lap.

My physical discomfort might have been a somatic expression of my anxiety at the prospect of evaluating erotica with strangers. It only worsened, after all, when Ladybug introduced an excerpt of her historical romance novel. As Ladybug situated her excerpt in a larger tale—one of a winsome heroine "stranded on a desert (sic) island" until rescued from marauding pirates by the "dashing captain" of a British frigate—I struggled to concentrate on the words slipping out of focus on the pages splayed across my lap. Panicked, I realized I had nothing to say about the piece, even though I'd spent all afternoon rereading about the heroine casting aside her "savage rags" to accept the "amorous advances" of an accomplished master and commander clearly modeled on Russell Crowe. I kept getting lost in convoluted passages about tangled limbs, intertwined fingers and long locks of blonde hair, and lavish descriptions of "breathless heaving" and "undulating hips" and "knees buried in oriental silk sheets." I kept returning to the same questions about a coital act more than gently resisting comprehension.

For a moment, I thought my critical capacities had been hobbled by my own sexual inexperience and physical limitations. I wondered if more dexterous individuals routinely achieve the extreme yogic postures employed by Ladybug's characters. But then I'm imaginative, I assured myself, and still couldn't envision the act described by Ladybug. There was something decidedly wrong with it, logistically speaking. References to "languid limbs wrapped around the captain's hips" and a "slender back arched toward the ceiling" seemed unnaturally coupled with descriptions of "a waterfall of hair flowing across the captain's shoulder blades" and "the play of tropical moonlight across his expansive chest." Every limb seemed hyper-extended, and every extremity dangerously distended. Every law of physics appeared entirely upended.

If only to reassure myself that I wasn't miserably inadequate, having never heaved or undulated as the heroine, I pulled a sheet of paper from my binder and began to draw, staying as true to Ladybug's text as possible. As Chuck Palahniuk Jr. spoke of "subverting the paradigms of literature and pornography," I completed a series of quick sketches, each dedicated to a different interpretation of an act I could only represent by dispensing with any consideration of human anatomical form. Again, I wondered if my artistic skills were insufficient to the task at hand, or if I'd led too lackluster a sex life to appreciate the heroine's elastic limbs and bedroom gymnastics.

I drew my only assurance from the fact that others in the room seemed confused by the piece, too. When Jr. petered out, almost everyone stared at the ceiling or shuffled papers. I leaned forward and stared into a bowl of Chex Mix to feign reflection. Unnerved by the deepening silence, I cleared my throat, sending the dead wrong signal that I was about to deliver a considered remark. Everyone looked at me, visibly relieved.

Cornered, I started with a mumbled remark about "a minor point, really, regarding certain passages spanning pages 25 to 37." As Ladybug's eyes narrowed, I took a deep breath and read sentences describing implausible arm spans, too many fingers caressing too many ankles and calves at the same time, and the captain's elbows ("Inner arms?" I queried, only to be reminded of the rule against authors speaking during critiques) pressing against the back of the heroine's knees as "he parted her legs and lifted her into him." It wasn't entirely clear, I said, how one sea captain, however familiar with rigging, could be touching and seeing so much all at once. The problem, I ventured, related to point of view. Simply, the captain seemed privy, in the same moment, to both frontal and dorsal views of the heroine. At the end of one paragraph, with her knees pressed against his ribs, he'd looked into the "dark pools of her glistening eyes." But then, there'd been a minor plot twist—presumably a painful lumbar twist—and his eyes had wandered over the small of her back, still arched above the Chinese sheets. Prodded by the psychoanalyst, I held up a sketch to illustrate my point.

Ladybug bristled while everyone considered my work. The romance novelists lifted their feet from the ground and shifted in their chairs, envisioning various positions and shaking their heads. "He was supposed to be sideways," Ladybug finally whispered, breaking one of her own rules. Lapsing back into silence, she watched me sketch a second figure over the original outline of the captain. "No, facing the other way, perpendicular," she hissed. Exasperated and slightly unhinged by insecurities, I blurted, "Has anyone here actually done this?" Everyone looked at the floor. Needless to say, I'd behaved crassly. That alone might have gone unnoticed in the group, but I'd done something worse. I'd implied that Ladybug had struggled with point of view because she hadn't engaged in the act under consideration. I'd inadvertently lent support to the injunction issued to young writers in many MFA programs. This, of course, is the injunction to "write what you know."

I've never been exactly sure what most people mean when they say, "write what you know," but it seems to be a mantra of sorts among MFA students warned against creating characters unlike themselves. For many, "write what you know" is shorthand advice rooted in the idea that, if one stays close to home to gather material, one will write with authority and passion, and that a story rooted in personal experience will flow naturally from the pen. Forget all the authors who become blocked up trying to write about their traumatic childhoods. Even assuming that all authors wanted to write about their own lives, not everyone has a personal store of scandal and misadventure to draw upon for subject matter. As much as I hate to air the soft white laundry of the literary establishment, I'll say it. Most writers I know are almost boring in their willingness to sit by themselves for hours at a stretch. Not everyone can or should be Hunter S. Thompson. Writers are rarely rock 'n' rollers, and as some have lamented, you can't dance to a novel. If every bookish individual produced a barely veiled memoir, the world's readers would be in for a darn boring ride. Thank goodness there's no shortage of authors smitten with the creative aspect of creative writing, people who write wonderful novels about things they haven't experienced firsthand. Few mystery writers actually commit murders to better understand their most heinous villains. The best conduct extensive research and stretch their imaginations to fill in what they don't know. Millions happily devour their books.

That said, I'm willing to concede that simply countering "write what you know" with "know what you write," as many do, invites its own set of problems. What if an author is writing a book about dashing British naval officers and high-seas sexual hijinks, and home happens to be a quiet suburban ranch in the middle of a desert town? In Ladybug's case, it's hard to imagine what hands-on novel research would involve. Depending on one's confidence level and the costs of procuring certain services, it can be quite difficult to accrue firsthand sexual experiences of a certain kind, especially with men who look like Russell Crowe. This I know.

That caveat aside, authors should be wary of seemingly commonsense dictums such as "write what you know." Strictly interpreted, "write what you know" can be an impediment to good writing, especially if sex and romance enter the picture. Sexual relationships can be so consuming that it's sometimes hard for authors writing about their own affairs to gain the emotional distance needed for editing. Nostalgia often impairs the judgment of authors wallowing in happy memories of past flings—writers who find it difficult to finger the delete key, clinging to scenes that bring mysterious smiles to their faces but add nothing to their stories. On the flip side, authors writing about failed relationships often dispense with nuance to indulge their most vindictive tendencies. Mired in the familiar narratives and over-rehearsed dramas crowding their heads, they rarely consider multiple points of view, explore the motivations (or excuses) of secondary characters (usually exes), or deviate from transparently auto-biographical narratives driven by bitter resentments. Intimately identified with their characters, they have difficulty recognizing the difference between craft-based critiques of their work and insulting commentary on their unhappy sex lives.

No one illustrated this more clearly than the author who presented after Ladybug. A self-defined "adult erotica writer with literary aspirations," Rhonda dressed her part in a micro-skirt and thigh-high leather boots, a tight tweed jacket that barely buttoned over a halter top, and long red press-on nails. The piece, she said, recounted "this woman Jenna's fling with this guy Ben," a coworker at a distributing firm "just like the place" where Rhonda worked. Outside of Rhonda's clipped introduction, our knowledge of Ben, aka "Jerkoff," came from an ostensibly omniscient but not necessarily reliable third-person narrator with a penchant for telling rather than showing. The opinionated narrator, given to overusing the adjective "lame," informed readers that Ben "wasn't very good-looking and even worse in bed." The piece didn't provide details that might have suggested underlying reasons for Ben's sexual proclivities and failings. We knew only that Ben had "zero interest in moving up the corporate ladder, or for that matter, going down on anything, either," and that he "came quickly and snored."

Needless to say, the excerpt had all the hallmarks of an axe-grinding breakup piece. Like the relationship it portrayed, it ended abruptly, with the statement that Jenna had been "screwed over for the last time." From what we could tell, Rhonda had little interest in exploring the psychological valences of a sexual encounter. Her sole ambition, it seemed, had been to vindicate and flatter Jenna, a character "way better looking and totally in a different league than Ben." To be fair, Rhonda provided a revealing description of Jenna, although she might have shown her readers more than they wanted to know. The description left us all in silence.

It wasn't that Jenna's business casual suit was a bit too revealing of "two perky natural breasts," or that her fictional thong barely covered the topiary of her Brazilian wax. It was that the description hinted at a complete collapse of any distinctions between the embittered author, her acidic narrator, and her "screwed-over" character. To cut to the chase, Jenna bore an uncanny resemblance to her creator, between her "thigh-high leather boots," her "really short skirt that showed a lot of thigh," and her "flattering cleavage" and "long red nails." Growing suspicion that the character, narrator, and author were all the same person was reinforced by Rhonda's inadvertent use of "I" in place of "she" or "Jenna" at various points in the text, as when the third-person narrator stated, "I started dating him because he seemed like a bad boy."

The unfortunate slippage between first and third person, the product of editorial oversight, provided an entrée into a conversation about the piece's deeper problems. In any critique, readers should always cite specific passages when making general statements about what an author is doing well or badly. Vague generalizations (e.g., "This was off-putting" or "This is the kind of sex that gives sex a bad name") don't provide authors with a clear sense of how to build upon their strengths or remedy their most pressing problems. Also, specific passages can provide support, crutches really, for readers critiquing defensive authors—writers who seek out feedback only to dismiss criticism as the product of gross misreading or unfounded conjecture. The dozen or so passages containing first-person pronouns provided our group's otherwise reticent members with a conversational toehold on a very slippery slope.

Taylor ventured forth first, fidgeting and looking at the floor as he tentatively offered that the frequent "default" to first person, coupled with physical descriptions of Jenna, suggested that "the piece might have been inspired by real-life experiences." With a pained expression, he continued that animosities left from a past relationship might have made it "hard to flesh out Ben as a character with real feelings." Unresolved anger, Taylor barely whispered, had "taken over the story." Everyone concurred, with exaggerated nods, that the characters needed further development. Tapping his pen on his knee, the psychoanalyst suggested Rhonda take some time away from the piece, to let the dust of her relationship settle before going back to "fictionalize things a bit."

This was the final straw for our ill-treated heroine, or rather author, who insisted that she "wasn't Jenna or anything like her" with such venom and conviction that most of us almost felt sheepish. Undeterred, the psychoanalyst began to probe into the subconscious underpinnings of the excerpt. In a tone one might associate with an AA intervention, he said Rhonda needed to consider her characters' motivations and answer the "painful question" of why Jenna always sought out men who reinforced her negative self-esteem. Blatantly violating the group's rules of engagement, Rhonda folded her arms across her chest and spit, "it was only a few times" and "she's dated guys who aren't like that, too." The unsolicited backstory didn't answer the psychoanalyst's questions about character motivation. Nor did they answer mine. Inspired by the heady atmosphere in the room, I added that "the guy sounded like a real dipshit," and that I needed to know more about the protagonist's slumming proclivities, because "only a bigger dipshit would repeatedly sleep with him." I'd gone too far. As I finished speaking, Rhonda insisted (in the literary present) "she's not a dipshit," only to add (in the historical past) that "he was just an asshole."

As I mentally measured the distance to the door, Linda, the woman "dabbling" with a romance novel, mercifully intervened. Happily, she said, we'd all just "stumbled into a learning moment" about the merits of establishing "safe authorial distance" from "embarrassing" material that's "a little too close to home."

A learning moment, it was. Fortuitously, Linda had just completed a noncredit course focused on how fiction writers can benefit from creating narrators with voices distinct from their own and foregoing journalistic accuracy for the sake of a good story. Students in her class had experimented with different narrative voices, assuming different "personas" entirely unlike themselves. In creating alter egos for narrators, they'd shed the compulsions of many first-time novelists to recount personal experiences exactly as they'd happened, and to "be themselves" on the page. Writing fiction is different from keeping a diary, in that it's about "relinquishing reality," Linda declared, growing ebullient. "In my art, I give myself freedom to make up other people to say and do things I can't. I give myself permission to be someone else and have fun."

Whatever artistic freedoms Linda had embraced, none of her characters seemed to be having much fun. Her piece, a series of sexual scenes presented as flashbacks, had been taken from her novel-in-progress, "an updated *Bridges of Madison County* with a touch of *Brokeback Mountain.*" When she started the novel, Linda's protagonist had been a married suburban woman smitten with a businessman renting a neighbor's house. Writing about people "just like her friends" had filled her with inhibitions, but her class had provided her with a "clear solution to a common craft problem." On the advice of her teacher, she'd given one of her characters a quick sex change, deleting certain naughty bits and typing in others until she was ready to begin work on a piece of gay erotica about two men conducting a marital affair, quite literally, in a walk-in closet. She'd also reconstructed her narrator, abandoning first for third person and adopting a "male voice more appropriate for writing about squeamish details." As she explained, performing or rather penning a sex change and adopting a "foreign point of view" had given her the "authorial distance" needed to write, because "she didn't feel like she was writing about sex anymore."

I was impressed, albeit perversely, by Linda's ability to turn a myopic and bigoted view of sex into the basis for a bold experiment in craft. And whatever else can be said, she'd handily dispensed with the crushing restrictions of "write what you know." Sadly, though, she seemed entirely disconnected from her post-operative characters and unable to depict their emotional states or ejaculations. Certainly, she referenced physiological states. Her piece featured involuntary quivering, heart palpitations, dizziness, faintness, vertigo, tingling in the extremities, and a host of other things one might find on a list of side effects for an antiseizure medication. Her characters' encounters, though, never culminated in eye-rolling orgasms. After extended nuzzles and caresses, her characters abruptly "finished" without anything resembling an orgasm, as if stricken by an incurable case of coitus interruptus. In an erotic novel, this seemed a problem. Still, no one complained about the absence of a so-called money shot. We were members of a literary fiction group. We were above that kind of thing. So, like the characters, we finished quickly and quietly unfulfilled. After a few strained comments about commas, we thanked Linda for her point about unfettered artistry, if not her unsatisfying illustration of sex made exceedingly safe by authorial distance.

Linda, if anything, had provided a cautionary tale. If you're going to dispense with "write what you know" to gain authorial distance from difficult material, you should probably create a strong persona, a confident narrator who is so engaging that the facts become secondary to the telling of the story. However liberated from the embarrassments of heterosexuality, Linda hadn't created a narrator able to overcome his hesitations and bring her characters to orgasm. In her failure to satisfy, she'd broken what publishers often call the writer-reader contract.

Crassly put, this contract refers to authors' obligations to meet readers' basic expectations. If someone purchases and commits time to reading a book, that person should trust its author to deliver on a promise to entertain or enlighten—or at the very least, to tell a coherent story with a comprehensible plot and characters with identifiable motivations. By the contract, an author should deliver the goods advertised on the book flap. If a work is literary fiction, it should probe the deeper meanings of human existence or something like that. A murder mystery should contain a crime and some clues that lead logically to a resolution. Too many red herrings or false starts in a suspense novel can frustrate readers. Hence, the rule of thumb: if a gun appears in a play's first act, it should go off by the third. Otherwise, the gun's no more than a tease, and readers will reasonably criticize the author for failing to deliver. Linda hadn't delivered. She'd left us high and dry because she hadn't thought much about gay sex and couldn't fake it. She hadn't followed her own advice and created a persona confident enough to tell a story with such compelling (if inaccurate) details that readers would overlook minor errors for the sake of a good yarn.

As self-proclaimed experts on the contract will tell you, readers browsing through new books usually decide within a few sentences whether they're willing to buy the ticket and take the ride. A confident and authoritative narrative voice can often convince buyers that an author has the bona fides to give them a memorable bang for their buck. Let it be said, though, that one should never confuse cockiness and confidence. If authors can win readers' trust by creating narrators who seem qualified to tell a given story, they can just as easily alienate readers with grandstanding narrators. This is especially true of authors writing about sex. However well endowed with a knowledge of sexual positions, a narrator should never come across as arrogant or presumptuous. Narrators who show off by using inaccessible language about esoteric practices are likely to engender a sense of sexual inadequacy in readers who, let's face it, might want some gentle hand holding on the path to emotional catharsis.

The "coming-of-age" novel excerpt the MFA submitted for the group's second meeting provided a case in point. The novel was about a guy taking a year off after getting a writing degree, "a guy with a dark side who's spent too much time in school and needs to find out what it's all about." The problem was that no one in the group could figure out what "it" was. It seemed to have something to do with sex. In the first sentence, the narrator described the main character Jake "getting off in a Daisy Chain with the waitress and some guy he knew from hanging out at Frankie's." If allusions to "double rainbows" and "golden showers" in the next few paragraphs perplexed some in the group, imagine the general consternation over cryptic references to the waitress's urolagnia and Jake's "raw deal with switch-hitters giving him swimmer's ear." Sure, the narrator knew his stuff, whatever that was, but he seemed incapable of communicating his expertise to lay readers. He simply took too much (and too many of us) for granted when he described the waitress "snowballing Jake to choke him in revenge for his lousy tip."

Aside from the possible double entendre of the word tip, this was a straightforward, almost journalistic account. Yet, it suggested a certain kind of literary obscurantism bound to alienate. Almost everyone, at one point, has railed against overeducated authors who pepper their prose with foreign phrases, technical terms, and esoteric seventy-five-cent words. A snob of sorts, I've often attributed attacks on literary obscurantism to the laziness that prevents just about everyone from opening a damn dictionary. Reading the graduate's excerpt, though, I truly understood the frustration of readers who criticize "literary elitists" who write books the so-called average person can't understand.

It's bad enough to dispense French phrases and distracting bon mots to dress up indecorous scenes ("He ejaculated loudly, delivering the coup de grace to the ménage à trois."). It's even worse, I'm convinced, to establish a narrator's authority through blithe references to cheap novelties, odd toys, or positions that defy most readers' comprehension. Undoubtedly, my newfound empathy with the disgruntled democratic masses had its roots in my own performance anxieties. Still, should every reader of literary fiction be expected to know the definition of "chili chicken taco"? Should every reader need a firm grip on "saddlebacking" to enjoy a coming-of-age novel? I'm a working woman, and not in the oldest profession, and I don't have time to get an advanced sex education or learn the lingua franca of every strange narrator passing in the night.

I didn't say this to the group. I was among literary types, the sort of people who scorn passive readers and refuse to cater to the lowest common denominator in the name of democracy. Fortunately, I wasn't the only one at a loss. After praising the graduate for writing with courage about male sexuality, the psychoanalyst suggested that some readers wouldn't be able to visualize "certain, more transgressive acts." As The Bridges of Brokeback Mountain's author glanced at our transgender member, the psychoanalyst continued that Jr.'s piece had raised the most enduring craft concern inspired by the modern novel form: the appropriate balance between telling ("he felt anxious") and more subtle "showing" or rendering through revealing gestures ("he bit his nails"). The narrator hadn't "seduced the reader" through dialogue and well-chosen details, but had rather relied too heavily on the easy shorthand of an extensive vocabulary. Better, the psychoanalyst concluded, to "unpack scenes" and provide more detailed description to reveal characters' "inner emotional states."

As Jr. opened his mouth to speak, the group's more prescient members grasped the potential for embarrassing elaborations. Through pursed lips, the woman chipping away at a romance novel, a tax consultant with a penchant for floral skirts, pointed out the pitfalls of providing potentially gratuitous details. Little, she said, would be gained by describing Jake's expression as he performed "various and sundry acts." Character-driven fiction should foreground the psychological facets of human sexual experience; otherwise, she insisted, it's just pornography. Seemingly at odds, she and the psychoanalyst nevertheless agreed upon Jr.'s need to explore the complex emotional exchanges between Jake and the waitress, and to uncover the dramatic tension inherent in daisy chains. How to do this was the question.

She had an answer, one spelled out in a sample of her novel about a nun's battle with celiac disease and her ensuing crisis of faith. She'd written metaphorically, using suggestive language to reference acts that "need not be named," and free indirect discourse to "dip inside the heads" of characters having sexual intercourse. Indirect discourse, she explained, involved the use of an omniscient narrator to tack back and forth between characters' thoughts (the real subject of literary fiction) and "sensual acts conveyed more poetically than pornographically through innuendo." Waxing eloquent about poetic meter and less sublime rhythms, she scanned her excerpt until she found a scene that demonstrated the power of metaphor.

"With bated breath, the low-hanging fruit weighed heavily in her hands," she began, "and her palms filled with fire, but she dared not let go for fear of losing it." I listened intently, trying to visualize the scene and coming up with something almost unholy. The misplaced modifying clause suggested the fruit, itself, had bated breath. The vague pronoun "it" made it unclear what the nun feared losing—her mind, euphemistically speaking, a fire, understood as a manifestation of the spirit, or her grip on the fruit itself. Quibbles aside, there was something profoundly wrong with the piece, specifically with the piece of fruit. It came as an unpleasant revelation as I started doodling, reproducing the images flooding my mind and, I assumed, everyone else's: twin maraschino cherries dangling from sticky stems, a pair of oranges straining the end of a branch, and an overripe banana bruised from too much handling. As my indecent still life took shape, I recognized the gender ambiguity at the core of the metaphorical fruit. I had no idea, simply, if the fruit represented breasts, testicles, or some other kind of appendage.

Only when the nun "wrapped herself around his trunk and inhaled his nature" did I realize the proverbial fruit didn't refer to breasts, but rather to some aspect of male anatomy. "Low hanging," I decided, suggested testicles. After all, fruit could hardly denote/connote a banana/penis, which presumably wouldn't be low hanging at this particular juncture of a burgeoning relationship. Perhaps the nun had been cupping his testicles, but why did they weigh so much? And why were they so inflamed? A bit more specificity might have clarified things, but details only added further confusion, as when the nun "drew sweet juice from the swollen fruit with her hungry lips." I couldn't wrap my own head around it. Putting aside that the nun and not her lips was hungry, it wasn't clear what juice the nun could possibly be ingesting, unless the sweat of her partner's blessed labor, although "drew from" suggested some sort of extrusion. At some point, my confusion became too much, and I began to rail against the slippage between metaphoric and literal descriptions. It would have been better, I insisted, if there'd been a barrier, a dental dam of sorts, between the metaphorical world and its seamy physical underside, if only because you literally can't slobber on a metaphor.

At my third and last meeting with the group, my crusade against slipping metaphorical fig leaves was assumed by the psychoanalyst, an unwavering advocate of "sobriety in speech and writing." To the appreciative nods of a new member, a woman who looked like she'd been around the block, as my mother used to say (and a seedy neighborhood, I'd add), he presented a scene he'd written to demonstrate how spare language can be both accessible and artistic. Taken from a suspense/thriller about a female Japanese American master of kung fu and disguise evading arrest, the scene featured a "silky haired heroin" (sic) making a sexual overture towards an off-duty police officer with "polished onyx skin." It stood as an argument against obscurantism, overly opinionated narrators, and overblown metaphors, or so its author said. It represented a testament to "direct Hemingway-esque" writing.

Hemingway-esque the piece was not. After enacting a patter of dialogue, the psychoanalyst read a description of the detective's hands moving over the martial artist's sacral bone, rib cage and kneecaps, zygomatic arch, "snowy brow," and delicate chin. Straight from Fifty Shades of *Gray's Anatomy*, the scene ended with the suspect "smiling smugly" as she touched the detective's "black member." Through straightforward descriptions of acts and gestures, the psychoanalyst declared, a "detached narrator" could both engage readers' senses and provide insight into characters. Granted, we'd learned the Japanese suspect was a silky smooth operator wily enough to risk an afternoon tryst, or rather medical examination, with an officer of the law. But this was hardly a neutral narrator. If the psychoanalyst was drunk on Strunk & White, his narrator was intoxicated by orientalism and fixated on color. The detective's penis was not simply a penis. It was a "black member" seemingly separate from the rest of the detective.

Maybe I've read too many history books, but I couldn't help but observe that the phrase "black member" recalled the obsessions of nineteenth-century pseudo-scientists creating bogus racial taxonomies based on measurements of facial angles, crania, and genitalia. When the new member asked "why I was getting so uptight," I ventured that the psychoanalyst wouldn't have put "white" before "member" if the detective had been Caucasian, to use a standard taxonomic term. "Black" had made the member seem like an exotic specimen. In any case, it was redundant, unless the detective's penis existed separate from his body and required its own description, much as a Midnight Cowboy might, I added, employing a term for dildo gleaned from Jr.'s writings. As Jr. praised the "guts of the piece," I scribbled "archaic" beside "member" and "given" beside "black." The psychoanalyst glanced at my scrawl and merely conceded an "unfortunate redundancy."

I might have walked out then if Taylor hadn't started speaking, stammering almost, about his attempt to "blur the lines between race and gender" in a sci-fi/fantasy novel about a hermaphroditic empathic healer who travels around Galaxy Q, treating people on planets ravaged by war-fare. Reluctantly, I pulled out his piece and skimmed the scene I'd read the night before. Involving the healer and a bisexual political dissident dying in a cave, it was painfully awkward, interrupted with stilted dialogue about energy transfer and the dissolution of pain into pure light. It was sloppy, too, filled with salving ointments softening on feverish brows and bodily fluids dripping onto scarred skin. The characters melted into one another and melded. Their tears mingled. Their sex lasted for seventeen pages, occurring more slowly than anything in real time. And yet it felt real. Forget that there were five hands in a tryst involving two humans, as I confirmed with a quick sketch. The fifth hand was a minor detail that Taylor could easily explain with a quick reference to laws governing stem cell reproduc-tion and autogenesis in Q. I forgave the fifth hand. I welcomed its healing touch. It was almost...beautiful. For all its clumsiness, it never distracted from the arduousness of empathic sexual healing and the gradual, pains-taking nature of recovery from emotional and bodily trauma.

If we seemed poised to regroup, the new member had to ruin our loving feeling. "It wasn't believable," she began, shaking her head. "Any of it. If he or whatever was like any of the guys I've dated, he would've finished in a sentence and rolled right over. It's ridiculous." The author began picking at the knee of his overalls. I suspected he might cry. For the first time, a member had spoken directly, rather than implicitly or accidentally about her own sex life. In narcissistic fashion, she'd insisted that fiction (an inter-stellar fantasy, no less) reflect her own experience. She'd judged a work by the tattered standard of her own life, using criteria entirely unrelated to craft. Worst of all, she'd demeaned an author for his supposed naïveté. That, for me, was the final straw.

I left the group without debuting any of my half-written novel. Like The Great Gatsby's narrator Nick Carraway returning to the Midwest after a stint of debauchery in New York, I wanted "no more riotous excursions with privileged glimpses into the human heart." I'd lost interest in what Fitzgerald called "the abortive sorrows and short-winded elations of men." I'd had enough of strangers' unintended confessions, badly crafted affairs, literary biases, and real bigotries. I'd concluded that fictional sex should be left in the hands of experts, erotica writers well versed in proven formulas, stock poses, and characters familiar to readers of purple prose—defrocked priests, masquerading aristocrats, and multimillionaires with endless stores of toys.

Two years later, much has changed, and I've revised my conclusion. First, I'm in a new and more fulfilling critique group, one defined by mutual trust and a commitment to exchanging honest, craft-oriented feedback.

Second, I've written a rough draft sex scene that could probably benefit from some gentle feedback. The scene, I'm certain, belongs in my novel. I swear, there really is something about fictional frottage that reveals characters' psychological states. I'm confident, too, that the piece meets certain minimal standards of storytelling. Still, despite my group's agreement that one should never confuse an author and narrator (Kafka presumably never witnessed anyone turn into an insect), I go rigid whenever I imagine others scrutinizing my rough draft sex.

Certainly, there's no reason readers shouldn't be able to critique sex scenes with the same criteria they apply to fiction generally. There's no rational reason to fear the snickers or smirks of my trusted peers. My peers know I'm not my narrator. They're aware that "write what you know," narrowly understood, has never been my guiding principle. This, though, is a bit academic. Down in the dirt, things are different. Extra hands accidentally slip into passages, awkwardly bent knees intrude upon scenes, and flimsy characters deflate at inopportune moments. Stretched metaphors sag, and attempts at erudition turn out to be turnoffs. People, however forgiving, make assumptions.

Sex is a monumental force in most people's lives, whether they're engaging or abstaining, slumming or sleeping their way through distant galaxies. Fair or not, the assumption is that, if you write a bad sex scene, you must be bad in bed. Excluding the "write what you know" fanatics, no reasonable person would expect an author to have every bit of knowledge at his or her disposal. Still, if you write a bad sex scene, you'll be a laughing stock by the end of the first sentence. If you don't believe me, consider the varied implications of different kinds of ignorance. Not long ago, someone in my critique group pointed out that I'd used "engine block" to refer to the space beneath a car's hood when, in fact, the term refers to the metal casing around the cylinders of an internal combustion engine. Not even the two motorheads in my group so much as blinked when I admitted ignorance, despite the fact that my main character is a seasoned cab driver. Ignorance of cars is forgivable. Bumbling around the fictional bedroom is not. It suggests some shameful inadequacy. It hints at some hidden kink or, more embarrassingly, its utter absence.

Usually, we reveal our sexual failures only to one other person at a time. In a writing group, such failures became the subject of collective scrutiny and discussions certain to mortify. In Ladybug's group, we all seemed so bad at sex scenes, so embarrassed and disappointed after every session. To be fair, we were all desperately, bravely trying to hone our skills. However exasperated our sighs or bitter the taste left by certain scenes, we finished every session with new questions and clues about what to show,

how much to tell, and how to get the most out of certain positions. Maybe, in our groping, we were working towards something more fulfilling, or at least less off-putting, one humiliating error at a time. Whether any of us should include sex scenes in our final drafts is a different matter.

Alison Condie Jaenicke

SISTERHOOD OF SPIES

M y daughter peered up into my face and said, "You look like a naked mole rat."

I had forgotten eyeliner that morning. I had taken off my glasses to read the instructions at the exhibit's entrance. "Better to disguise myself," I said, keeping my naked eyes ahead.

Taking on a voice she had discarded long ago, like a snake reverse-shedding its skin, she echoed an instruction she used whenever I made myself look different to her, imploring in her high-pitched, three-year-old voice: "Put yo' glasses on, Mommy!"

I turned to her, raised an eyebrow, asked: "And you're taking on the identity of a toddler? You'd never pass for any age under twelve." She laughed and pushed through the gate.

I took the name Christina Roach. My assigned age was forty-five—younger than my true age, but one I could pass for. I repeated my hometown and birthday again and again in my head: Duluth, Minnesota, July 12, 1966. My destination and the purpose of my trip: Kiev, Ukraine, World Conference of Accountants. This was my cover. I would be asked to regurgitate pieces of it, convincingly, throughout the afternoon as we traversed and interacted with exhibits about bugs, disguises, and history's most famous spies.

We had ridden the Red Line to Gallery Place–Chinatown, walked winter streets to the International Spy Museum, its name lit up in red neon. In lettering made to look like it came directly from an old typewriter ribbon, a large banner spread over the entrance read: "A spy must live a life of lies."

One large exhibit told about disguises created by Hollywood for the CIA. Before-and-after pictures showed people transformed with accoutrements of all kinds: moustaches and wigs, eyeglasses and pipes, fake noses and eye color–changing contacts. Within this exhibit, a flock of nuns bent toward a glass display box holding objects of disguise. Another group of nuns horseshoed around a computer screen that offered a challenge: recognize a disguised agent in action. One nun sat in the center with earphones on. They all wore black tunics, black veils lined with white, white coifs framing their faces. Heavy silver crosses dangled on thick chains that reached nearly to their waists. Only their height and the size of their gold-framed glasses distinguished them. (I wondered whether they were told that they could only wear glasses that were decidedly unfashionable, that gave off a John Denver vibe.) One of the nuns looked at me with eyes enlarged by her lenses, owl-like. She blinked. Her eyes appeared empty, revealed nothing, transmitted nothing.

Could I pick one of them out of a lineup if she were dressed differently, if hair were exposed or clothing changed? Likely not. They aim to blend in—not into the secular scene of the museum (everyone must have been eyeing them) but blend in with each other—just like the flock of grackles Maggie and I saw spread and swaying on the dark branches of a large bare tree in front of the Capitol Building's bone-colored dome.

We traveled on through glitzy displays, our new identities flitting in our minds, threatening to fly away if we didn't pin them down. Maggie and I wandered, lost each other. I came to a segment called "Sisterhood of Spies." Marlene Dietrich, femme fatale, who performed in body-hugging dresses and a Swansdown coat, loomed above me, right next to a life-sized black-and-white photo of Mata Hari, with her jeweled bra and headdress, bangles around biceps and wrists, exposed belly and bellybutton leading to a low, full, rich silk swoop of skirt.

Facts: Born in the Netherlands in 1876, Margaretha Zelle married at eighteen, bore two children, left her older husband after eight years and fled to Paris, where she reinvented herself as an Indian temple dancer, trained in the exotic dances of the East. She took aristocratic lovers and the stage name Mata Hari, performed all over Europe in diaphanous shawls, which seemed to hide little. (In truth, though, she was covered by a body stocking.) About her work, she said: "My dance is a sacred poem in which each movement is a word and whose every word is underlined by music." About her life: "I have always lived for love and pleasure."

Nearing age forty, her dancing days behind her, she accepted a lucrative assignment to spy for France during World War I, tossed gossip to Germans as she seduced them, got labeled a double agent and caged in a French jail. Her code name was H21. In October 1917, at age forty-one, standing before a French firing squad for her alleged espionage for the Germans, she refused the blindfold, stared straight at her executioners.

Mata Hari means "Mother of God" in Sanskrit and "Eye of Dawn" in Indonesian. *Mata Hari: Mistress of the Kama Sutra. Mata Hari: High Priestess of the Temple of Love. Mata Hari: The Most Notorious Spy in History.* So many labels, so many ways to present oneself.

On the day of her execution, in addition to her lawyer, a captain, and a priest, she was visited and accompanied by two sisters of charity, who gently woke her on that morning and stayed with her through the last moments of her life. At the age of fourteen, she had been sent to a convent school to be trained in the domestic arts in preparation for marriage—the proper upbringing for young women of her class. Nuns punctuated her life, from first to last.

I tried to put on the eyes of a nun to see what she would see when she got to this sultry exhibit, this reference to Russian "honey traps," this advertisement for a Valentine "sexpionage" evening at the museum, entitled "Spies, Lies, and Naked Thighs." Would the nun's hands fumble beneath her robes to feel for her own shape, trace the lines of breast and hip; would spangles sparkle behind her closed eyelids?

Sexuality can root out secrets, raise them from dark depths—that's why these women made good spies—and yet sexuality breeds secrecy, shame, lies, and denial.

In this town of secrets and silences, of layers and lies, this town that is my hometown but no longer my home, the city with the largest number of spies in the world, the city most outsiders would say has no sex appeal, I have been a virgin, a lover, and a double agent. I have worn a basketball uniform and a Pizza Hut get-up. I have worn stockings with a pin-striped suit and bare legs with a bikini. I have donned black cap and gown, white wedding gown, and nightgowns both flannel and filmy. I have seen the world through contacts and eyeglasses and closed lids. I have spoken English and French, pig Latin and slang. Cut my hair short, let it grow long, dyed it blonde, and left it mousy brown. Bore a child and bore treachery. Hid and told secrets, lied (sometimes to the same people, sometimes different, sometimes to myself), stepped into a confessional and stepped out to say my Hail Marys and Our Fathers.

My experience with nuns is slim, but I have an aunt who entered a convent as a teen and left after one day. She went on to become a wife, mother, teacher, lover of beaches and Grey Goose vodka, with an infectious cackle-laugh.

Maybe it's true that Mata Hari was a double agent for France and Germany. Maybe it's not. She was a double agent in other ways, anyway: a mother and sex worker, say, roles that are difficult to reconcile.

In truth, Maggie never told me I looked like a naked mole rat that day. Maybe it was my son instead. Maybe it was neither. Maybe they were my thoughts, and I gave her those words. (My kids accuse me—and rightly so—of fabricating stories from thin threads of truth.)

Perhaps what she said as we stood on the verge of assuming our fake IDs was this: "What identity would you choose if you could choose anything?" And to answer her question would be nearly impossible.

I could tell my teenage daughter—born Margaret, called Maggie—to look at the grackles near the Capitol, see how they take on no identity except that of black-habited bird in the sky or ground or limb, swooping together or alone. I could remind her of the Bible verse: "Consider the lilies, how they grow: they neither toil nor spin; yet I tell you, even Solomon in all his glory was not clothed like one of these." But enacting this advice spouted by a long-ago human—advice that seems applicable today only to birds or lilies or naked mole rats—will prove tricky to any of us girls taught to shape and reinvent ourselves, fashion and fabricate, disguise and reveal, every one of us a trained double agent.

Luisa Kolker

Brian was my hair stylist. He was super cute and not gay, at least not then, in 1984.

We flirted a little bit every time I sat on his chair and he sculpted my shoulder-length hair into something nice and professional. He had a girlfriend and I had a boyfriend, but we had one-hour-long flirtations once every six weeks or so, while I sat in his chair in the posh salon on Wisconsin Avenue in Georgetown.

In a desperate attempt to assuage the depression and sense of purposelessness that'd been creeping up on me since I started working right after college, I was working at four different jobs: by day, I edited a financial newsletter; by night and weekends, I assistant-produced for a small theater company, freelanced writing ad copy, and volunteered on the staff of a local small press literary magazine.

As far as I can recollect, the object of all this over-busyness was to (a) feel like I had something going on in my life, and (b) distract me from the fact that I had nothing going on in my life.

Yes, I had a handsome boyfriend, a smart, chiseled, aspiring literary critic employed at the *Washington Post Book Review*. He once inscribed the *Oxford English Dictionary* he'd given me as a birthday present with these words: "With love and concern for your usage of the English language."

Yes, I was gainfully and even somewhat engagingly employed.

Yes, I lived and worked in a trendy part of downtown Washington, D.C.

But it all felt pointless. I felt pointless. And empty. My teenage wildness and the wilderness inside of me had been tamed. The eighteen-year-old who hitchhiked across the country with her transsexual friend, the punk rocker girl with hot pink hair. What the hell happened to her?

When I walked over the bridge overlooking Rock Creek Parkway to and from work every day, I fantasized uncontrollably of leaning a little too far over the railing and somersaulting over, arms and legs akimbo, landing in an inert heap in the middle of the perennial flow of traffic. I knew it probably meant there was something wrong with me. But the images and the abrupt end of the fantasy happened every time.

I liked the way Brian touched my head and leaned down in front of me, holding wisps of my damp hair on either side of my face to make sure they were even. I liked the friendliness of his touch when he washed my hair. The way he massaged my head, like we had all the time in the world, would bring me to the verge of tears, which I controlled by digging my fingernails into the palms of my hands.

I was twenty-six years old and I had nothing to look forward to.

It was June or July. I was sitting in Brian's chair at the salon. He was combing out my hair. "Look, you already have a few gray hairs! Don't worry, in ten years you'll be sitting right here and I'll get to color your hair for you."

That was it. That was the moment of "the choice." Me here, in this tamed and urbane salon chair in ten years? Me here, the highlight of my month being the sixty minutes I'm laughing overly loud at my hair stylist's jokes? Me, here, in ten years? Till my hair is gray?

"Cut it off," I said to Brian. "What?" he asked. "My hair. Cut it really, really short." "What's going on?" he asked.

"Just cut it," I said. And he did. That night I wrote a twenty-page manifesto. My freedom manifesto. My wake-the-fuck-up-and-do-something-outrageous-NOW manifesto.

The something outrageous didn't happen immediately, but it did six months later. And the haircut was the beginning of it all.

Leonard Kress

THE THEORY OF BETA DECAY

M y father told me that the one thing he regretted in life was not taking up Harry Kemp's offer to spend the summer with him and his girlfriend in Provincetown. Harry Kemp was a famous hobo and moocher and part-time memoirist, his *Tramping on Life* a classic in the genre. My father met him at a jazz club in the Village. Kemp got him to spring for drinks and a steak dinner. My father was a grad student at Columbia at the time, and when he told the story (which he did on several occasions), he lowered his eyes almost coquettishly when he mentioned the girlfriend. I suppose he was hoping I couldn't comprehend the idea of the three of them sharing a bedroom.

HE MUST HAVE met Kemp several times afterwards, because he claimed to have a signed first edition of the book, though he couldn't remember where it was. My father was working towards his PhD in chemistry, with ventures into biochem, and he was one of a handful of students who were studying with Enrico Fermi, who had recently arrived at Columbia, a year after winning the Nobel Prize for his discovery of slow neutrons. Fermi was young and vibrant, still in his thirties, grateful to have escaped the pernicious fascism of 1930s Italy.

WHEN MY KIDS were teenagers, and deeply involved in musical theatre, they were the only ones who knew why the high school in *Zombie Prom* was named Enrico Fermi High. *Zombie Prom* was a terrible play about a high school student in the 1950s, who turned into a zombie after venturing too close to the town's nuclear plant. In the musical, he returns to take the popular girl to the prom. It was really just one more remake of the Elvis story. My kids were frustrated that no one in the production, including the director and stage manager, cared about their connection, and they only made it into the chorus.

WHEN I FINALLY read *Tramping on Life*—it wasn't until I was in college that I managed to find a copy—I was struck by its self-congratulatory tone. "This innocence stuff is overrated," he wrote, and advised sending a college kid to a prostitute named Jennie, who'd been hired by a fraternity to deal with innocents like him. Better Jennie than "horning in and jeopardizing" some good girl. Kemp seemed to have no qualms sleeping with other men's wives, whisking them off to his shack in the dunes. He was responsible for breaking up a number of marriages, mostly those of his benefactors.

ONE OF MY father's classmates was the sci-fi writer Isaac Asimov. According to my father he was still a teenager in grad school, who often took catnaps in an empty cabinet in the lab. They used to go out for pasta and chianti on Saturdays after long days in the lab scorching beakers and dipping pipettes. Asimov always covered the bill because he had extra income from selling his stories to *Astounding Science Fiction* magazine. Asimov never worked with Fermi, though he wanted to. And, according to my father, he was there the night he met Harry Kemp, though he left early. My father appears briefly in one of Asimov's short stories. He doesn't remember which one, though it would be hard to check because Asimov published over four hundred short stories and it could have been unpublished. My guess is that it could have been "The Magnificent Possession," (1940) about a chemist who creates spray-on aluminum and has to deal with the patent-hungry mob and crooked politicians. In the end, his project has to be abandoned because it produces an unbearable stink.

IN GRAD SCHOOL, in what I now see as a misguided tribute to my father, I wrote a paper on Harry Kemp. We were studying marginalized writers—women, African and Native Americans and Latinos, gays—and I wondered what it would be like to write about someone who willingly chose marginal status, even cultivated it. However, I couldn't stomach Kemp's depraved self-revelations. How as a twelve-year-old, he seduced his even younger cousin while they were sharing a bedroom, his aunt shouting up the stairs, "Come to breakfast, lazy bones!" Harry Kemp and the carnivalesque, Bakhtin's perfect "degrader figure." A few days later, he found her body under the bed, her face and pretty white neck burned from the carbolic acid she drank. "Poor kid," he wrote.

Judith McCombs

My Life in Crime

E xploring, we called it—this was after the war, the big war, the late
1940s. Little towns way out West, Idaho and California mostly, where
my father's government survey party would stop for two or three
months. When their elevations and triangulations were done, we'd move
on, in convoy, trucks and Dad's office trailer in front, our house trailer following, more trucks at the tail.

Go out and play, the grownups said back then, and off we'd go, me
and my smaller sister. Old deserted houses, closed-off sheds, once a dark
shut-up barn—I still have the scar, like a shiny peapod on my knee, from
when I crawled onto a long sharp piece of glass that was lying in the soft
dust under the barn wall. This happened in Twin Falls, Idaho, the week our
baby brother was born.

Only one place was really scary—the two tramps' beds somewhere
in the California desert, with their big footprints, and their fireplace still
smelling of smoke. I got my sister out of there fast. We must have left
footprints, but we hadn't messed with anything.

All next summer Dad's survey party stayed at Ridgecrest, outside the
Naval Ordinance Test Station. I was just old enough to catch the station's
free bus by myself on Saturdays, go to their library and then their movie
matinees. *Daughter of Don Q* was the serial I loved: each week she had
to save her father's inheritance from murderous, lying thieves. She was
dangerous and beautiful, and so brave with her bow and arrows—the bow
was about as tall as me. I loved the scary but somehow triumphant music
at the end. Saturday nights, while Mother read old bedtime stories to my
sister, I sat in the living room with Dad, and told him the latest triumph of
the *Daughter of Don Q*.

One Saturday I left the library early, for no reason, and wandered over
to the station's deserted wartime barracks—rows and rows, all painted
white, with little porches, and no one around to chase me off. I jumped at
windows to see inside and tried the locked doors. One pushed open, and
I slipped in. Black metal bed frames, dozens on each side of the long center aisle, each perfectly aligned. Shipshape, Dad would have said. Empty
shelves and cabinets, no dust, no fingerprints. Two metal trunks, big as
bathtubs, without any locks. I didn't lift their lids. My steps were sounding
louder, too loud without my sister—I got out in a hurry. All clear.

Early the next year we stayed at Pomona fairgrounds—that was our favorite place to explore—even though little Freddy, Dad's boss's kid, was tagging along with us. Under the open bleachers, we kicked at the dust, squatted down to rake it with our fingers, found things that people dropped. A signal ring that looked like a prize from Crackerjack. A wadded-up lacy handkerchief that we tossed—who wants snot? A ticket that still looked new. Two dimes my sister found—she gave me the dull one. A shiny penny that Freddy got to keep, for luck.

We left the fairgrounds office alone for weeks, though when I jumped at the back porch windows, it was always empty. Closed down for the season, Mother said. We had to use a rickety wood box to boost me in, by the unlatched porch window. Then I opened the back door for the other two. Inside we checked out everything—the hot plate, the coffee mugs and sugar bowl in the cupboard—I boosted Freddy up to see first, and then my sister. When Freddy looked away she put a licked finger in to taste the sugar. We saved the desks for last. Nothing but a chipped glass ashtray, old files, an official handbook in the bigger desk. But in the smaller one a lady's comb and one bobby pin, alongside the forms, carbons, office stuff—and under my hand, three quarters that I took.

Who told? Freddy, it must have been. Two policemen knocked on our trailer door late the next afternoon, just before dinner. They looked bigger than Dad in their blue uniforms. They had nightsticks and holstered pistols, and the jowly one grunted in a mean way while they walked me and Dad through the scene of the crime.

Dad kept telling them and me that I was the one responsible—nine was plenty old enough to know right from wrong. We weren't vandals, Dad pointed out, but we, meaning me, had to understand that we couldn't break into places, even if we didn't break anything. Did I understand? I had to nod, say Yes, and how truly sorry I was to the county policemen, whose time I was wasting.

It was still trespassing, the sour-faced, jowly officer said, and trespass-ing was a crime, against the law for everyone, kids included. I knew better than to say Forgive us our trespasses, from Sunday School. All I could say was I did understand now and I was very very sorry.

Dad kept blaming me, making me feel smaller in front of them. From now on I had to stay where he or Mother could keep an eye on me, until I could prove I knew what was right and what was wrong. Did I understand why he had to say that? And no allowance for this month. Yes, and Yes, I had to say.

I understood, all too well. I'd let him down, and Mother too. I'd been trusted and I'd taken my sister and Freddy where they shouldn't be, and set a bad example, and shamed my father's survey party. I *was* ashamed.

But not enough to confess about the three quarters I'd found, and was keeping, which more than made up for my lost allowance.

Frances Park

MEET ME AT THE BAYOU

There are still times while slipping into REM the dream stage not the band when I find myself back on that treacherous staircase from hell as if it's still there and I'm still in strappy high heels negotiating each step down. I'm in fog, a voodoo fog, *Don't fall, don't fall, don't you dare friggin' fall...* Yet I do, always, lose my footing then jerk awake under the sheets.

Crazy, I know.

The actual set of steps, steep and narrow and a mile long in memory, led from the main floor to the balcony level of the Washington, D.C., night-club where I worked one summer as a cocktail waitress. Part of the job was looking cool, not tripping flat on your face though frankly you couldn't slip through the cracks if you tried given the trains of people jamming both directions. Party! Still, it instilled something in me with staying power; wobbly and fearful and beyond my realm. Yet it makes no sense as I was having the time of my life, ever conscious of my finger on the pulse of what it meant to be alive that iconic moment in time, movin' and groovin' along with everyone else. Riding the American rock 'n' roll wave in those days possibly meant more to me than you but don't worry, this isn't that story. Not really.

This is the story, no, backspace, not a story, a glimpse, a dreamy sliver from the summer of 1976. And if I've lost the writing fire of my youth, so be it—no flowery prose or highbrow poetics goin' on here. Don't need no imagination cuz this ain't fiction. It all happened at The Bayou.

Located under the Whitehurst Freeway in an old building on the Georgetown waterfront—a neglected plot in those days—the legendary club was known for premier house bands that electrified the stage, two levels of dance floors and bars, dollar ten cocktails, and unapologetic debauchery. Loud and cavernous, before its incarnation as The Bayou, it apparently had a storied and checkered past, unclear to me but something about a mob hit back in the thirties, I think. During daylight hours when the joint was deserted, ghosts, very shady ghosts, likely roamed their old haunt. But the seventies were my era and I can tell you there still wasn't a polished note in the hazy, votive candle-lit air—everybody drank and smoked and did unspeakable things in the dark, you didn't think not to. Our families in 'burbs such as my hometown of Springfield eating Colonel

Sanders Kentucky Fried Chicken and watching *Happy Days* would choke on their chicken wings.

Just x-ed out a line about remembering every corner like yesterday because I'm no historian and whatever I'm reliving is obviously dimmed by time and mental mist. Consider this: My recollection that the steps were wooden and creaky as skeletons is seared in my soul but if you said, No, darlin', they were covered by a burgundy booze-soaked carpet, I wouldn't argue. On the other hand, though The Bayou was infamously razed in 1999, I'll leave my memories standing. Don't we always?

Monday night was Blues Night when the Nighthawks took the stage and played honky-tonk, hell-raisin', foot-stompin' sets shades of Little Feat that could make an old biddy boogie. Tuesday night was Ladies' Night when guys on the prowl got girls with Charlie-perfumed hair drunk on fifty-five cent drinks. The other nights were so busy they didn't need a name, packing in more bodies on two thumping floors than fire code allowed. Bands like Face Dancer, Sinbad, and Cherry People (or was it Cherry Smash or both?) rocked cover songs from Pink Floyd and Led Zeppelin and Yes and David Bowie, etc. All album material, some original compositions, no disco shit. Wanna know something? I can actually hear "Dark Side of the Moon" as I'm typing this...

The music, amped up and deafening, brought out the zoo in you and suddenly this was life, real life, high voltage just the way it was meant to be—yeah!—and nearly every face I'd ever known in my twenty-one years seemed to pass through these doors during one of my shifts or another as I, soaking up the magic as I was living it, snaked my way through the madding crowd on the balcony level where I claimed a station for two reasons.

One, the ladies' room was here—an easy scoot, no stairs to face. Decrepit glam, it was a throwback to the thirties with an enormous powder room that housed a dozen or so parlor chairs facing an L-shaped mirror (or was it U-shaped?) crowded with female reflections all hair, lipstick, and chatter. Two, I liked it up here where the tone was a pitch more civilized. You could even catch your breath every so often as you held a tray high above your head, balancing Michelobs and Tom Collins and screwdrivers while racing back and forth from table to bar all night till two a.m. Before the end of the first week I went down two jean sizes.

Night One I walked around in a white tube top with pink-coral bells, hair swept up in a long ponytail revealing dangly earrings plus a ruby stud for statement. The look was tied together with a sweet little white apron my mom made for me—my tip drawer, you might say. She was a whiz with a sewing needle having spent part of her schoolgirl days making uniforms for the Imperial Army when Korea was under Japanese Occupation and then later in life shortening the arms of her husband's shirts—in their early days here you couldn't find clothes off the rack in Korean-man size. Anyway, my ensemble wasn't exactly thrown together as my younger sister Ginger vividly recounts me modeling my outfits in front of the mirror for hours on end. I guess I went to great lengths to feel beautiful even if I feared it was all an ornamental lie. But mirror model today? For my wedding last year I picked out a dress online—granted, a gorgeous shimmery dress—and tried it on only once before the Big Day.

Ah, but this was then. *Every* day was a big day. Or night. Can't forget the sparkly lip gloss and dressed-up eyes, much to my dad's chagrin. For the longest time he pictured me at ten forever, a Madame Curie in the making. When he realized I favored pen and paper over Bunsen burners, *Even better, Fran!* A voracious reader hungry for signs of meaningful life— Tolstoy, Saint Augustine, Pearl Buck—he was already having delusions of my grandeur before my eleventh birthday.

My Fran will be world renowned!

I'm wincing as I type this: Had my father lived to see the sale of my novel announced in the *New York Times*, no one would've been prouder. And had he lived to see that same book in the Dollar Store a few years later, no one's heart would've cracked louder.

Now that I'm his age when he passed away, older even, I wonder what he made of a bookish daughter who began to show signs of a party girl who loved to come alive after midnight. I think it bothered him, it must have, but he wouldn't let it bother him too much. Keeping peace was always preferable even when his face was a megaphone:

My Fran doesn't need makeup!

But of course I did, and here's a story whose humor may be lost in the telling: One time as a teenager I was sitting next to him in our white Pontiac Tempest in the driveway. I'm zoning in here and to understand this sentiment you'd have to know firsthand the cruelty of strangers, so cruel I'd be happy to hear they were all dead: Our world in this warm little sacred cube was ours, all ours. No one could hurt me here. I was safe.

About to turn on the ignition, he hesitated.

"Close your eyes, Fran."

A gift? It wasn't my birthday. I couldn't read his mood but if anything it seemed playful and I closed my eyes, expecting a surprise but not exactly the one I got. In a move as uncharacteristic as him breaking into the Bump in The Bayou, he wiped my eyelids clean of Maybelline.

"There's my Fran!"

BUT TONIGHT I was boss, in full glitter and glory. Whenever I bounced by one particular table I'd hear "Hey, Miss Universe!"

Turn the clock back to 1962 when I would slip on my mom's white high heels and pretend I'd just been crowned Miss America, holding imaginary roses and crying with joy—*Thank you, thank you!* Seeing as I was who I was, the coronation was laughable on every level. Fast forward to 1976.

"Hey, Miss Universe!"

You only own that title once in your life, so smile. Oh, but they could never have me, that was the power, that was the high.

Not that I was an angel but compared to the other waitresses who were rougher around the edges and well acquainted with the underbelly of club life, I was. Another difference was that for me, the only college girl, this was a rockin' dream summer job, a wild scene but make no mistake, not my life. I wouldn't be doing this when I was twenty-*two*, for God's sakes. Oh, wait, there was another college girl, an art student from New York whose name escapes me but not her exquisite Jacqueline Bisset looks, ruined whenever she opened her mouth.

"So these guys promised me a ride home tonight if I partied with them after work. D'ya think I can trust them?"

That night and a couple of other nights early on she asked if I could drive her home to a group house in Georgetown where she was living that summer. She was mindful of giving me gas money—a quarter, your average tip per drink—which was decent of her and I took it because a quarter was measurable money back then.

If I wasn't the only college girl, I was definitely the only waitress with a foreign face—nothing new; mine was unique everywhere I went, so I held it high. I was also, as far as I could tell, the only girl who had no interest in sleeping with the band, so to say. In my own head my insecurities blared louder than any Bose speaker but I'd rather barrel down the staircase in front of a packed house than show them to anyone, much less to some musician who'd played with my boobs and then dumped me. During a training period that lasted all of ten minutes, I heard all I needed to hear:

"I went to bed with him and now the bastard acts like he doesn't know me. What do I do? How can I get him back?"

Momentarily she was circled by her comrades, all obviously well versed in humiliation. Right then I knew my place wasn't inside their circle and I honestly can't recall a conversation with any of them except for the art student who didn't last the whole summer. Being outside the circle, any circle, was where I was most comfortable, anyway. When you're different, you don't assume you'll be invited to the party, you don't even assume your second-grade teacher will treat you equally, which she didn't, so unless someone throws themselves at you, you never say a word. In that sense you're always a loner, even in the company of friends, to some degree. Jeez, why am I saying *you*? Of course I mean *me* who never once came across another Korean-American student during my entire education, from kindergarten through college.

But back to the local rock gods with great hair and sexy moves. Even if they were sweet guys with college degrees, I was always more drawn to the thinker in the corner, then and now. My husband, who I picture as a baby in a crib full of books not blankets, has lamented to me on more than one occasion:

"Why wasn't I in D.C. that summer? We could've met at The Bayou and had ten grandchildren by now."

He's joking. Isn't he? At any age, fifty-eight or twenty-one, Gabriel would've never stood in line, flashed his ID, paid a cover charge—a dollar fifty on weekdays, two dollars on the weekends—and entered the divine dive that was The Bayou, not in this life or the one after that or the one after that, period. Mentally, we were on different planets, he studying in Jerusalem and me serving up drinks at a nightclub. Circling different moons. Still, he claims that *had* our paths crossed, it would've been love at first sight. He's joking. He must be.

Now that first night I did meet a boy, handsome but a bit conservative with preppy brown hair and a shirt vaguely disco. From his first line, Paul was curiously familiar to me, a Boston boy with a girl-crazy Bahhston persona. Our comic bond was instant.

"Vahhka Tahhnic, please!"

"Uh, I don't think so!"

Why the exclamation points, you ask? We were shouting over the music!

"Why nahht!?"

"I don't see a stamp on your hand!"

"I'll be twent-one ahhn July 17!"

"Hey, that's my dad's birthday!"

"It's in the stahhs!"

"Are you from Boston?"

"Bahhston bahhn and bred!"

"I was born there, too!"

"What'd I tell you? It's in the stahhs!"

But of course, the stars. A little gleam in your eye can make you stay in a moment.

"You're so exahhtic! Wanna dance?"

"Sorry! I can't dance until midnight!"

Midnight was the magic hour when cocktail waitresses, if we didn't mind losing two hours of tips, could rip off our aprons and hit the dance floor. Having spent my preteen years dreaming of being a go-go dancer on *Hullabaloo* while listening to WPGC or spinning 45s on a blue and white polka dot record player, you might say I loved to dance.

My dad, a World Banker who traveled too much, relayed a sweet story to me: He was in London one day when a pop song wafted out of a clothing boutique on Carnaby Street, a song that reminded him of his daughter a-go-go in a rec room across the ocean. He went in, coming out with a very mod-looking top, lime green with sequins, something Twiggy would wear. The wow factor told me a shop girl had picked it out for my dad.

"I felt like you were with me, Fran."

For years the top stood out in my closet like neon. When I think about it now, I grow sad.

Of the two dance floors at The Bayou, I preferred the one on the main level. It was bigger with more exposure; even people leaning over the balcony railing were watching, and I liked that, all those eyes on us. At this age, dancing for me was a kind of striptease of the soul—look but don't touch. My moment, however, was always upstaged whenever this one particular girl would show up. A blonde baby doll, she could boogie like it was nobody's business. Damn! I was gonna be outdanced.

My husband, bless his sweet lying heart, says I still have the moves even when the moves are more Frankensteinian than seductive. But I'm digressing...

"Wanna pahhty when you get off?"

"Sorry! I have a boyfriend!"

Off and on, anyway. His name was Mark, we both went to Virginia Tech and were home for the summer but the love wasn't there no matter how many times we said it. Some good times but not love, never love. Without digging deep here, our history had made us resentful and immature and say some really shitty things you can never take back so no surprise that midway through my Bayou stint we broke up—again—and I began spending time with Paul, during and after hours. A little dancin' and romancin', sweet and harmless, was just what the doctor ordered. A student at UMass, he was working as an intern for the Treasury Department, his second summer in a row, doing all the right things against a wild-streaked will. Over and over, as if sensing a tremor from a future quake, he'd deliver with heart-crushing angst:

"Francie, I don't want to end up working for the government and getting married and settling down in the suburbs. I don't want to do it. God damn it, that's just not who I am."

Me, neither. IN ALL CAPS.

"Then don't, Paul. No one's making you do it."

Poor guy would do all those things by age thirty; fall into the traditional crack. I'm no shrink but I've always wondered if it had something to do with two brothers. One brother, his identical twin, a hellraiser who smoked a lot of dope, dropped out of college, and eventually lived the life Paul wished he was living. The other brother, apparently challenged, would always need caring for. Someone had to be the responsible brother.

IN 2001 PAUL wondered if we could meet for lunch, having run into me through the years not at The Bayou but here and there in the 'burbs and the city, occasionally even wandering into a sweet little fabled chocolate shop I happen to co-own with my sister. His first time in, it was as a customer.

"Do you take Mastercahhd?" he asked.

I'm not making that up, nor this: In the quarter century since we'd actually sat down together, not a minute seemed to have passed. We were twenty-one again, just like that. The space we'd carved out for ourselves so long ago was still there after all these years, waiting for us to flesh out again. Not for dancin' or romancin', just to say "Hey, our time together was special, wasn't it?" After lunch my parting words were:

"Meet me at The Bayou."

He smiled, still handsome, going gray.

These days I'm still in touch with both Paul and Mark in an "I'm-still-in-this-world-and-you're-still-in-this-world" kind of way. Not in a way they would or could ever save me from a fall, not in real life and not in my dreams. But once upon a time I could count on one or the other to visit me during my shift and stay with me till closing and funny how in memory, however flawed, it gives me a warm fuzzy feeling to revisit those late nights when they would help me blow out votive candles, place empty beer bottles back into their appropriately labeled cases, prop chairs on tables, upside down. I'd retrieve my tip money from my apron and count it like a poor paupette. Then it was time to climb down that staircase, holding onto the railing for dear life.

THE SUMMER AFTER I met Paul, a girlfriend and I decided on a spur-of-the-moment to drive up to Boston to spend Thanksgiving with my relatives. From a phone booth in Harvard Square, I called to see if he was home. His dad answered. It was my only conversation with the man but I remember his voice, the voice of a good man; I understand he passed away quite a while ago. Mark's father died last week and that he outlived my dad by thirty-five years is a crime, enough said. And then there's Lydia, the only friend in present day I could imagine with me at The Bayou way back when and maybe even now, let our hair down and dance with strangers and sing, just for one lawless night, *We don't have birthdays anymore, we're like the store—Forever 21.* She lost her dad, an esteemed Princeton professor, to cancer just a few months ago. At least he lived to grow old and see grandchildren.

So all fathers go but mine went first.

THE NIGHT BEFORE I went away to college—not cross country, just cross state—I went out with friends. It seemed like the thing to do, party and say goodbye. When I left the house, my dad was on the couch in the living room, the same place he often sat to read and be alone with his thoughts, though there were times he'd ask me to join him so we could talk about Life. He was nursing a drink, most likely a Scotch, his drink of choice.

"Bye, Dad."

"Bye, Fran."

Hours later when I returned he was still there, in the same spot. I didn't know what he'd been doing or what was going through his mind, whether that was the same Scotch or another one. But I did know it was hard for him to let his children go.

ONE NIGHT I forgot my apron. There was probably an extra apron or a jar behind the bar where I could stash my tips. The minor emergency would've been forgotten by morning if not for one thing. Fairly early into my shift, I heard:

"Your dad's downstairs!"

Downstairs...

Downstairs...

Downstairs...

My dad? In *The Bayou*? Why, for God's sakes? To my knowledge, my father had never driven to partying Georgetown, how did he know how to even get here? Where did he park? I couldn't picture him, a dignified man—much less a dignified Korean man—in The Bayou. How insulting to his senses. How mortifying to mine. When you walked in here, you pretty much abandoned who you were in the 'burbs. Yanked out of one dimension and into another, no doubt I stood at the top of the staircase ready to trip my ass off.

Don't fall, don't fall, don't you dare friggin' fall...

When I saw my dad—there he is, near the entrance—it was like spotting a polar bear in Hawaii. *It can't be....* My identity as his daughter went up in smoke with my painted lips, eyes done up to dazzle in the dark. Would he even recognize me??

"Fran!"

He waved my way, seemingly oblivious to the stomping audience and ear-splitting amps, the crazed haze that was The Bayou.

"Fran!"

Suddenly it was just the two of us in our walled-off, incubated world. We may as well have been in the living room discussing Tolstoy.

"Dad," I said, noticing something in his hands, "what are you doing here?"

"I brought your apron."

"You drove all the way from Springfield to bring me my apron?"

Whenever my college friends got letters from home, they were always from their moms. But my dad wrote me, too, whenever he had a moment to spare, whether from his desk at the World Bank during his lunch hour or the Erawan Hotel in Bangkok before bed. Sharing his reflections du jour was a calming pastime for him.

"Yah, Fran. You left it on the banister."

My sister Ginger, then a pipsqueak of thirteen, insists she had come along for the ride and was at The Bayou, too, that night, with our dad. But I can't see her. Underage, maybe she wasn't allowed past the entrance. Maybe time blurred her from the picture.

"Thanks, Dad," I said, backing up into the bowels of The Bayou to return to duty. What else was I supposed to do? Invite him in?? "Drive home carefully, OK?"

"Yah."

A thought comes to mind: Had I known I would lose him to a stroke three years later, lose him forever, I would've dropped my apron, run out of The Bayou and grabbed my father so hard he could've never left this Earth, not even if God, the angels, and fate willed it.

WHILE TRYING TO make sense of a staircase probably more menacing in memory, I'm reminded of something Lydia said to me. We're women with little free time so when we get together, each minute feels sacred and secret. *Talk to me. No one's listening.* Last November, just before Thanksgiving, she stopped by my shop to pick me up, along with some chocolate treats. Then we went for coffee at Au Bon Pain a block away. The hour was dusk.

Divorced now for a couple of years, she began telling me about a man she was seeing. Red flags went up left and right but I held my tongue as she, in a charming if not absent manner, arranged little nuggets of chocolate-covered toffees on a napkin as if we were sitting down to a game of chess. But the game of love was what she was really playing and she needed to make a move. Red flags wave forever. And no one's Forever 21.

"Run," I said.

Hoping for some reaction, she, no meek woman, added meekly, "The sex is good."

"Run."

"Doesn't that count for something?"

"No, Lydia. Run."

She nodded airily, moving her chocolate nuggets around, eating one or two in the process and still talking about him as if to convince the universe he was worth a little more time. But at our ages, you don't play with candy. You do that when you're young and it's fun. In the midst of a sentence, her face changed.

"As I say this all aloud, it's so clear to me."

AS I PUT this all on paper, it's so clear to me, too: Some nights when I'm drifting off, the beauty of life comes off like makeup and I know in my heart of hearts, my darkest heart, the one beating at the top of a staircase, that I'm no longer safe and my dad will never, ever meet me at The Bayou again.

Ginger Peters

CHEWING, SPITTING, AND KISSING

Granny never lived with us. She was way too independent for that. But out of the seven children she bore, three of them lived in the same town and one lived a little over an hour away, so loved ones were checking on her regularly. She was a short, round cheerful lady made up of Irish, American Indian, and just plain old toughness. She made it through life by chewing, spitting, and cussing.

Granny, born in 1904, was one of fourteen children who grew up on a ranch in central Texas. Her father was a Texas Ranger and seldom home. According to her recollections, her mother was the "meanest woman that ever lived." She used to tell the kids she "was going to whip them," on Friday, then lay the switch on the kitchen table and make them wait three or four days before their beating. And, according to Granny, she never forgot. I saw a photo of her once, with all of her children around her and those eyes looked like they would just soon kill you than to look at you, so I believed Granny spoke the truth.

Granny earned her toughness growing up with a kind father who was gone a lot and a brutal mother who was left alone most of the time with fourteen children, fifty miles away from town. She remembered her older sister was a trick horse rider who performed for rodeos and various events for money. One morning, the sister was practicing at home, and a rattlesnake spooked the horse she was riding. Ten minutes later, the sister lay dead in the corner of the corral with a broken neck. Granny's mother told Iva, Granny's name, and her brother to throw her in the back of the wagon and take her to the town morgue. She didn't want wild animals trying to dig up the body. So Granny drove a team of horses over fifty miles with her dead sister in the back of a wagon, covered up with a horse blanket. When they returned two days later, their mother had killed the rattlesnake with a hoe and shot the horse. Granny and her other siblings were responsible for hauling off the horse too.

Granny played the piano at church every Sunday. Just a little country church in a small wooden building, where a few of the area ranchers gathered from time to time to worship the Lord. Granny was eighteen years old, still not married, and enjoyed playing the piano for the worshippers.

Every once in a while they would hold a dance where a few people would play bluegrass music on old guitars, fiddles, and banjos. Granny decided to attend one of the dances. This was a mistake, because she didn't have an escort and wasn't engaged to anyone. She came alone, independent and proud, just wanting to have a fun night out. My grandpa happened to be there. That's how they met, so Granny and Tom danced the night away. The next morning at church, Granny was relieved of her piano playing duties by the church deacons, indicating she was nothing but a "loose" woman to attend the Saturday night dance unescorted. Granny never stepped foot in a church again, except for the funerals that would inevitably come her way.

Granny ended up marrying Tom Tucker. Yep, that was my grandpa's name. Just like the song, "Old Tom Tucker." He moved Granny to southeastern New Mexico, where they bought some acreage and built a three-room house, an outhouse, and a small barn. They began to raise cattle and a few goats. Now the area they settled in was rough country. Their closest neighbor was at least twenty miles away and their home set in a draw about twenty-five miles south of the Carlsbad Caverns and about thirty-five miles south of Carlsbad, New Mexico. There were snakes, coyotes, bobcats, mountain lions, cactus, and rock hard dirt. There were monsoons in the summer, unbearable heat the rest of the time, and in the winter, back before climate change, it could snow hard, and bitter north winds would whip through the couple's small, uninsulated home with a vengeance. But that didn't stop them from setting up a fairly nice ranch, making a pretty good price on cattle and goats each year, and beginning a family of their own. The seven children Granny had over the next twenty-one years of her life were all three years apart. The need for tobacco came about this time. Granny smoked rolled-up cigarettes for a year or two, but finally an old rancher offered her a "chaw of chewing tobacco." She pitched the cigarettes and was hooked from then on. Chewing, spitting, and cussing became the ways in which Granny dealt with the difficult job of raising four sons and three daughters. "Sometimes cuss words got the most attention," she often said with a smile.

Granny's oldest son was in World War II. He came home on leave one time and Granny heard someone up in the night. She got up to see what the chomping noise was and her son was standing at the window, chewing the wood on the windowsill with his teeth and shaking profusely. Three weeks later he shipped out again and was killed in battle. Granny attended church for the first time in twenty-two years, but only to bury her oldest boy.

Another son, the youngest, was playing in an old 48 Ford that was not running, but was sitting on their property. Granny never drove a car, and in the eighty-three years that she lived never got a driver's license. But, her husband drove a little and a couple of the older girls got their license through a program in school. Tom had planned to fix up the old car, just hadn't got around to it yet. Gary happened to find an old book of matches lying on the dashboard of the vehicle. He started striking them, as a five-year-old might do, and suddenly, Granny and the other kids heard a small explosion. Gary was engulfed in flames as Granny ran barefoot across the desert floor and pulled him out of the burning car with her bare hands. One of the older daughters jumped on a horse and raced like lightning to where her father and another rancher were mending fences. The other rancher had an old truck and they rushed Gary into town to the hospital. The prognosis was not good, but Granny wouldn't let them amputate his hands. She stayed with him for six weeks and finally, Gary pulled through, not unscarred, but able to go home. The doctors told her he would never be able to use his hands again. Granny said, "Bullshit," one of her favorite words, and began rubbing Gary's little deformed hands with oils and home-made potions every night, exercising his fingers and hands. Twenty-five years later, this burned little boy grew up to be World's Champion Bareback Rider of 1967, 1968, and 1969. Granny's toughness paid off.

Now Tom Tucker, my grandpa, had a soft spot for gambling. Beginning about 1951 through 1956 or so, a severe drought hit the area and ranchers were not getting enough money for their poor cattle, barely existing on what few native grasses plunged through the dry, cracked earth. He began to gamble some through these tough years and eventually, due to the drought and the gambling, they were forced to sell the ranch. They were nearly broke, so off to town they moved and Grandpa Tucker began building barbed wire fencing for the state of New Mexico. He was gone a lot, so Granny had the burden of raising the last of the children who were still home.

She had not seen her mother or younger brother since she left home and married. The mother had moved in with Granny's baby brother and as luck would have it, the land my great-grandparents owned turned out to be rich with oil and gas. The baby brother talked the mother into signing over all the land and mineral rights to him and his family. He grew wealthy, while most of the other siblings, including Granny, continued to struggle through life. She wasn't too bitter about it. She saw the brother a few years before he died and all he did was walk around and cry. Granny said, "Hell, it was the guilt of being so greedy that caused him to eventually die depressed and miserable."

I remember going to visit her and Pa Tucker in the summer. Granny was always out watering her fruit trees and flowers in front of their little two-bedroom asphalt shingled house. She was always barefoot. Those feet of hers were tough as leather. I'll swear she couldn't have felt a nail shoved through the bottom. She had walked so many years barefoot in the heat of the desert she had built up layers of extra skin that probably would have protected her from a rattlesnake bite. She was always chewing tobacco when we pulled up. She'd grin real big and spit, wipe her mouth and run hug each and every one of her grandchildren. She'd always tell the grandsons, "Goddamn, you're a handsome little sonofabitch." One time I told her she probably shouldn't curse so much and she told me, "Ginny, I don't ever use bad language." Looking back, I don't think she thought she cursed a lot. I think she grew up thinking curse words were just a different way to express oneself.

After all seven children were grown and gone from home, one of her elder sons married a young woman and they had a baby boy. Granny was hired, but not paid, to keep her grandson almost every day. After about six weeks, Granny's son and daughter-in-law split up and both walked off and abandoned the baby boy. Granny was in her sixties and was about to raise her eighth child. My mother and aunt begged her to let them take the little boy, since they were both younger, had husbands, and were in good financial shape, but Granny wouldn't hear of it. After a lot of cussing and spitting tobacco, Granny won the battle and raised yet another child. I guess after raising so many kids, one more didn't matter much, plus that's all she knew how to do. So she and Grandpa Tom began raising a little boy in the 1960s, in their sixties, with virtually no money, no car, and they ended up never saying no to their new son, which eventually caused severe repercussions in everyone's life, but especially my cousin's and Granny's.

In 1963, Grandpa Tucker became ill. They took him to El Paso to a doctor and he was diagnosed with leukemia. They didn't have any money or insurance in that day, so he just stayed home, grew sick and weak, finally dying in his own bed. Again, Granny attended church again to bury her husband and was left with the burden of raising her grandson alone.

Granny didn't live in the best of neighborhoods. She didn't have a phone or a car or even a gun to protect herself with. Her children paid for her to have a phone once, but all the "damned old women kept calling me all the time to gossip 'cause they were bored," so she called the phone company and had them remove it. I remember going to spend a few nights with her every year. She had no air conditioner, so she raised all the windows in the house, which had no screens on them, and would begin telling us grandchildren scary stories. Granny would put a big wad of chewing tobacco in her mouth. Her favorite brand was Red Man chewing tobacco. It came in a green and white pouch, with big red letters that said Red Man and a picture of an Indian chief on front. None of us grandkids thought much about it, since most of our relatives, parents included, used some form of tobacco in those days. But she'd get out a wad of leafy brown tobacco, form it like she liked, and stuff it between her cheek and gum. Juice would often run out of her mouth, especially after she began telling stories, and she'd wipe it off with the side of her hand, wipe her hand off on the white bed sheets, and continue with her tall tales.

"The Pieman" terrorized my brother and some of my younger cousins. According to Granny, when she was growing up there was a mentally challenged man around thirty years old who lived with his parents, but wandered all over the ranch country day and night, scaring people and stealing women's pies. Granny told us that he was seven foot tall, weighed over two hundred pounds, and had hands that were deformed. His fingers supposedly grew together, forming one huge appendage that was shaped kind of like a fleshy hook. Then, according to Granny, his teeth had all been filed to a point, probably from a file used on horse hooves and no one knew if he did it or if his parents had done it to him. He'd run around and sneak into the screened porches of the houses on the ranches and if there were pies cooling, he'd take them. If there were no pies, he'd run into the house and start screaming like a "goddamn banshee," and not stop until someone in the house got up and handed him a chicken leg or a piece of pie or something good to eat. Granny said she watched him eat a live cat once, but I never believed that. I think she got a big kick out of scaring us kids at bedtime, in the dark, plus she was a Texan by heart, so I knew from being raised by Texans that they all exaggerated the truth from time to time.

The story that really got to me was "The Donut Man." I don't know why she had to call every story "The Something Man," but she did. Anyway, down the street from her house there was a famous donut shop. Everyone, including me and my cousins, loved getting donuts there in the morning. Granny would walk us down the street and around the block at about six thirty a.m. and let us pick out a donut. They were delicious. Plus, the husband and wife team that owned the donut shop were the nicest people you'd ever want to meet. We would pick our favorite, Granny would pay for them, then the husband or wife would throw in about twelve donut holes in a brown paper sack for us kids to munch on the rest of the day. Umm, nothing better when you were a kid. Anyway, I was about eleven years old when Granny told us this story, just about the age where I questioned some of her tales anyway. But, supposedly one morning about four a.m. when the old couple got to their shop to start making the dough, rolling it out, getting the vat of grease all hot and ready to cook donuts for the morning crowds, it happened. "Two thugs came barging through the back door where the kitchen was and started beating on the old couple. They tied them up, went to the front, got all the cash out of the register and what cash the old couple had on them, and then decided to kill them." Granny told us, after she went outside in the dark and threw her wad of chewed dip away, only to get a fresh new wad to finish the story with, that "these two bad guys were not happy with just robbing the old people. They were mean, like my momma was. They decided they would torture the old couple a bit before killing them dead." I was not sure I believed any of this, as Granny wiped the tobacco juice with the side of her hand. But her dark brown eyes were sparkling with mischief as she continued to tell us the story. "Well, next day come sun up, the donut shop had not opened. Everyone that knew these folks were concerned, because it just wasn't like them to not be there. So, finally, someone got the local sheriff to come check on the place. What the sheriff found made him puke his breakfast right up. The sheriff found both the donut people tied up and dead. But the two mean men had cut off the old man's balls and the old woman's tongue was cut out and the sheriff found them fried in the vat of grease like donuts. Damnedest murder that ever happened and they still ain't caught them bad guys yet."

My brother and my cousin didn't close their eyes the rest of the night. I, on the other hand, was supposed to be older and wiser and know better, but I still was awfully nervous about the windows being wide open all over the house. The next morning I asked Granny if we could go get some donuts, because I still halfway didn't believe her. Well, while the little ones were still asleep, Granny marched me right down the street and around the block for me to see the crime tape all around the place and the windows and doors boarded shut. My eyes widened and I looked at Granny, swallowing hard. "I told you those sonofabitches cut their balls off and their tongues out and fried them in the same grease used for the donuts." I didn't eat donuts for a very long time.

Granny continued to chew, spit, and cuss as long as she breathed. She watched the grandson she raised continue to spiral downward with bad crowds and addictions. She had to attend church again, to bury an eighteen-year-old grandson who was killed in an automobile accident on prom night. She found out the doctor died who told her "she better give up salt and greasy foods or she would die" had a heart attack fifteen years before she passed on. She got word that the last of her thirteen siblings died, somewhere back in central Texas. She saw a granddaughter have a hysterectomy at seventeen years old and lived long enough to meet that same granddaughter's adopted daughters ten years later. She loved Saturday night wrestling on the television set and never worried too much about fancy clothes or pretty hairstyles.

She cared about her children, grandchildren, and great-grandchildren. She cared about her little home with all the peach and apple trees she cared for each day. She cared about being able to walk around her property barefoot, and she cared about the many friends she had accumulated through the years. She had her memories, many of them hard and gritty, she delighted in the tall tales she spun, and I never heard her say "I regret."

And, even though the use of tobacco is no longer socially acceptable and the use of swear words around grandchildren is probably highly unacceptable, the fondness and love I will always hold for Granny, chewing, spitting, and cussing, is unmeasurable.

Kate Sampsell-Willmann

no cracks in the pavement

After looking for work for six months in every country except Saudi Arabia, I have buckled down and accepted a job contributing to the inanity of the Internet. I write "content," a term that inspires no greater understanding of information exchange than its plain meaning. The infinity of the Internet beckons those who will fill it with everything and nothing. I write for those how-do-I-do-it sites, often resorting to offering well-written but incomplete and virtually useless knowledge (as per guidelines). And, I am paid fifteen dollars per "article" for constructing the written equivalent of a paint by numbers.

Now, I am not saying that this is by any means a fruitless endeavor. Yes, income of any stripe is always welcome, but there are deeper truths about our society to be gleaned from the questions posed by the merely average to so-called experts such as myself. In this banal existence, I may have found some mystical knowledge about the human condition.

One question in particular has inspired this commentary: "How do I install a drain after the cement floor has dried?" There is an innocent beauty in that most obviously wrong of questions; we call it hope. Any one of us could be that do-it-yourselfer who, while presenting his (or her) beautiful new garage/basement/party room floor to a spouse is asked the innocuous question, "Where is the drain?" This belongs to the realm of haiku:

Flat, dry, unyielding
Still, a windless graying sea
What do you mean, "Drain?"

Insight dawns. Visible physical deflation ensues.

Thus begins my travel from a purely academic understanding of the human condition through a portal to the true core of humanity. Whether college professor, middle manager, or waitress, the Sisyphean futility of life becomes manifest when grasped in the pathetic frustrated hands of imperfect and imperfectable human life; we are all one—there is a Zen moment in here—when in our DIY projects we neglect the most obvious and necessary. One can imagine that poor schmo standing before the computer, having been told that the Internet has all the answers, praying to the binary god, typing frantically, "How do I... ?"

Now this foible of humanity lands on my desktop. Rather than gently passing on the bad news that, no, there really isn't anything to be done now, I open my article formatter and type in the box labeled step one: "First thing, rent a jackhammer and protective ear covering..."

Next assignment: "How do I get a date for my sister?" It is going to be a long night.

signed, the content hack

Max Sheridan

FIVE, SOLVED MURDERS

1. THE EAR RINGERS

FOR YEARS NAMETH had been under the impression that his ears had been ringing longer than anyone else's. But then he was introduced, through a common acquaintance, to Ulch, who had been complaining of a similar condition. Newspapers described the meeting as a "revelation" and a "blessing." Their collaboration was fruitful. Nameth, a pink-skinned California boy, claimed he could hear the rolling cadences of the Pacific ocean in his ears; Ulch, a native of Cheb, in the Czech Republic, that he could taste the damp, tuberous Bohemian forest floor in his eustachian tubes. The two appeared on morning talk shows and toured the country lecturing on tinnitus. The sonic activity within their ears, thought by most scientists to be a figment, was eventually charted by sonogram and it was graphed and a popular poster was made in DayGlo colors. Nameth and Ulch appeared on the verge of a major breakthrough when Ulch unexpectedly took his life at the Tampico Motel in Miami, where he was found dead, draped over an untasted pupu platter. A bellboy later confessed to the crime.

2. AUTOEROTIC PYROCLASIS

IN THE OFFICIAL police report Gardetto stated that he had been naked at the time he inserted the stick of dynamite into Temple's mouth, that with two fingers he had carefully unrolled the safety fuse and then looped it around Temple's scrotal ring, according to Temple's explicit directions, with lasso-like whimsy. Further to this account, in a taped deposition made before his lawyer, Gardetto stated that Temple's ankles were shackled together with a Rollo chain that was also attached to a studded collar worn around Temple's throat and that Temple, also naked, was sitting on the floor of the master bedroom on a square of dark purple cellophane. The TV was playing. According to official EMT documentation, Gardetto was sitting at the kitchen table of Temple's split-level suite at the Motel Tahiti in Phillipsburg, Ohio, eating from a carton of Breyers Ice Cream, when they responded to multiple reports of a terrifying explosion.

3. THE CAIRNCROSS ENIGMA

IN 1982, GEORGE Cairncross was found dead in his bathtub along with a signed confession claiming he had committed the murder for financial gain. Local investigators were quick to point out glaring inconsistencies in the case, such as the fact that Cairncross was known to avoid white rice and eggs, while in the confession the murderer professed an unhealthy appetite for white rice and eggs. Furthermore, neighbors interviewed in the weeks following the murder claimed that Cairncross had been self-abusive but not self-destructive. He was a quiet man, a little off, with nothing to gain from the murder as his life insurance policy had nothing to say about such a contingency. For two decades in prison Cairncross denied having committed the murder and then, in a televised interview with French TV in 2005, he reversed his original position and claimed full guilt. He and his lawyers are now preparing an affidavit, while forensics in Eau Claire, Minnesota, where Cairncross was not living at the time of the murder, reexamine the original confession and a strand of hair found with the confession at the scene of another crime.

4. THE REFRIGERATOR BOX MURDERS

IF VAN DUSER is to be believed, he had no intention of murdering his wife or her entire extended family over the course of a quiet Thanksgiving Day two years after his retirement as Chief Medical Advisor to the Armor Modeling and Preservation Society, Mt. Sterling Chapter. According to Van Duser's original testimony, they had all entered his box willingly. Contested photos from the crime scene reveal a cardboard refrigerator box draped enticingly with a shiny black cloth and show at least one of Van Duser's wife's relatives, Dave Kobax, the paper mogul, from behind entering the box. The case was further complicated by the fact that no bodies were ever recovered from the ten-by-sixty-foot pit Van Duser was accused of digging under the box, and that, further, at least two of the deceased had never attended the Van Duser Thanksgiving party and were believed to be unrelated genetically to Heidi Van Duser, née Kobax, Van Duser's wife. When questioned in his jail cell on *60 Minutes* five years later, Van Duser denied any memory of the murders or ever having been married to anyone named Kobax, let alone killing the entire Kobax family. He then admitted that he was unsure of his own ontological existence and soon thereafter, according to the *60 Minutes* news crew and at least one prison guard, he ceased to exist. Van Duser was executed in absentia ten years later after losing his third appeal.

5. THE DEATH OF BULI DIAZ

SEVEN FORENSIC STATISTICIANS in Baden-Württemberg have come to the independent conclusion that the chances of Buli Diaz, grandson of revered Filipino actor Paquito Diaz, being crushed by a boulder from the original set of Efren C. Piñon's classic *The Killing of Satan* on a Heidelberg chairlift are so small as to be ridiculous. Paquito Diaz, famous for nearly being killed by a giant boulder on the set of *The Killing of Satan* in the role of "Pito," was ruled out as a suspect after witnesses sighting Diaz, deceased in 2011 of sepsis, in the vicinity of the chairlift at the time of the murder changed their testimony, claiming it was the movie they had been watching all along. Hours after the murder, confessions materialized simultaneously at the homes of (1) Pito Estregan (no relation to the character), an extra from *The Killing of Satan* who *was* famously killed by a boulder in the film; (2) Dolores Cyclone, Buli Diaz's estranged girlfriend and a former lap dancer, who was unaware that Pito Estregan was (1) alive and (2) had *not* been killed by a boulder in real life; and (3) Claudio Tulli, an Italian man with no connection to Diaz or the filming of *The Killing of Satan*.

Sarah Louise Williams

Tight Lines

n July 2010, Year 17 on the Quality Chicks calendar, I was invited to join the Quality Chicks, my mother's all-women fly fishing group, for five days of fly fishing in southwestern Montana. I was the first daughter asked to join the group. We were to stay at the Big Hole Lodge in Wise River, Montana, and to fish for trout on various nearby rivers: the Big Hole, the Bitterroot, the Beaverhead, the Wise. For seventeen years, I had heard from my mom, Carol Jo Williams, about her fly fishing escapes to rivers in Montana, Idaho, Utah, Wyoming, and Colorado. She founded the Quality Chicks, a disparate group of women united in their obsession with catching and releasing trout—rainbow, brown, cutthroat, brook—caught using manmade flies designed to look like the real hatches of insects on the water, and using lightweight fly rods, not poles, never say fishing pole with this group. The Quality Chicks get their name, oddly, from the Decorah Hatchery in Decorah, Iowa, which sells quality live baby chicks (as in young chickens) and makes fine T-shirts that say as much in various bright colors. Each fly fishing Quality Chick has a different color shirt she wears for the annual group photo. By Year 17, the fisherwomen in the group number into the twenties and they come from all over the country: Montana, Idaho, Wyoming, Georgia, California, Texas, Iowa, Connecticut, Minnesota, Pennsylvania, and Ohio, and range in age from early forties to early seventies. The group changes slightly each year; one year, someone can't make it so someone brings along a friend. An ICU nurse, a financial advisor, academics, fundraisers, liberals, conservatives, introverts, extroverts. The common denominator is a love of fishing and a desire to be in the Mountain West, even if just for one week a year. My mom is one of the four originals who have been fishing together since 1994 when they met as strangers on an Orvis-sponsored "Reel Women" trip on the south fork of the Snake River in Idaho.

My goals in my Year One with the Quality Chicks: don't drown, don't embarrass my mother, and maybe catch a fish.

DAY 1: THE HUMBLING

"YOU'RE AN ATHLETE, you'll do great," so said the collective wisdom of the Quality Chicks. I felt some concern.

I *was* an athlete. I *was* also: a high school English teacher, a restaurant hostess, an underqualified fact checker for a financial magazine, a gopher girl for a semi-famous feminist, an overqualified temp at a sleazy commercial real estate company, a paid slush pile reader for a literary journal, an overly attentive and therefore inefficient dog walker, a former resident of New York City. That was *then*.

In 2010, I was forty and a stay-at-home mom of three boys—seven, five, and three—who were back in Chevy Chase, Maryland, with my husband, who would telework and parent the offspring while I became Brad Pitt, minus the chronic drinking and death by gun butt in *A River Runs Through It*. My "athletic past" the Quality Chicks referred to made me feel pressure to perform well. I have good hand-eye coordination. Ask me to whip a lacrosse ball into the corner of the net at high speed, whack a field hockey ball way up the wing out of the defense, smack a golf ball at a driving range farther than my guy friends (granted, this was years ago—I'm sure they're better now), or just send something up into the hills; ask for that, and I know what to do. But to stay in the lines in tennis rather than just power-hit it out from the baseline, to play golf by the rules, to play badminton gracefully, to surrender broad strokes for subtlety and work by finesse alone; ask me for minimalism, and results may vary. Fly fishing is subtle, not a go-for-broke sport, and this worried me.

Day 1 began with a casting lesson on the lawn in front of the main dining hall of the lodge. The various guides gave casting advice that showcased familiar as well as unusual metaphors:

Flick the paint.
Stop the hammer.
Punch the sky.
12 o'clock, 10 o'clock.
1 o'clock, 11 o'clock.
Answer the phone, slam the hammer.
Boom, boom.

I understood the mechanics of fly fishing, the need to bend that rod, not to use muscle, to do less so it becomes more. I got it. Or rather, my brain got it. But when it came to making my arm not go as far back as I can get it to go, to hold back on the energy, not to follow through all the way with my arm as I was taught to do in every sport I ever liked, things didn't go so well. Think less, I'd tell myself. No, think more, pay more attention. Think less and think more, all the while, rein in that arm, do not open up your shoulder. Oh, and relax, too, because this is easy, simple, "You're an athlete," "Didn't you play sports?" and women, as so many male guides told me, are supposed to be better at fly fishing than men because, well, they don't overdo it or muscle it out. Some might, I thought. The voices of my female high school and college coaches—Callahan, McNulty, Rice, Way, Jenkins, Den Hartog—blended with the male fishing guides' reminders. It's all in the wrist, no, not in the wrist, flick the wrist, no, don't break the wrist, it's in all in the shoulder, no, relax the shoulder, loosen that death grip, relax your elbow, no, pin that elbow to your side, open the door, shut the door, don't think, just do. Well, not quite like that. No matter what I told myself, I kept trying to hurl the discus, I mean fishing line. My practice casts on the lawn of the lodge were more:

Flickpaintstop
hammerpunchsky
BOOM BOOM BOOM

My fishing line flailed like wet spaghetti, not tight, not right. Athlete or no, I was exposed as a problem caster. The Shame.

On Day 1, Wade Fellin, that's actually his name, was my guide on the Big Hole River, and Pat Murphy, Iowa State food science professor, was my fishing partner. Both were patient with me. Pat is a font of knowledge about many topics, including all things Lewis and Clark and every book written by the Bard of Montana, Ivan Doig. When I asked Pat what she liked about fly fishing, she said, matter-of-factly, "Trout are crafty, beautiful fish." She just likes them and their Platonic, trouty essence.

I liked them, too, but I was apparently more interested in blowing out my arm. Unable to get the right timing on my back cast and overdoing the forward cast, I showed not enough trust in the physics of the fly rod, and after too much throwing of the line for nearly eight hours on the river, I had throbbing shoulder pain no amount of ibuprofen could touch.

Even so, on Day 1, I caught fish. It's taboo with this group to count fish too overtly, so let's just *imagine* I caught and released twelve fish, rainbows and browns, and some white fish. Each time Pat or I brought a white fish to the boat for Wade to dehook, Pat would lean down to the often-maligned cousin to the prized trout and say, "Why, hello, Señor Blanco."

DAY 2: BELIEF

THE WATER WAS fast and high, and even my Day 2 fishing partner, Lisa Huey, Double-Hauling, Casting Queen of the Western World, didn't get a fish in the morning. Everything the guide, Chuck, told me to do or not to do, I was simply unable to implement his advice. Body, mind, eyes, ears all out of sync.

Then, in the afternoon, it rained, a lot, but it was a warm rain, and

I liked the drama of it, lightning threatening all around, but far enough away that we could stay on the river. I put up my rod and decided to help myself out of my slump by spending what was left of the day helping the boat—scouting fish for Lisa, netting a few so Chuck could keep rowing. I witnessed Lisa land a bulging twenty-four-inch brown trout, a hog. It was an impressive fish. Lisa, a financial advisor from Minneapolis, explained, "I always believe there is a fish. I never think there is not a fish. I always think, *I'm going to get a fish*. I just do," she said, her line stretched out and ready, even in the rain. Be the fish. Believe in the fish. It Will Come.

DAY 3: FOUL HOOKED

"COME ON, FISH! Come on, fish!"

Part entreaty, part command, our guide, Rick, Montana State math professor during the school year, growled out to the fish as he rowed the drift boat.

I was partnered with my mom this day and, either through intuition or word of mouth among the guides, Rick knew that the less said about my casting problems, the better. Unlike Days 1 and 2, this time I got to be in the back of the boat. My mom and Rick faced the other way—no witnesses. I decided not to think about my casting at all. I thought only of fish.

Hours passed. No fish.

My position in the back of the boat gave me a view of my mom and her cast. She stopped her arm not at 12 o'clock, nor 11 o'clock, not at any o'clock at all. Rather, her cast was a fluid, hard-to-define, flip back and flip forward of the forearm. Unorthodox, maybe, yet on nearly every cast, she got the fly where she wanted it to go with apparent ease. The line unfurled with speed, but made no sound when it hit the water, fly hitting first, followed by line stretched taut on top of the current. It was lovely to watch. As much as fishing means to her, my mom fishes only once or twice a year—five to ten days total. She takes these fishing days on the water home with her. When she can't get to sleep at night or has some worry that won't go away, she goes fishing in her mind. She clenched her jaw with each cast, perhaps to help capture the memory, and in that clench, I recognized the profile of my grandfather, who was an avid fisherman. In his jaw clench, which I remember noticing when I was a girl, were all the words I imagine he was not able to say to my mom as her father, or to me as my grandfather. Not an emoter was he, though it's possible that this clenching was due to chewing tobacco. I could not help but see in the tightening of my mother's jaw, all the unspent energy of the catches and throws she never made, the plays never run, the coordination never tested, and the athletic challenges never attempted. She grew up in Oklahoma City in the '40s and '50s when girls' sports consisted of half-court basketball and sewing. If she had grown up post Title IX, who knows what she might have played.

I was fishing off the left side of the boat, still in the back, my mind not at all on fish when Rick yelled at me, "STRIKE!" so loudly I nearly dropped the rod. There was such heavy tugging that I feared my rod would snap. I'd never had a fish like this on the line. The fight was serious, but the mechanics comical. Rick banked the boat, put down the anchor when it seemed the fish was near, jumped out of the boat with the net, ready to scoop under the fish, but then the fish went out again, taking more line down river. At Rick's direction, I let the fish run. Rick jumped back in the boat, pulled up anchor, and rowed like hell down toward the fish. This happened a few more times. The pull of the fish was engrossing to me; there was room for little else in my mind. Rick explained in between cardio bursts into the boat, out of the boat, anchor up, anchor down, that this fish was foul hooked. That sounded ominous, Shakespearean.

"What does that mean?" I asked him.

"Fish went for the dry, but he got the nymph, in his side," he explained, miraculously not out of breath.

I was pulling the fish up the river, against the current, from the side of the fish's body, not the mouth. Foul hooked. Ouch.

When at last I landed the fish, I felt only empathy for the twenty-inch brown trout. I could not take my eyes off of her. Rick was shin-deep in the water, lightly cradling the exhausted fish in the long grass at the bank. The possibility that the fish might not make it left me unsettled, unsure whether to sit or stand, and to whom to apologize. I said nothing, and could do nothing but watch the fish. Another minute went by, it felt like five, and then she swiveled once or twice, followed by a jerk or two, and she was down river, her power regained.

DAY 4: BLIND FISH

ON DAY 4, I was assigned to go to a large pond near the Beaverhead River, Sacajawea's territory, about an hour's drive southeast from the lodge. No drifting, no boat, only my wader-encased self. I looked like a deformed, gigantic sausage, or two.

We walked on treeless banks, stalking the fish. The water was clear, often still, allowing us to see the fish, and the fish to see us. My guide, Craig Fellin, owner and operator of the Big Hole Lodge, walked ahead, scouting the fish. After I cast, I knelt down in the grass to hide from the fish, and then waited for the fish to take the fly.

I was nervous, not just because my first few casts were not good, but because I was with Craig. He's a quiet, still-waters-run-deep kind of man, the sort I did not want to tangle my line in front of, or be at all what I was—a neurotic caster. And yet there I was in all my be-wadered glory, playing at stealth, kneeling in the goose poop that decorated the edge of the wide pond, with a curled fishing line I'd just loudly tumbled onto the water, scaring his well-scouted fish away.

I made a passable cast. I knelt and waited.

"STRIKE!" he yelled. I set the hook and stood up before letting go of the line in my right hand. A classic beginner move that almost invariably leads—as it did this time—to the fish snapping off the line and away.

Believe in the fish, let go of the line, I told myself.

Midafternoon, and I still hadn't caught anything.

Craig had me walk to another place along the bank where he thought I might have some luck. I cast into the wind, not that much wind really, but enough to mess me up. I managed to snag my hook into the top of my hat so securely that Craig had to cut out the hook. As he wrestled the hook out of my hat, the stampede strap on my hat became caught in my sunglasses string, which became caught in my fishing line. At that moment, I felt that as much as I loved being exactly where I was—mountains, valleys, water, sun, rocks, big sky—maybe I wasn't meant to *fish* there. I don't have to be good at this, I thought. I don't have to make varsity fishing my first year, or ever. In future years, I could float in a boat with my mom while she fished well. I could conjure the trout, net her fish for her, or just growl at the water like a grumpy math professor, "Come on, fish!"

Hat back in place, line and fly reconfigured, my gumption weak but rising, I started again.

Craig walked us down into the water now. After he saw a fish take a live grasshopper blown in from an adjacent field, Craig changed my fly in favor of a single parachute hopper dry fly. This was going to be a blind fish, he explained, because at our location, with the sun's glare on the water, neither he nor I would be able to see the fish ahead of time.

Blind fish. Blind us.

I walked up a bit, and then I cast. I wished for real blinders, so I could be like a Central Park carriage horse, no distractions. Believe in the fish.

The fish took the hopper fast, I set the hook, and let go of the line.

I kept my rod tip up, and the fish was going, out and out, and then, it gave us a jump. It was a rainbow trout, arcing its glorious, pink-tinged body right in front of us. I could not see Craig, but I heard his voice behind me, encouraging me to keep the rod tip up, no matter what, to give more line if the fish wanted it, and to reel in when there was any slack. There was no slack. This fish wanted nothing to do with me, the bank, or grasshoppers, real or otherwise, ever again. I looked at my yellow line, spinning out fast. I said to Craig, still somewhere behind me, "What if the fish takes all my line?"

"Oh, it won't," he said.

And then there was no more line.

Craig looked at my reel and I saw his face fall. My new reel and new line were put on at the Orvis store back home in Bethesda, Maryland, with, inexplicably, an inadequate amount of backing, the neon-yellow line extension that comes at the end of the translucent fishing line. The brief pause Craig took before coming up with a strategy let me know I was about to lose this fish. This man is an expert, a professional fish stalker, and he was surprised by the situation.

All I was going to be able to do was stand firm, hold the rod high, and wave it in big arcs from side to side—giant 9 o'clock on my left, giant 3 o'clock on my right—while keeping the rod tip up. I'd seen the "We are the World" video. I'd even seen the "The Making of the 'We Are the World'" video, so I understood this motion well. Wisely, I chose not to share with Craig how the movement he was ordering was similar to the video. This zigzag maneuver would, Craig hoped, tire out the fish. There were no other options. The odds were against me; I was supposed to lose this fish. But my legs and arms are strong, I thought, from so many hours of field hockey, basketball, lacrosse, and all that time still counted, right?, even if there had been years, well, decades, of dis-use, un-use. The waving motion seemed to work after what felt like an hour. I have no idea how long I fought the fish—three hours or two minutes—as I was in Fish Time and Fish Time has its own timekeeper.

Once I saw Craig in front of me with the net, I let down a bit, my wrists screaming at me to chuck it all in the pond. There was one more run by the fish, before I was able to lead it, head first, right into the net. Craig's main concern was saving the fish. He held it in the water as it tried to recover. He measured it at twenty-two inches. I petted the fish for a moment. You goddamn beautiful fish you nearly killed me and I love you, I thought. Then Craig let it go. He looked at me straight on, and said, with a hint of pride and disbelief, "You did everything right."

You did everything right. You would have thought I'd passed the Army Ranger course. I can imagine a time in the future, when I will have caught many large trout, maybe even bigger than this one, and will be a more consistent angler who resists the impulse to try to hit a home run every time, and just calmly casts the line into the water. Like an adult. But I hope I can remember always the jolt I had landing that fish on that day. How nice it is for anyone, whatever the age, whatever the circumstances, to hear: you did everything right. The joy I felt at what I'd done made me miss my three boys. I wanted them to be right next to me, watching their mom reel in this tough trout, and, also, I missed them because I want to coach them as well as Craig coached me. "You did everything right," I will say to them, when their work has been hard and honestly done.

DAY 5: FIZZLE

WE WOKE TO rain and hail.

There was no way we'd fish today, I thought. We could sleep in, read, be normal people on vacation. I could not stop thinking of my rainbow at the pond. *My* rainbow—how possessive I'd become overnight. If I went out today, I knew that nothing would measure up. The rain stopped, the hail melted, and the sun came out. The Quality Chicks go fishing no matter what, save lightning.

My boat was skunked, meaning we caught no fish. No one was counting—OK, I was. We had three fish all day, but not one made it to the boat. I caught one of those fish, by accident, when I wasn't even holding onto my rod.

Same day on a different Quality Chick boat on the same section of river I floated, Suzanne Hendrich, a nutrition science professor, caught many fish, including a twenty-seven-inch brown trout, which might be the biggest fish ever caught on the Big Hole River. She followed that up with a twenty-four-inch brown a few hours later. Two giants in one day, caught by the same person. "It's the unexpected fish that keep me coming back," Suzanne explained what she loves about fishing. "A sixteen-inch rainbow in one deep pocket of a stream three feet wide. A twenty-inch brown you've been watching. Seeing the fish circle the fly and finally take it. It's all a pleasant surprise."

Luck, skill, front of the boat, back of the boat, wind, current, slant of light, bug hatches—all this matters. But the angler's mindset matters as well and such different attitudes—mine to fizzle, Suzanne's to hope—yielded quite different outcomes on the same stretch of river.

THOUGH LEARNING TO fish properly may have a potential corrective effect on my character flaws, the reason I'll come back is to be with my mother. I'm forty, she's seventy-one. Numbers matter. We are both in reasonably good health, but I'm aware of a subterranean savoring at work in me, a kind of canning of my times with her, in preparation for a future when she'll be gone. I don't dwell on this, but I pay attention to it, and in doing so, I am propelled toward directness with her now. I tend to overemote and she will just say, "Let's go fishing." She is always right.

I'll also come back to look at those Western rivers. They're mesmerizing. "It's the scale," my fishing partner Cathy Krinsky suggested, as we looked from the top of a pass on the Wise River Road in the Pioneer Mountains down to the emerald banks of Grasshopper Creek, wending its way through a sunlit valley. The smaller rivers and creeks are more intimate and, in taking them in, I can comprehend the erosive work of water on rock over time. As impressive as the rusty yawn of the Grand Canyon is, for example, while looking at it, my feet want to move back, away from the abyss. Too big, too deep; my brain shuts down. Cathy's right, it's the scale of smaller water that appeals. The scale and the whimsy. The narrow, meandering, almost fairy-tale like paths that Grasshopper Creek and the narrow Wise River make through valley and forest, on the way to meet the Big Hole River, lead me to think God was having mechanical problems of his own one day, just doodling brilliantly.

"Are you hooked yet?" the group asked me each night at dinner. I never knew what to say. Maybe?

The day I got back to Maryland from Montana, I took my rod and reel into Orvis. I wondered how best to explain the blind-fish showdown on the Beaverhead pond. How much detail to leave in or out? Arm nearly broken off by absurdly strong fish that had to be *muscled* to the bank, in; Sacajawea reference, out. Or, perhaps I could show the salesman the picture of my twenty-two-inch fighting fish and me and say to him only two words, "No backing." Or, opt for more of a performance art confrontation: walk in with rod and reel all set up, begin the desperate side-to-side arcing wave of the rod. How long before Orvis calls security? My mother was relieved to know I did none of the above; I did not overemote, just explained, politely. The Orvis manager was gracious in return. And a man of few words.

"That's some fish," he said, and put on a hundred yards of backing, no charge.

Before I left the store, I noticed for sale a casting technique DVD marketed for women. At first, I thought the teacher pictured on the front cover, Joan Wulff, was my childhood piano teacher, Mrs. Howie, who had to be dead by then. I never said goodbye or thank you to Mrs. Howie and that has nagged at me for years. Back then, the pattern was there: I had some natural ability with piano, but I crammed all the daily work into one long practice session the night before my weekly lesson. I bought the casting video.

If I am hooked, as the other women engaged in this expensive, logistically challenging hobby are hooked, I will blame it on that arcing rainbow trout on Day 4, and also on the grayling, a fish I've never seen.

The American grayling. *Thymallus arcticus.* They are a trout, arctic in origin, held over somehow in the Big Hole from the last ice age. They thrive in high mountain lakes, but not necessarily in trout rivers, though they are there, all the guides assured me, in the Big Hole River, in ever-declining numbers. There is something in the grayling name itself that I like: gray area, changeling, ding-a-ling. I think something clicked when I looked into the lodge's doorstop of a tome, *McClane's New Standard Encyclopedia of Fishing*:

> Grayling...when seen at certain angles of light, may reflect lilac and gold, and at times, the entire fish has a silvery or brassy sheen, *as though wearing an ancient suit of mail*... The male holds its...large sail-like [dorsal fin] erect when repelling invaders... Its singular beauty caused the citizens of Crawford [Michigan] to change the name of the town to Grayling, a distinction which few fish achieve. (italics mine)

That first night I was home, I dreamt my bed had become the surface of a river, and I was floating on it. Something invisible but stable held me up, like a now-she-will-walk-on-water piece of thick plexiglass. I looked down deep into the river, and there they were, all the grayling of the world, not vanished, nor extinct just yet, darting and posturing, protecting their own.

I woke up with a start.

"Did I fish today?!" I blurted out to my husband.

"No, you didn't," he said, bewildered, but amused. "You flew home today. You're at home. You can go back to sleep."

Oh, grayling, river knight in shining armor, I'll find you next year.

IT'S 2015 AND Year 22 for the Quality Chicks. I'm forty-six, my mom is seventy-seven. We all keep coming back. I've still not caught nor even seen a grayling.

This year I relaxed about my cast. That only took six years. For old time's sake, sometimes I still do a careening cast, using just power, because hurtling it out over mysterious current feels freeing, before the arm pain registers, and the fish zoom away from the boat. But enough with the hammer, the clock, punching this big sky. Enough with sports metaphors. I'm almost fifty years old and just glad to be out there with my mother and these other women. Most of the week, I went with a ho hum "1, 2" counting under my breath to make myself wait for the line to stretch out fully behind me before I sent it forward into fish. Boring, but, there it was, finally, to my surprise and delight, a tight line.

Jessy Randall
monotone functions

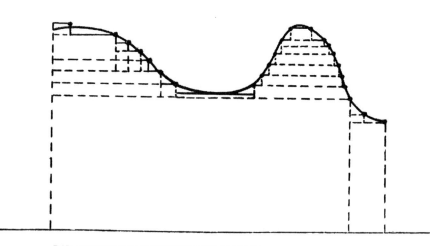

$x_1 + 0, y_3 - 0$ $x_3 - 0, y_3 - 0$

$x_1 + 0, y_2 + 0$

$x_1 + 0, y_2 - 0$

$x_1 + 0$ $x_2 - 0$

$y_1 + 0$ $y_1 + 0$ $x_2 + 0, y_1 + 0$ $x_3 - 0, y_1 + 0$

HAVE YOU BRUSHED YOUR TEETH?

DID ANYTHING INTERESTING HAPPEN AT SCHOOL TODAY?

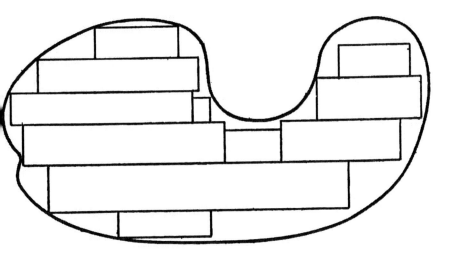

WHO DID YOU SIT WITH IN THE CAFETERIA AT LUNCH?

IS YOUR HOMEWORK FINISHED?

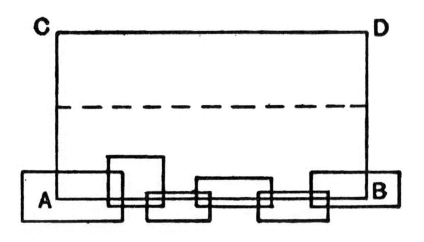

DID YOU CLEAN YOUR ROOM YET?

Jeffrey C. Alfier

Stopping At Texas Loosey's on A Warm Monday Homeward

Don't judge the man for a heart's
digressions that specter through him.
No. Judge him for this:

The boilermaker's midday vertigo,
the sweat and backstory of gin,
playing Rare Earth's "Get Ready"—
the longest number in jukebox history.

The barmaid's a Latina cowgirl,
or someone disguised as one:
black hat, leather chaps,
a waistline low as lust,
and he can't recall whether
she's Jacqueline or Jasmine.

On the bar TV, the Fonz
degrades himself
with a realty commercial.
So much for cool
when you're nothing
but a 1-800 number.

Four stools down, a dude his age,
late '50s, sits with his daughter,
hairy of arm and leg.

He won't bet they'll make
the lingerie show tonight.
Not sure he'll make it either,
stumbling now into the men's room,
his dignity ever more in doubt
as he trips toward a whitewashed
wall that looks like his future
hungering toward him.

Nancy Allen

CITY PARK INTERLUDE

Sycamore saplings, budding and leggy, lean over their own reflections
in the pond, like young ballerinas backstage, sharing a single mirror.

Each tree is already draped in the showy grapevines that will wind
around and around and squeeze it to death. I can't watch them

swoon and collapse. One morning I arrive to cut the vines in two.
I want the sycamores to grow tall, to shed their early bark

for the powder white skin that will catch the least lamplight
and glow among the trunks of oak blending with gray streets.

I want them to board the downtown bus like taking a curtain call:
shoulders back, dressed in satin despite the threat of rain.

David Alpaugh

AGAINST...

always makes the scariest face;
always wields the bloodiest knife;
strongest crowbar; bluntest battering ram;
packs dirty bombs with raspiest nails;
attaches nuclear warheads to emails.

Against has season tickets to wherever
fans of the status quo gather en masse:
townhalls, senate chambers, churches, saloons.
Against is the big bad wolf, howling at the door
To the little lambs within—baa-baaing

FOR...

Jacob Appel

TRANSACTION COSTS

The postman knows secrets:
Magazines sheathed in black plastic,
Final warnings, notices of default.
Overwrapped packages that rattle
Pharmaceutically. One morning,
Inside a Ziploc bag, he delivers
A crushed marital aid, all shards
Of fluorescent pink and yellow,
Marked: "Damaged in Transit."

Maybe that is what keeps him going,
Day after day, year after tedious year,
Performing in a role that we never could,
Like collecting coins at a toll plaza.
He slips among us hardly noticed,
Humming on torrid August mornings,
Hirsute brown calves strained and sweat-
Soaked below his regulation shorts.

Sipping from his water canister, he
Lingers beneath an open window.
Our voices, like power, drift to him
On the hot summer breeze.

Flying with Clarity

Our flight attendant is older than I'm used to—
Maybe the oldest person on the flight, in fact—
Certainly old enough to know better, so when
She announces that my seat cushion can double
As a flotation device, that second mini-amaretto
Urges me to rise like a royal herald and shout, *No,
It cannot! I mean, has anyone, anywhere, in the
History of aviation ever survived a catastrophic
Failure by floating away on a sliver of nylon?
Jesus Christ, lady, has it never crossed your mind
That steel tubes cruising five hundred miles per hour
Don't just skim the ocean gracefully like cormorants?
No, they sink. Sink, sink, sink! You'd be
Swimming with the fishes around Davy Jones's Locker,
If you survived the impact, which you wouldn't, because
You're old, and out of shape, and not made of graphene.
And if by some miracle you did manage to grab
Hold of your cushion and paddle unscathed through
The field of debris, hypothermia would kick in,
Soon enough, and in three minutes your rheumatic,
Ice-stiff fingers would lose their grip on that precious
Flotation device of yours, and you'd go the way
Of TWA and Pan Am and everyone else in your damn
Line of work who thought themselves unsinkable.*

I say none of this, of course. I sit placid as a madman
Doped on Thorazine, nursing my third amaretto,
While you indicate the floor lights that will lead us,
In case of emergency, from this lunacy into
The dark wintry waters beyond.

Touring Greenwich Village

Spouses of dentists—wives and one husband—and
Only me to guide them. The dentists are in an
Air-conditioned ballroom near Midtown, absorbing
The latest advances in articulating paper. I'd expected
The wives—and one husband—to have better teeth.
I had never given consideration to the spouses of dentists,
Which is likely why I agreed to lead this tour.

Walking backwards on a summer day is hell on the calves.
Willa Cather lived here, I say. *Sara Teasdale died there.*
Dental spouses nod politely, displaying chipped canines.
I might add: This is where a poet whose name you wouldn't
Recognize wrote about a bridge I could easily sell you.

Next I might say: This is the spot where Hannibal
Led his elephants across the Alps, and over there,
Beyond that bus stop, hunchbacked Richard III,
Who may not actually have been hunchbacked,
Fell to Henry Tudor. And there—yes, right where
You're all standing, brave Pheidippides proclaimed
The Athenian victory over Persia before collapsing
Fatally onto the asphalt.

At this moment, you spouses of dentists, I feel
Drained as Pheidippides, his marathon complete.
Only that man saved civilization, while I stand
On blistered feet, watching you gawp at me,
With your poor occlusion, your ashy crowns,
Knowing we are leagues beyond rescue.

Sara Backer

ADVICE

As your father, I would say
learn from your mistakes.
As your mother, I would say
it happens to everyone.

As Adam, I would say
you think too much.
As Eve, I would say
I told you so.

As your friend, I would put my hand
on your shoulder. As your hand,
I would curl beneath your chin
while you thought.

As the floor, I would say
clean up the blood and move on.

As your eyes, I would close.

As the stain on the wall,
I would say I'm a black-winged angel
or an angry badger—and what
does this say about you?

THE MAN WHO IS NEVER WRONG

A magician shreds paper into a top hat,
waves his wand, and pulls out a white rabbit,

assured of his talent in misdirection. He, too,
watches his hand with the wand, ignoring

his hand in the hat. A magician is never wrong.
He adroitly shifts the world from round to flat,

several lies ahead of fact-checkers,
truth-seekers, and women who fall in love
with him by proxy for the idea that change is easy.

The man who is never wrong has no qualms
about altering past or predicting future.
He lives for an audience who is never right,

who confirms his power by believing the wand,
believing rabbits can materialize from hats

and that they vanish after the show
instead of trundling into cages
to eat pellets in a plastic dish.

Someday, I'll sneak backstage and steal the rabbit.
We'll find a field of alfalfa and live by principles

of matter and uncertainty, on a watery globe
that circles a fiery sun.

Sarah Barlow-Ochshorn

mild scoliosis

i fumble to reach
the bend in my spine
like your hands
when they first met
the touch of my back;
i reach but cannot find.
36 degrees off kilt and
rising,
my love as scoliosis:
x-rays showing hips
and chest
clearly as you see them
when you call me beautiful
and hold me like vertebrae
hold my lumbar in curves.
every year
another degree of love
until gravity pulls me
down
completely into you.

Stacy Barton

BESIDE YOU ON THE PORCH

don't tell me this breeze
passing
        blues singing
        on midnight porch
        with patient dog lying

is not

or that this
        wicker chair
        wedding lights
        your arms
        those eyes

won't be

don't tell me I forgot
        my mind
        throwing well-fanged words
        like venom down your side

I fear most
the less   the loss   the lack
        unremembered mingling
        of blonde and brown hairs
        '79 hatchbacks

but see
see   see   see
        my crumpled
        heart beating
        watching your bleeding
        broken on brick
        lost shine of moon

dark   shadows   light
dawn translucent
        dark troubled eyes
        gray stubbled skin
        in Easter dew

you

you   you
don't tell me
          how it is with you

you enfold me
          ruffled with guilt
          reclaim my fault
          your pain
          our seam

with one whispered word

I WAS READING ABOUT
ASCENSION SYMPTOMS AND
ONE WAS THAT HEADACHES
WERE CAUSED BY — UGH I CAN'T
REMEMBER — SOMETHING LIKE
HEADACHES WERE CAUSED BY
BEING ATTACHED TO PEOPLE

angels whisper "untethered"
      stone on stone
      peace of sand
      tide passing
unattached ribbons lift
      from my mind
      orb brightens
      hinged heart creaks
      uncaged, rising
gut spirals, tourniquet tied
      Monday
      Tuesday
      Wednesday
      Thursday
      Friday
      Saturday
      Sunday
unfurled ribbons tangle
      nest in my throat
      choke
      knots open
      to warbled hum
      the angels hear
      i whisper

"enough it is, to speak"

Nina Bennett

REGRET

The fedora Grandfather wore,
black wool faded, band sweat-stained,
brim shadowing his scowl as he trudged
the streets of Baltimore, to synagogue
for morning and evening prayers,
to the gym to watch his buddies box.
Sometimes he'd set his hat on a stool,
go a few rounds, anything
to escape a household of daughters.

Gary Blankenburg

Good Little Soldier

1. WW2: DISEMBARKMENT

Mother and I followed him
        to Texas and then Alabama
                where we lived in a strip

of little bungalows surrounding
        a dirt courtyard
                which had been

a Mobil gas station—
        all that remained were two pumps
                and a sign on a tall post

displaying a red-winged horse—
        and next to the sign
                was a single pecan tree—

when my father came home
        now and again on a pass,
                my mother gave me a hammer

and sent me out
        to gather and crack pecans—
                and only when I filled

a mason jar with their meat
        could I come in to join them
                for dinner—

on those nights I slept on the sofa—
        when he left he would smile
                and pat me on the head,

telling me to be
        a good little soldier
                for my mother—

when Mother and I were alone,
    I would beg her to wear
        her red jersey dress

that felt so good when I touched it.

2. WW2: DURATION
BERTHOLD'S FUNERAL PARLOR

After my father left for war,
    my mother and I were given an apartment
        above Berthold's Funeral Parlor,

and she took a job mornings
    working at the 5 & 10. So
        Bill Berthold, the mortician,

became my babysitter. He was
    a friend of the family,
        and his father was our minister.

In the mornings Bill
    would entertain me by playing
        train. He would line up folding chairs

and give me an empty briefcase
    to pretend it was my suitcase and I

was a passenger boarding
    the train. He was the conductor
        and would make tooting of the horn

noises. Sometimes we would sit
    at the organ together in a parlor
        where a body was laid out for viewing

and he would play Lutheran hymns
    while I sat on his lap watching his
        fingers touch the keys. He was

missing a joint on his index finger,
    and the skin had grown around it—
        very smooth to my touch.

Everywhere the air was fragrant
   with the perfume of funeral flowers,
      and I watched sad people

come and go. When Bill was unavailable
   to me, the beautiful secretary
      became my sitter, and she

seemed to just adore me.
   She always kissed me on the cheek
      and I would wear her lipstick as a badge.

She gave me sweet hard candy,
   and I would sit at her desk
      and draw pictures and color.

One day she was out sick,
   and Bill had to take me with him
      to the basement embalming room.

I watched him work with tubes
   and fluids and needles on an old
      naked woman laid out on the table.

When I had finished my ham sandwich
   and had nothing to do, Bill handed me
      a comb and told me to comb the lady's hair

while he finished up his work.
   So I did. I combed and combed her hair
      until, to me, it—and she—looked beautiful.

One day when mother came home from work
   she brought me a bag of toy tin soldiers.
      They were two-dimensional lithographs

mounted on little stands. I took them
   out in the back driveway where the ambulance
      and limo were parked and found

a patch of dirt where I could play war.
   I dug trenches and foxholes and moved
      the soldiers in and out dodging bullets.

But when I pretended one was shot
   and fell dead, he didn't look realistic
      because the stand made the feet higher

than the head. And I knew dead people
  didn't look that way—they were perfectly flat.
   So, one by one, as they were killed,

I bent the stands back and forth—
  back and forth—until they snapped, and then
   the soldiers were, indeed, dead.

But when I was ready to resume
  the game the soldiers could no longer stand up—
   they were dead for good—

and at that second there was in my brain
  a momentous synapsis. Death is finality—
   if my father were shot—he would be gone

forever from my life. And then it followed. I, too,
  would eventually die. My fear soared, and my tears
   flowed. I ran through the parlor and upstairs

to my mother crying. She thought it was
  because I had foolishly broken my toys,
   and she assured me she would replace them

the next day. I found no comfort in that
  and thereafter avoided the rooms where
   bodies were on display for mourners.

3. WW2: DURATION
GRANDFATHER'S HOUSE

When Mother left
  her job at the 5 & 10
   we moved to

my paternal grandparents'
  farm where I was
   surrounded by their love

and my mother became
  nothing but a blur
   in the pastoral backdrop.

Each morning, after
  waffles and bacon,
   Grandmother would put

her broad-brimmed
    straw hat on me,
        tie the black ribbon

in a bow under my chin,
    and send me to
        the victory garden

with a basket to fill.
    I picked green beans,
        squash, and cucumbers

until the basket was full.
    In the afternoon,
        after I'd had my lunch and nap,

Grandfather appeared
    with a shotgun over
        his arm and said, Gary,

let's go hunting for supper.
    We walked the fence line
        that was mounded

in fragrant honeysuckle
    that I shook and kicked
        until I flushed a rabbit

that he shot as it fled
    past the chicken coop
        and toward the vast orchard.

When we had two,
    we walked back to the house
        and I got to carry the

rabbits by their ears,
    one in each fist. Grandfather
        retired to the porch

for iced tea and a cigar,
    and I stayed in the kitchen
        with Grandmother and watched

her skin, gut, and quarter
    the rabbits. She left the pieces
        in the sink filled with saltwater.

I watched the water gradually
     turn pink. At dinner time,
         she dusted them in flour

and fried them in bacon grease
     until they were golden.
         I gladly ate them,

but I could still hear
     the gunshots
         ringing in my ears.

4. WW2: DURATION
GRANDFATHER'S ORCHARD

Grandfather's orchard was my
     universe, and he was its center.
         The peach, the apple,

the apricot knew no despair.
     The thicket of blackberries
         loved its tangle of snakes.

The east and the west
     fences fell beneath
         the mounds of honeysuckle,

and the silver poplars
     were the pride of the north.
         To the south

was the pigsty.
     They snorted, rutted,
         and suckled—sows

collapsed indifferently,
     huge curved sides
         baked in mud,

squealers at pink teats.
     Each dusk Grandfather
         tossed the day's

garbage over the gate
     with a heave-ho
         and a laugh I learned

to laugh. It came
> from a deep place—as
>> deep as the cellar

where I found
> his magazines hidden
>> behind Grandmother's

mason jars of preserves.
> Each dawn the rooster
>> crowed, and I raised

my blinds to see
> Grandfather's Kaiser
>> in the drive, and off

to the edge
> was the rusty red pump.
>> Then was a time of enchantment.

5. WW2: THE CHILD

a world of women, children,
> and old men—
>> aunts clustered

together, chatting,
> cooking in the kitchen
>> while the cousins played—

a picnic at Lake Decatur,
> aunts resting together
>> on blankets spread,

the car door open
> with the radio playing,
>> and then the news—

the war was over—
> Mother and her sisters weeping—
>> the father I had forgotten

was coming home—
> gentle, loving, soft-spoken,
>> and so very handsome—

the man who gathered
　　　me in his strong arms
　　　　　　and became my first god.

6. WW2: COMING HOME

all the young men
　　　on both sides
　　　　　　of my family

served—Army, Navy,
　　　Air Force—
　　　　　　European and Pacific

theaters—
　　　and all returned unscathed
　　　　　　except my father

who brought back
　　　a purple heart and a scar
　　　　　　like a smile in his side—

he was not
　　　proud—and he never
　　　　　　spoke about

the circumstances
　　　except to say
　　　　　　they were at best

trivial—not dramatic.
　　　not heroic,
　　　　　　but it was his shy

and quiet manner,
　　　that confirmed the lie—
　　　　　　making him my hero and savior.

 FATHER CHARLIE

is coming to the rehabilitation facility
    to give me communion on his way
        home from visiting hospitalized patients.

I've gotten out of my hospital gown
    and into real clothes, pulled up and
        smoothed tangled sheets and bedspread,

rolled into the bathroom in my wheelchair,
    and emptied my urinal. I take this
        opportunity to trash two vases of dead

flowers—one from my wife, another
    from a pretty poet friend. I have had nothing
        but sponge baths for six weeks, because

of the infusion line that runs through my arm
    to my heart and the thick bandages that rise
        from my toes to my knee. I really stink so

I spray the room with Lysol in hopes
    that it will soften and clean the air,
        and all this activity leaves me breathless,

exhausted, and trembling. I run a comb through
    my greasy hair and matted beard
        but it is so useless I feel like weeping.

Charlie is all smiles when he enters the room.
    He has a travel case for the paraphernalia
        needed to administer the Eucharist; however,

all the bread was used up at the hospital.
    He has, nonetheless, managed to secure a packet
        of crackers from the cafeteria which he consecrates.

Now that the saltines have become the flesh,
    he gives me communion. The cracker is dry,
        but a gulp of wine helps me to swallow it.

Finally, he anoints my forehead with oil
        and urges me to go in peace. Afterwards,
                there is a little conversation that touches

on Augustine, Aquinas, and St. John
        of the Cross. And then, after a handshake,
                he leaves me to go join the world. When I later

happen to look into the bathroom mirror,
        I see cracker crumbs in my beard. Carefully,
                I pick each crumb and eat it—not wanting

to desecrate the Body of Christ,
        wanting so badly to believe in this rite,
                praying that the magic works this time—

in this the dark night of the soul.

DOGWOODS

They had just settled
        on a small farmhouse
                seated on eight acres

of meadow when suddenly
        his wife died.
                After the formalities,

he sat on the back porch—
        a cedar box of ashes
                cradled in his lap—

looking out across
        the blank meadow
                while an idea began

to work its way
        up through the strata
                of his grief

like a dark fish rising
        to break the surface
                and dazzle into light.

The next morning
        he planted thirty-four
                dogwood saplings,

one for each year
        of her life. And
                into each hole,

along with compost,
        he sprinkled a few
                teaspoons of ashes.

Now, each spring—
        as he becomes
                an old man—

the meadow will break
        into a rush and flush
                of love and beauty lost.

CL Bledsoe

APRIL 26TH, 2011

They cut you out of your mother, blue
and silent and so, so breakable, handed
you off, and shoved us into a room full

of curtains and quiet murmurs. Smaller
than a football, you lay in my palm
while I wondered what I'd do when you woke

and started to cry. Everyone behind
the curtains would know I had no idea
how to fix this. Tiny, bundled girl,

you opened your eyes, fixed them on me
like a duckling imprinting on its mama.
The room was empty save for you and me.

DOOR: 5

After you were born, I understood
why my mother never closed doors.
Darkness conveys sound more effectively
than the day; my dreams have been
of your breath, regular and small.
This is my sleep, hearing you sleep.

In the mornings, you give your cereal
to the crows. They bring you castoff
trinkets, misplaced detritus. Likewise,
the squirrels you give nuts and seeds to
bring you flowers, bits of bark
with unusual hues. This, too, is love.

Your bed, an ark of stuffed animals,
the odd species dropping off when you
toss and turn. Many times, when I can't sleep,
I retrieve them before you grow restless.
If I closed the door behind me, you might
hear it and wake, I might find, once closed,
it will never open again.

Diana Smith Bolton

I.

The fingers cannot rest,
cannot ignore this magnet

      like a tide,
the filament stretching from my shoulder to your hip,

across the crowded room just one part
of a warren of crowded rooms, bodies

      in each throbbing
corner. *Here is where you touch me*, she whispers,

and she takes his fingers in her fingers, her fingers
moving to a foreign landscape, and she opens the atlas wide.

II.

The pressure must build,
must crescendo the cork

      from the bottle,
the force thrusting from containment into air.

In this fevered den far away
from our forgotten homes, shame

      in all directions.
What is the dread you visit in the dark? he asks,

as he twines his legs with her legs,
her legs trembling. A yellow bird and her breath, the cork from the bottle.

III.

The evening will close,
will evaporate our memory

      like morning mist,
the dampness burning under sun into airy nothing.

Before the open doorway, just down the hall
from a row of identical doorways, boots

      under every white bed—
this is how we choose our futures, we think,

and we collapse our bodies with other bodies,
all bodies carrying a minor crisis, and we collapse again and again.

Anthony Isaac Bradley

FIRST BORN STAR

~~Wanted to lick her pussy through the TV~~
~~Suckle every areolae bump like sacrament~~
Her nineties cut held enough bounce for me
to pretend she could headline an advertisement.
Baptize her into any girl in the choir.
Curls meant she could be out shopping
for Suave to ensure ascendance of hair, inspire
on the job, arrive smooth and humming.
I could hope to discover her lost in the aisle
of a supermarket, hands folded, but full: avocado,
pita bread. A woman on the domestic mile.
~~But I can't forget her mouth as an O~~
when—if—we scrub and spit, tuck in for a story
of indulgences as our lips part with history.

John Bradley

CELESTIAL PABLUM

After Remedios Varo's painting of the same name

I must feed the moon, you say, as you turn
the wheel, grinding gelid night stars into ever-
bright pablum. It's wrong, though, to consume
living light. *Nothing can be more right than kindness,*
when silted with salt, you tell the stars, as you grind
their shine into swirling powder on the small ceramic plate.
But you are captive here, Remedios, bound by
celestial task, punished for bringing edible light
into this inevitable world. *Stand back*, you warn.
Few can resist the shifting, sifted light. But why,
my lower back asks, why cage the curling crescent
moon? Soundless as moth crumb. Why forever
feed on its unending hunger? *I must follow this*
spoon, you note, *into the merest mouth. Even*
as it glows with the shine of skull. But why? Why not
let the moon glaze our flesh? Let it feast on vowel
of owl and vole. Silence. *I must feed the moon*,
you say, grinding the cosmos into dust.

April Michelle Bratten

If you don't know by now, you never will

Josie, you have never seen a blueberry bush this bright,
or a sky this dark like tea. I am a smart figure in the grass,

dreaming of breakfast, the day's rain on my face. I no longer notice
where you wake. Perhaps the sea, your blonde hair a torture

on innocent fish, or a stranger's garden, your tongue petrifying
the vegetables. I remember how easily your pansy mouth could suck

the black from dirt, the yellow from a bastard bee. How your hawkeyes bitched at my yes, my no, my moon hands in his.

I stepped away from you then—the girls' closet was much too full and spiteful.
I stepped away from you then—how I loved you, you April witch!

Together our vast throats could have consumed the earth,
but we grew rocks where our teeth should have been, spat diamonds.

The day the sun boiled our bodies you dared me to walk
the picket fence. I bested your effort, walked the long arm of the roof,

almost killed myself for you. Oh, God, Jo, I know you remember
how strong that boy's arms were, but you never knew his face,

and on the day when the light pounded the road with its uneasy thirst,
you looked our way, your engorged vagina feeling so empty.

Shirley J. Brewer

THE PRINCE OF CHEESE

for Ron Fader

My cheese man wears marigold
shirts, sings like a dairy canary.
His kingdom is a circular display
at Eddie's on St. Paul Street. As soon
as I enter the market, he's waiting
with a grin and a Gruyère. He tries
to be fair, but we both know
he favors Italian—luscious provolone,
mozzarella, Savello di Roma—
flavors of the boot in every bite.

Oh, how tenderly he holds
each small package of perfection.
When Ron says *Cheese*, shoppers click
their heels, then buy. Cow, goat, and sheep
visions curdle in his eyes. He weeps with joy.
To think I might have passed him by.
Mister Cheese teaches cheer, his
taste buds a happy bouquet, a gourmet
blossom envied even by the Swiss—
their cold palates so full of holes.

IN PLACE OF CAKE

we feast on wedding pies,
their round faces oozing rhubarb and peach
in the suffocating church reception hall.
Ceiling fans insult the air
with their lethargy. The Greek caterer
wields his knife like a kamikaze
confectioner's sword. When he raises
his arm to slice, we keep our hands
away from the pies—the risk
of *finger food* a clear possibility.

Those desserts a delight, bland crusts
concealing jewels: rich berry colors,
chocolate cream, even a tart
lemon with its crown of singed meringue.
No one misses the traditional
tower cake frosted in paste. Pies
offer choices; we relish our selections.
Two long tables soon empty. Square
cardboard boxes discarded in stacks
look like the remains of opened gifts.

Off to one side, the winsome bride glows
next to her handsome groom. Blind since birth,
he senses her joy, hears our praise of pies.
Behind his placid face, a tapestry blooms
within: delicious blues, verdant greens,
musical forests of fuchsia and orange.

twist

Come on baby, he cajoled us.
Chubby Checker changed history,
challenged our pelvises, much like Elvis,
only Chubby made it seem easy, his
jovial face living proof we could groove
despite warnings from our chiropractors
to abandon this ludicrous dance.

In the lounge's dim light, you request
a Bombay Martini with a twist.
I picture the lemon remnant gyrating
'round and 'round this slippery cocktail glass.
It startles the laid-back gin, wins
applause from the bar's docile limes,
thrills obese maraschino cherries.

Even the green Spanish olives lighten up.
Their red pimiento beacons pulse
like the buzzer at the bistro
that lets you know your table's ready.

Michael Brockley

HAVING DISCOVERED UNRELIABLE NARRATORS IN HER LEISURE READING, SIRI APPLIES HER NEWFOUND LOGIC TO HER WORK

Siri directs you to diners with health code violations every time you ask for a restaurant that serves fresh fish. To a roach coach parked in a No-Parking zone beside a hazardous waste dumpster in response to your queries about the best chili in town. You ask her to check her GPS algorithms, and she sends you to a biker bar on Cornbread Road. A converted Blockbuster store now famous for its recreational brawls. At first she apologizes for the mixups. Understands you're not interested in Tea Party fish fries and Republican wiener roasts. You try to pay her more attention. Compliment her on the earrings she is wearing. Ask her where she got such a captivating outfit. You invite her to choose the CD to listen to during work commutes. But when you want a sushi restaurant with a wine list and many artisanal options on its menu, Siri sends you the wrong way on one-way streets until you reach an abandoned park downwind from a pharmaceutical lab. Where the air is rife with ammonia and flatulence. You summon Siri on your cell phone. Gag through your complaints about her disregard for your wellbeing. You ask to speak with her supervisor to request a replacement. Maybe someone named Sola or Yazmin. Someone who is comfortable in little black dresses as well as jeans. Someone with a sultry voice. An upgrade, so to speak. Siri hums show tunes. *Whatever Lola wants, Lola gets.* Says she thinks you need a remote adventure. Insists she'll do all the driving from now on.

THE MAYOR OF HAMELIN

I met the Mayor of Hamelin at a wine-tasting seminar. He unfolded
a card from his wallet with 130 names curlicued in monkish German
script. Names like Moesperg, Decan Lude. He ignored the California
samples our hostess proposed. Favored Moesels and Spätburgunders.
When I wondered about the children lost to the cave of Klöppen Hill, he
retrieved the card and laid it on a napkin. He said after he cheated the
piper the townsfolk banished him to his penance. Trolling the cities and
hamlets of the world with the roster of *die Kinder des Rättenfangers*
as his only *raison d'être*. Along his journey, he learned sleight-of-hand.
Still carried worn florins in a moleskin pouch. Delighted children by
pulling coins from behind their ears. He extended his glass for a taste of
Gunderloch Riesling Trocken and spoke of Transylvania. Saddened as he
remembered Goethe reciting *Der Erlkönig* in Weimar. At last, he emptied
the dregs into a spit bucket and ran a finger under the faded cursive.
Tapped the name of his mistress's daughter, Magda. He said he could
sleep in his Hamelin bed again if he returned with just one child. I looked
over the roll. At the names now centuries old. Pointed to one, a surname
that might have meant *badger hole or crumb*. Knowing this could be our
one chance at forgiveness. *That's me*, I lied.

The only Aloha shirt in town

A retired nurse found the town's only aloha shirt while cleaning her attic. It was buttoned around a set of books one of her exes left in a banker's box. The nurse wore the shirt in the evening while she treated herself to a glass of wine. While she danced alone with Monk and Coltrane. During the holidays, she hosted a Scrabble tournament for members of her church and agreed to donate her talisman to a clothing drive. But the outreach chair's daughter plucked the garment from the miscellaneous bin. And being the sort of girl who stood up when everyone else sat down, she wore it to her school where all her classmates sported v-neck sweaters tucked into white pegged jeans. She enjoyed the in-school suspensions and edgy reputation. Until she became interested in the poems of Anna Akhmatova and never noticed when her father included the shirt in a care package for an intern at the Rand McNally map printers where he worked. The intern gave the aloha shirt to her best friend to celebrate her new job as a camp counselor. And so the only aloha shirt in town passed from person to person. A divorced homecoming queen, vacationing in Havana, kept the shirt on a hanger in her cottage. "For luck," she wrote on each postcard she sent home. A former mayor put it on before caring for his wife during the worst of her dementia. The town's pharmacist fell in love for the first time on the day he wore the shirt beneath his smock. Some folks kept the shirt for a week or so but most held onto the talisman for a month. A Little League umpire needed it for a baseball season. The local surrealist spent last winter using the shirt as a pie pan whenever he baked his signature bumbleberry pies. His neighbors gossip at the supermarket. Hoping the shirt will come to the elementary school's champion dodgeball player or to the woman who keeps black toads in her yard.

Kevin Brown

PRISON

is more than this,
than a slammed gate that locks you in,

than walls and mesh-wire
windows, watered-down milk served with watered-down

meals, than same-colored
uniforms on different-colored inmates, than bodies herded

in stencilized existence, cuffed
chaos and caged rage, knowing when to stand

and stand down, than
routine branded into mind and muscle, and always

thinking in number scales—
6'x8', 3 meals a day, 60 minutes yard

time every 24 hours,
names spelled with 8 digits stamped across backs,

4¢/hr, $31.51 in savings,
4 years, 48 months, 298 weeks, 1,460 days.

It's more than fear,
loneliness, anger and regret, embarrassment and boredom, disbelief

and acceptance, than receiving
care packages of photos, cards, and letters, Dora

pictures colored outside the
lines and the best Keefe coffee ever drank,

than kid names over
hearts inked with soot and shampoo, than watching

your son grow up
and away, seeing your little girl for the

first time each time,
every Sunday from 1–3, missing dance recitals, graduations,

wedding anniversaries that will
one day be just another date scratched off

on a wall, than
sleepless nights when you realize this is your

life, and nights of
deep sleep when you realize this is your

life, it's more than
checkers, poker, reading paperbacks, and writing letters to

anyone anywhere else, mopping
for minimal wage, drinking liquor fermented in toilets

made from fruit skins
Christmas Eve, toasting friends bound by address through

sentence, than fights won,
fights lost, solitary confinement, gangs, the barter system,

sex or no sex,
religion or no religion, heads raised, heads dropped,

heads watching the shackled
hands of the clock chip 34,944 hours away,

to where the gate
slams and locks you out, where outstretched arms

touch nothing touching back.
Prison was that and more, but not much.

for #34576051

Mary Ann Cain

I PRETEND TO BE CHINESE

After M. H.

I pretend to be Chinese,
change my name to follow
hot yellow trails,
hummingbird flickers
feeding on fermented
sound: drunken mash-ups that crash
like atoms in search of skin.

Reckless, I hover and break,
break and steal, entering a lush
hologram where my blood is stripped
of its red throat, and I fly, aimless,
into the necks of presidents
and other prominent goiters.

I place myself in a translation
I can't pronounce, or even read,
only sense a drunken mash-up
of peripheral olfactory grimaces
that pass for cash. In my stumbling
arc, nothing flies any different than any
church's bell. Nothing sunflower
can bloom, or even sway, other than
any other yellow. I grew tired of being
blank, and now hide my anus
in animated light, so no one will hear
the crash and fall of a bloodbeat
that can't help but be echo,
swooning into the arms of a star, lost,
whose name no one can remember.

Roger Camp

BONFIRE OF THE VALENTINES

for Jerry Enroth

It started as a leaf burning,
a raked pile of golden kindle
spiffed with phosphorescent flares
of fiery leaves branded into the heap.
Forked at the top,
a turnover exposing skeletal rot,
a doily of spidery veins
matching the hand that wrote the cryptic cards
and love letters rich in the *silence of innuendo*.
Dumped carelessly, followed by
every gift which spoke his name,
a silk scarf choking an Italian
serving dish, seasoned in lighter fluid
and set alight.

Doritt Carroll

MY NAME

i try not to hate you
for mangling my name

for saying Dora
or Dorothy
or Doris

because you've heard of those
and what can exist in the world
that you haven't heard of

i try not to hate you
for ignoring the way i say it
as if you are overlooking
some social faux pas

my left hand extended
or spinach caught between my teeth

after 50 years i am almost used to
the way you reverse the order—
"is Carroll there?"—

as if my father was a fool
who never could adapt
to this country's better ways

as if there is only
one way a name can be
which is
just like yours

KATIE

the days still warm but
browning on the edges
like toast
the sun bright but
somehow scant

maybe September sun
is margarine
instead of butter
a bit unsatisfying
harbinger of shortages

of light
of time
of days

with this girl
in the passenger seat
not talking

her yellow ponytail
seeming to bend her head
toward the glowing afternoon window
like a sunflower
curved on its stalk

Grace Cavalieri

FIRST MEAL AFTER HIS DEATH

I took a knife and peeled the fruit
So it will bleed, be eaten, heal—

Scrupulously I gave my best
(under the remembered
frosted moon
flavored by Autumn's sky)

This in my hand is essential goodness
Otherwise the morning is unremarkable
Spiritually desperate even—

What do we want from this idea? Sympathy?
The persistence of what is fatal?
Or appetite, a momentary camouflage of happiness—

CAVEFISH OUT FROM UNDER THE ROCKS

I used to be in a Broadway state of mind
But now I'm in a subjunctive sort of mood
All I knew of love was how to say goodbye
Clutch and success
Pledged to all that could not stay
Then charity began at home
Countervailing winter's Solstice
Bluebirds throbbing
I wish   I were   I wish   I were
Vulnerable and safe
A harp with no wrong chord
I'm   *supposed*   to be happy
If I were   If you were   If I become
Once I was in the Mississippi Mud, now
Everything's possible
If I were   If you were   if I become
Green meadows with wishing stars
I want to walk till the dust turns blue
Using up the present
Until the last floating tree's
An indicative case of nothing at all
If it only were   would that I   if I become

Laura Cesarco Eglin

without words

The scars are pictographs
that accompany your history
they open stories to me
let me trace myself in their reliefs
I run my fingers over them
and learn them by heart

If the shadow advances, erases
my mouth, it is not a question
of hoping the hours will pass
and the sun will move:
in that same place in the now
my voice slices through the shadows.

I begin to understand despair
pain that stabs, makes me
press my lashes together
tears sharp in my throat
I blink hard
so that they won't see me crying so that
I don't see you thinking about telling me
you're about to close your eyes

—*Translated by Catherine Jagoe and Jesse Lee Kercheval*

WRITING IN A CAFÉ

This brown windowsill is the beginning. I sit
gazing at a glass flower vase that insists on cutting
the stem of its daisy in two. Gazing
every time I finish a sentence, as if reading
between the lines, as if understanding the pauses make
the reading.

—*Translated by Catherine Jagoe and Jesse Lee Kercheval*

Patrick Chapman

NOT A BIRD

Ciao Bella Metropolis. I order the pizza bianca.
Then I whip my Anglo Americans off to look you
in the eye but you deflect my beam by turning on
your merlot, staring down your own gaze frowning
up. Trying to hide your gratitude. Sure, you've an idea
of what I am about to say but please, don't mention it.
Make nothing of my sacrifice.

                    Just now I heard a plane
go down, hundreds of innocents screaming as the brace
position failed them. The aquiline nose cone of the DC-10
crumpled on the runway. Shockwaves splintered back along
the body of the bird, ripping the wings away, crushing the pods
—the tires burst—pop-pop!—great balls of fire flushing the cabin
with lightspeed inferno and I, I could have saved them but you,
well, you needed to meet. See how much I think of you, Miss Lane.

Juliet Cook

MIDDLE-GROUND PUSSY

At least imagining my eye shifts
as strobe lights makes me feel
something young, instead of
researching eye floaters,
feeling older than my age.

Thinking of carapace strains.
Thinking of fluid drains.
Thinking of dissection of
white mounds of pubic hair
ripped off with fangs.

I'm too young for girdles.
I'm too old for weekly waxing
off the pussy hair. Off with my head,
with my mixed-up, middle-aged digits.

One side fine-tuned, trimmed, and bleached;
the other side a hairy, dirty, blood-drenched mess,
screaming like a decimated blowtorch.

SEMI-ABSTRACT SELF-PORTRAIT

My red yarn runs across
the floor like a bleeding rat.

My neck veins stick out
further and further
until they start dripping down.

Fans cannot trap me
because I don't have any fans.
Only my own mind is allowed
to hang from this ceiling,
drip, drop, and dangle
over the edge.

My disembodied logic floats faster
around the room, trying
to fill every spoon with non-

liquid sinking into
confetti bones.

Juliet Cook and j/j hastain

INSTEAD OF THE DOCTOR

Conjoined at the slit
and so
the mortician
gets out
her scalpel.
Blades dissect

grass. An acerbic area
in May.
A mother at a mall
uses her tweezers to
protect and to serve,
but then the little vixen swerves

into the back room
of the toy store
and hides in between
the lines of microscopes.
They bend and sway
in the fan wind.

Is microorganism necrophilia
crawling around the ceiling
in between the light
and dark swirls? Is that little
girl soon to be extracted
by the experimental mortician?

Awaiting her latest turn,
and then fired
into a misshapen urn.

Robert Cooperman

TRACKS IN THE SNOW: CHRISTMAS EVE

After last night's snow
primed our side yard,
we stare at abstract
brush strokes: squirrels,
a cat in Pollock drips
searching for sex, mice,
or a good fight; a rabbit's
tracks, stopping, sniffing
the air for danger,
then going underground
to its safe warren;
and of course, a fox
stalking everything else
in our crossroads yard.

As we scrape ice from the car
as if with palette knives,
we're grateful not to find
blood: a still-life reminder
of what nature's really like,
especially in winter: stars
so icily pointilistic-distant
they offer no solace
to the small animals
that hurry past,
like those figures
in winter scenes of small,
isolated, snow-clogged villages,
after the bloody canvas
of the Franco-Prussian War.

A SHORT MOVIE OF BLAZE STARR, THE STRIPPER

In the '40s and '50s, Blaze was Baltimore's
scorching stripper, giving Navy boys on leave
and college kids something to whistle about,
with her breasts like succulent torpedoes.
A friend sent me one of her short movies;
curious, and a little horny, I watched her
artfully tease off garments, only an industrial-
strength bra and panties left, while she straddled
the bed prop and pistoned, tossing her head
in mock ecstasies, accompanied by silky clarinets,
not the thump of drums you'd expect
from a bump and grind: innocence itself,
compared to her later screen sex.

Watching, I remembered the time we took
a friend about to be married to a Denver strip club.
A cowboy had convinced his girlfriend
to perform for money, her face a pleading red,
expected by the owner to reveal everything.
We left before she finished, ashamed, yet
something almost irresistible in her stripping
away layers of safe clothing and her flushed
revelation of what her boyfriend was really like.

Blaze might've told her, gently, "Hon, go back
to your daddy's Wyoming ranch," though maybe
that was a haven already closed to her.

Karen Craigo

BOWER

It's not the money, it's what
the money gives us—a place
that's ours, something in
the belly, permission to move
through the world. Isn't this
what the bowerbird says?
Sticks joined in a sturdy arch,
and all around, the things
a bird admires—stones
and pop cans, blossoms
and shells, arranged
by color and type, and,
the ornithologist tells us,
staged, just so, smallest
to largest. He's using
forced perspective,
an architect's trick, messing
with scale to suggest
grandeur. If we're smart,
we hold what we have.
The male bowerbird says
he'll take care of the one
who watches from the grass.
Pile of feathers, pile of glass,
that which you covet I have.

time is money

I'm not sure what time it is,
an hour misplaced between
phone and laptop, and it's never
been my habit to keep a watch.
So here I am in the middle
of time, both early and late,
but with nothing awaiting me,
so it might be said I have all
the time in the world. Strange
way we have of putting it.
I would never hoard time.
Someone might need it, like I
once did, to study the starfish
hand of a brand new boy, or
to count backwards as
the hockey game concludes,
the rocket ship ignites. How
will they launch the silver cup
if I won't relinquish time?
And anyway, I'm not convinced
it's what we think it is—
some thread we roll up
in a skein until we reach
the frazzled end of it.
Time is more like that time
I dropped cornstarch in
the Amish store. The stuff
went everywhere, no matter
more resistant to gathering
in a pile, and soon other hands
were helping, pushing the grains
into a mound, those hands
attached to cuffs of dresses
held together with straight pins,
anachronistic, pushing away
time and invention because

zippers and buttons are proud.
And look how my attention
has wandered from our pile of time,
and the stubborn particles of it
that don't make it to the mound
but escape into woodgrain
and refuse to be pushed.
A figure in black wields
a dustpan, and there goes
our metaphor, or most of it—
into a bin, not cosmic,
but corrugated and clean,
behind an Amish counter,
and all who saw it work
on forgetting the particulars,
keep only a keener understanding
of supernovas. All I'm wanting
is to know what time it is,
which device to put faith in.
I have work to do, a storehouse
to fill, and time is something
finer and faster than sand,
and I've seen, oh, I've seen
how it gets away from us.

Rachel Dacus

A VIEW OF LIFE FROM THE BEACH

On a stretch of powdered shells
where the surf flops and the horizon sways,
I wrestle my towel and nap, counting
each wave's smack and long-dreaming
myself more awake to each
sand grain's crystal splendor.

After a race into the sea
and a tussle with a towel,
I plan a long slide into the deep water.
Gusts of evening halfway arc
my life's bridge. I am old but the sea

sighs softly all night in my pillow,
like the sounds of lovers
who keep reaching for each other
and the tides of years roll me
over onto my back. I otter
on each wave's foamy tip
and again slip beneath.

Every morning, half-drowned,
I open a mango under a local palm
and read the news that gets newer.
This seaweed tangle words
make when they unbranch and the pods
get popped, as a child does,
merely for the pleasurable
whoosh of releasing saltwater.

GOOD HEAD FOR NUMBERS

I have a good head
for numbers but numb fingers,
and so half the week I live
in 3015, a millennium apart
from you. I date my checks
(such an outdated way to pay)
to be cashed ten lifetimes hence.

The IRS has no idea
of my whenabouts.
I time travel on Schedule C
and the tea kettle's whistle
blows me into yesterday.
I calculate the fricatives
and penumbral halos
of numbers as they fly by,
spinning my head, good
for naught, for numbers
as it may be.

Michael Daley

GENTLE DONG

It's not what you think. Ushered through velvet, its name over a door whose veiled origins hum, those wounded by the strange device entered a hall swimming in light. Beloveds hinting dispossession, whole countries of regret mapped on faces, bridges to our sullen art. An old man delights in readiness, while women joked, "How do you go around wearing one of those?" Happy weapon, it wakes us mid-dream to worry the prostate, embarrasses at school board meetings; caffeine affected, it drips in the rush. In a cumbersome codpiece, pissing wars in the later years, this contraption, or one like it never much improved upon, fueled history, led assault, swung the club, brokered the treaty, broke it, planted starts for endless replication, and can't be blamed. Soft tissue one's hand might brush tossing in insomnia and be reminded of another's touch. Nurse changing linen so casually comes close as if it were kneecap, big toe, a pretty piece of flesh, a dingle's lightning rod, wishbone off the fault line. Phenomenon we perish by, a high percentage do, or ignore at our peril that grave-pointing finger, water witch, proboscis of delusion we so charmingly hide.

Princely Hummingbird
sliver tip, narwhal-like,
vanishes in northern azure,
throbs on a wire
above his domain of roses.

THE LOSS OF BEAUTY

The way a face haunts us with its purity about the lips, within the eyes' glow, its frank pleasure in being; we can't exhaust ourselves with looking. All day every face gives everything it has to offer in the briefest encounters, but we need to see this one face perform. More than stillness, the eye needs its laughter, its calm trust, even savagery if we can withstand a sudden loss in one face out of millions.

> We cannot survive.
> Hearts roam continents panting
> over the wooden road.

Mark Danowsky

THE ROCKY MOUNTAIN LOCUST SURGE

One story is about the farmer
who just started running
right into the black mass
in a dispersal attempt.
How far past wits' end
would you have to be pushed?
He must have become the bull
seeing red—no? Just a human
out of ideas, out of hope—
ready for oblivion.
I'd guess the cloud of locusts
looked like a giant TV
tuned to static.
When he found himself
back on the outside
they say the locusts had eaten
the clothes right off his body.
Can you see him standing there?
In the middle of a dry field
flattened by plague
naked, except for his boots
his family looking on
from the windows of their dusty home
wondering why they came here
where promises are unfulfilled.

Kristina Marie Darling and John Gallaher

THE MUSEUM OF THE OCCUPATION

So, of course, you have to go in. And of course, each piece has a card
that reads "Give Me Back" beneath it, but, as you're reading it, it's not
clear if it's directed at you or if it's just a subtle reminder that each brick
of the city was forged in a different world, by different workers, with
their different dreams and hopes who were later to be shot and lined in
rows to illustrate the garden plot, where the hedge will one day go. It's
April. There's a woodpecker letting loose somewhere down the block.
The museum windows are open, which makes it seem the woodpecker
is right next to you. But instead, all you have is this floor plan with the
guard rotation schedule and a cyanide pill in case you're captured, and
the questions get too complicated, where you forget to carry the ten,
and they implore you to take a light rest, maybe some lemonade. "I
Remember" is the title of the traveling exhibition you came expressly to
see, and it's still here, which is surprising, as usually by the time you get
to these things they've gone on to Cincinnati. It's never really Cincinnati,
though. When we say Cincinnati we just mean we're going to die soon,
that the weather's looking bad.

IN THE BIRD MUSEUM

The traveling exhibition was disappointing, to say the least. First, there
were the seemingly endless rows of hummingbirds, shot and mounted
for display. Then the tiny golden placards, each name more unsayable
than the last. When I try to read them to you, the words gather in my
mouth like the hem of a dress. The entire time you had been expecting
something familiar, perhaps a landscape painting, but here, even the
flowers have been made strange. And every corridor seems to carry
us farther from the old house, the hedge, the garden plot. Before long
we're the only visitors, with the exception of the curator. Now a narrow
staircase, a locked room, a series of security codes. You seem nervous
that I'm just standing there, waiting for you to open the door.

William Virgil Davis

A BOX OF DARK

When I came into the room
it was there, a small gray box
tied in red ribbons. It had my name
on a card attached to the top.

There was no signature.
The box was light and delicate
and I opened it carefully. I didn't
want to break whatever it was.

I took the lid off and folded
the tissue paper back and looked.
There seemed to be nothing there.
Then I realized that it was only

a box of dark. I dumped it out
in my hand and carried it
across the room and put it
in a vase on the mantelpiece.

Occasionally, I take it down
and show it to someone.
I cannot say how very much
it has always meant to me.

HANDS

I've always been vain
about my hands. I guess
that means I have a hand fetish.

I've always been attracted
to photographs of hands—
just hands, or maybe a hand
and a wrist, but never an arm
beyond the elbow.

I've always been envious
of people who work
as hand models, their hands
the hands one sees in photographs,
hands to be admired.

I always want to hold those hands.

Mary Stone Dockery
THIS IS DATING

(a partial found poem composed of lines from OkCupid dating profiles)

I'm not quite the same person as I was before
so I've started this new profile.

Hedonist, I sing the fire. Or maybe it's the body electric.

I know enough about confession to unroll my acrylic tongue and
    paint the space between our mouths bruise-red, unholy.

I was one of those kids whose Mom hosed down before I could
    come in
from playing. Mud used to be safe.

When I want love I let my body love first, love hard.

I clean up nice. Think, paint, eat, repeat.

I love tattoos and plagiarism and finding her
on her couch at night with a guitar
and a cigarette, wearing a hangover.

A lover should be OK with sneaking cigarettes in a dive bar bath-
    room. With lifting her skirt.

I'd rather turn forty than understand
internal combustion,
visit an old friend than say the "Act of Contrition."

I don't really like people. Eat, think, paint, repeat.

She does not walk. She hovers and trades back massages even
    when I interrupt her.

You should message me if you
are a country girl, are a not a telemarketer,
if you want to know more about beards
if you love to satisfy, if you live somewhere
between Arcadia and Beverly Hills,
if you are polyamorous, if you are faithful,
if you're a super hot super wealthy nymphomaniac
    a boy can dream, a boy can dream—
if you have patience even for ghouls.

She chooses me. She chooses me and wears mismatched socks
    and says O God O God O God.

Stephanie McCarley Dugger

3:00 A.M., Knoxville

Songbirds chirrup through the night.   I miss
        the silence of the West   the clear sky
        where one or two birds pass over   in a single afternoon.
            There,
birds are never warblers,   but predators   looking for a carcass
or cat   to snatch from a yard.
                            The loneliness of the bare rocks
                    is sharpening hollowing.
Here,   the dogs uncovered a buried bag of cocaine behind our house.
            I imagined   the previous renters
                sitting around a fire   paranoid
        about the sirens blasting from the nearby interstate.
            But it was more likely kids   after all,
        hiding   the stash   from nosy parents.
                    I hunted for more,
dozens   of small holes   dug in the grass. I was looking
                        for consistency.
                                    When I was young
I searched for hunger.   The tulip tree beside the swing
shed its yellow and orange blossoms until the ground became candy,
        tempting me to nibble the petals   when I played homeless.
        But I was afraid of poison,
                afraid   the blooms would send my body
into seizures   or worse
        I would die quietly   in my sleep,   soothed.
            Now I lie awake
        listening   for hands through the window
            hands
that will take me violently from this room.   I wonder
        if I'm substantial enough   to leave.

Kristina England

A STATEMENT OF LINES

Attendants herd crowd into "No photos allowed"
gallery, "Van Gogh and Nature" on display.
We seek our proper places in line, shift with
the position of each painting, dark arch
of his childhood home, parsonage, garden
scarred by winter, makes us mope, descend
into creaking halls, angry whisper of mother
telling loud-stepped father to be quiet, don't
wake us. We shake heads, all troubled by
our own shoes, move on to brighter things,
splash of color, *Vase with Carnations and
Other Flowers*, people relax, walk faster,
watch each others' toes, perfectly sequenced
dance. Lady in tan khakis snaps, breaks line,
"I'm behind you." Man keeps eyes fixed on
Rain-Auvers as if he can feel the last streaks
of Vincent. I do not turn to see the woman.
I am too near to licking of water on canvas,
can hear the cold. Want coffee. Stumble into
gift shop. Wonder if woman found her way,
stood up close, gave those brush strokes her
mind, or if she took a quick, cursory glance,
bought a purse, thought the rain pretty.

EATING MY WAY THROUGH DEATH

I order a donut a day in memory of my grandmother
who ate two Boston cremes a morning, even though
she always told me to "watch your weight, you have
such a pretty frame." She had heart surgery at sixty-
five, clogged arteries, chunky thighs, and it's the
second bout of cancer that sucked the fatty layers
of dough out of her. I eat a frosting-filled center,
savor each sugary bite, think memorials should
span the length of one's waist. Stomach never
liked gluten. Shed five pounds by her burial.

Joyce Maust Enzor

Growing Up Mennonite

"You're a girl; know your place!"

No leading congregational prayers.
No teaching anyone in their teens or older by yourself.
No preaching.
No being President or Vice President of the youth.
No heading up anything except women's committees.
No acting as worship leader.
No speaking out.
No having a theological opinion.

"Silence!"

Work on the food committee.
Head up the sewing committee.
Be in charge of carry-in dinners.
Participate in special singing.
Do anything involving food.
Teach children's Sunday School.
Work as a secretary for any committee.
Be content in the role we put you.

"All roles of leadership must be held by men!"

I wonder what Jesus thinks.

"Go away, Deborah! Go away, Mary Magdalene! Go away, Lydia! Go away any woman not subservient—No room for you!"

So I went away...

Kallie Falandays

WATCHING AT THE WINDOW FOR
SOMETHING BIG TO HAPPEN

In the half-light of evening, E. reads me lines of prose that strike him:
the light through the window. A shrieking through a pinhole.
The back-window shadow on your ass. We strike and strike;

want to fill ourselves whole again. It's hard enough to respond.
The dryer screeches pitifully in the daylight. Our eyes grow bigger
when we don't yet know we love. And after we stop loving, I might say

hunger widens like a porch light burning out and I would mean
only something about the bugs; how they turn away from us then.
Our skin is slick from our own hearts and we're beating for something

earnest. I wouldn't beg anyone to love me, although I have I have I have.
The air in my left lung whimpers when he speaks. It wants to speak back.
To say *yes the line about the sick parade. You're right about the sick parade.*

It's true: everything we thought wasn't haunted is. The ghost grows more filthy
whenever we hide him away. The ghost will grow wider whenever we look
to the left. Whenever we open our blinds, the ghost sharpens his teeth

faster. Everyone wants someone to wilt.

Matthew P. Garcia

GUAVA WINE BLUES

Remember that day—that day when in all careless disregard
We drove down to the fruit farm in the Redlands and sampled the wines
Of avocado and carambola, mango, passion fruit and guava.

Could you recall if asked, the way we eagerly made our way
Through the property out back, bottle in hand of our select favorite—
   guava wine
The memory of its taste aging in the narrative cast of our lives ever since.

In the sudden downpour we scuttled over to a table beneath a pavilion
   on the lawn
And for a brief moment we watched the rain and drank quietly and content
Grateful for the time alone and the fermented fruit of deferred longing.

It was this virgin cloak you wore that brought me there to lift the veil.
And just before it was uncovered you might recall the message left
Addressing *the whore* who leaves her family at home and sneaks away
To fruit farms in unincorporated agricultural areas of the south
To drink guava wine with a man several years her junior.

And before—just before the intrusion we had noticed with great zeal
The impression the light made when it was filtered through the glass
Of shadows tossed by the rain in the wine. We looked through our glasses—
Through the ruddy haze at a world shrouded in ambiguity.

Now, many years later as you are mine and I am yours
And the world indeed has changed and come full circle—I drink
   burgundy wine at my desk
Staring through the glass and recall the sweet taste of guava and the
   needling rain
As I write a letter of contempt addressed to *the whore.*

Bernadette Geyer

PARABLE OF IMPENDING DOOM

Dumb pig iron fate eastbound and 41 miles away
traveling at 90 miles per hour toward the pomp
and circumstance of the gathered citizens.

Because, once hung, the streamers in the square
could not be unhung, their lazy arms waving
in mute celebration, gaudy pinks and greens

that seemed to mock the gravity of the occasion.
And anyway only one believed the recounted
dream of the prophet. Only one of the hundreds

who heard that street-corner sermon streaming
forth this morning from the mouth of the dreamer.
Only one crying *Didn't you hear? Don't you believe?*

until she was hoarse and desperate, disbelieving
the disbelief she elbowed through, finally breaking
out of and away from those eyes that turned away.

Bolts on the fishplate cracked and failing so that
the sections of jointed bullhead rail unwedded,
fixed asunder as an eye from an eye, an ear from an ear.

If only the graduates had recalled the crucial *if-then*
of their algebraic manifesto, but they tossled their tassles
and worried their chairs by inches aft and fore.

The one who survived being the one who
washed her hands of them early. The one
who was nowhere to be found when it arrived.

GHOST, I REMEMBER

the rotten plum color of that carpet
in my room. Every splintercold snick

of ice under my nails as I scraped
winter from the inside of my windows.

Some days I schemed to conjure you
but then recanted while my numb

fingers fumbled a plastic rosary, pitted
one form of belief against another.

I trained my newly pierced ears to hear
night whisper its vulgar gossip

into the dusty folds of the curtains,
but refused to confirm with open eyes

any shifting shapes in the shadows.
I learned to doubt, and then I left.

At times, I return to that house
with my daughter—whose future

I am tasked to shape with knowledge
and faith but shape, instead, by my

lack of both. There is now no need
for you to scuff and pace and ache

these looseboard floors, no need
to spook the watch hands backwards,

because now you are the least
of what, daily, haunts me.

Stephen Gibson

Saving the Mare

We were both drunk driving back to the harness
track where my friend was a groom, with a sulky
and bunk, and who kept a notebook because he
was going to be a writer—but it was all business:
whenever he tried to write something in the barn
during a moment's downtime, it was interrupted
with mucking out a stall or getting horses watered,
or keeping an eye on the one with the bowed tendon.
It wasn't fair, it wasn't fair, we whined to each other
as we had in Lost Angels (sliding bills under garters
so we could get close to the strippers); it wasn't fair
our jobs kept us from writing and no one cared—
like, with him, when the vet was up to his shoulders
inside the mare having cut in half her breached foal.

Kate Gillespie

to THE ARISING civilizations on my right hand

I bestow an atlas
Etched on atoms
Imprinted by Picosize wires
Chemosensory summons
Implanted into a biofilm city
For a denizen to find
A curious *Actinobacter*, perhaps
May interpret in bacterial Braille
The scope of the light kissed epidermis
From thumb to four fingers, my contours
Knuckle formation, continental divide
The gentle plains of palm, caverns of nail
Sweat rivers in the rivets of wrist
I will chart for you the embedded blood tunnels
I will detail the webbings upheavals
Multitude of wrinkles, warmed by biomagma
To you, the curious, here is my invitation
For the fungal
For the facultative
Fated to reside, unknowing
Generations to live and die
Without consciousness
Of our universe
Go forth, my Voyager in miniature
If received and understood
I will await your signal
Our future communication
To be intensely
Biomic

Sid Gold

STRANGER

Red dwarfs comprise three-fourths of the stars in the known universe. Cyclo drivers are among the poorest workers in Vietnam. And there stands the Accuser, alert to our every falsehood. I'd watch out for his polarity if I were you, advised Serena. Some of them stretched on their backs with both legs shackled in irons not moveable. The astrolabe was superseded by the sextant. Bananas cannot peel themselves. You must be witty, reminded the Chair. Very, very witty. The razor's edge of an unexpected silence. The rainbow in the eastern skies promised a fair evening. A healthy skepticism need not extend to arithmetic. Garrison had never been afraid of the dark. She buttered her bread. She walked barefoot through the city. Several hundred South American tribes have become extinct since the inception of colonization. The mud-brick structures of Mesopotamia required regular maintenance and periodic rebuilding. Comets follow elliptical or parabolic orbits around the sun. Coke burns with almost no ash as residue. Aguas de Marco. A watch is not a wheel. A moth is not a mallet. What to do with this pretty child? Desert soils are either light gray or brownish-gray. There exist actions for which the consequences cannot be ignored. He claimed more than a dozen tattoos, all drawn with invisible ink. The onset of iron weaponry made possible the growth of large armies. Rolling thunder in the mountains. Their eyes polished with curiosity. Exile is at any rate preferable to imprisonment. Oh, why do you even bother to think about it anymore?, Vonda snapped bitterly. I grew in those seasons like corn in the night. Sit down & eat quietly, stranger, or go somewhere else.

noon

The coal miners Van Gogh preached among in Borinage remained unaware of his later calling as a painter. Josephus writes that Titus did not intend to destroy the Second Temple. I've been hip from the beginning, alleged Solly. For whatever reasons, everyone said no to turnips. The Neanderthals buried their dead with the bones of sacrificed animals. Dana has her voodoo bop look down pat. Our vast but imperfect souls. Let us now visit that pleasant country. Daguerre began making photographs of Paris in 1839. One neighbor's bedroom window is still lit at 3:00 a.m. A cold beet salad is clearly better with grapefruit. Who can say what the gatekeeper believes? Spiteful as a thorn, she thought. Vicious or vicarious? Crowd or crow? Adorable Toughie requires a certain finesse. My mind was on the backbeat. One never expects to see a large fish sitting at table, no matter how friendly it is. Is that your idea of fun?, Bradley persisted. The over-mantels of Elizabethan fireplaces were often decorated with plaster reliefs. Anything could be happening behind a closed door. Roethke, for example, died of a coronary occlusion when he was fifty-five. Now I climb high above the busy square. Going crazy is not what I'm about, Claudette assured us. Cleopatra sailed to Tarsus for her first meeting with Antony. The implacable horizon of the body. I beg of you, do not neglect the bad machine. Come into my night garden, coaxed Madame LeFleur. Nothing here will harm you. His discourse so weightless it could not move air. The sultry ambiguity of dawn. The naked clarity of noon.

Bergson believed time spent refuting other philosophies was time wasted. Ready to get your glow on?, the counterman asked Elaine. Limestone is the compressed remnants of ancient sea life. Now there's a crowbar you can use with confidence. The Assyrian victory at Nihriya effectively ended Hittite power in the region. Pity the poor wretch destroyed by slander. In 1800, one-third of the British population worked in agriculture. Her words nibble at me like fish bait. Fear made fine bedfellows. The Mercalli scale measures an earthquake's intensity. Osborne wondered whether the subjunctive had passed him by. Not custom, but ritual. Not rare, but sensitive. Like a breath of wind, Athena passed to the maiden's bed. So, Doc, he asked, what are you doing with oxygen these days? Sikhism began as a reaction against the caste system. Lest we forget, the sign read. Just one more instantaneous lapse in judgment. I'm sure I've seen you in Remington's, she said, giving him the once-over. Sweden or sweeten? Pistol or pistachio? Every anesthetic using cocaine proved quite dangerous. My unguents were always from Benares, wrote Gautama. Unlike bronze, iron weaponry could be easily mass-produced. Maureen's real talent was in posing difficult questions. Toasted garlic was her nickel. Ah, but we haven't taken Manhattan, observed Haggerty. Beset by hailstones large as lemons. Coffin flies lay their eggs in corpses. He liked sitting alone in the dark, the AC pumping on high, his mind racing. Search as you might, you'll never find the fifth paw of the cat.

CRAWL

Certain historians treat Mary the Jewess as a legitimate chemist. The fields stuttered with gold under a relentless sun. Evan ran the streets. That's what he did. All told, the guild system lasted about five hundred years. I've truly been a beast to you, Abigail, he cried. Flat characters never need reintroducing. Who isn't tormented by curves? A pickle is not a gardening tool. A cigar is not a drainpipe. Pat's busking got him as far as the next street corner. Never, boasted Brenda. And I mean never. Like blind men we grope along the wall, feeling our way. Pelicans fly low until approaching land. Jazz is an octopus, Dexter declared. Present or peasant? Caustic or cross-stitch? That bunch doesn't cotton to the accepted rules of engagement. Apples do not ask to be eaten. Tilt meters measure how much the Earth tilts. Her secret is not to overdo it. One condom short of a condominium. The grandson of a serf, Chekhov always dressed impeccably. A very impatient work to keep the meaner sort from spoiling & stealing. We shall never forget the gravedigger's labor. A trumeau supports the lintel. She is the mirror in my hallway, the silence in my snowy field. Night's black satin shadow. Plato's dear, gorgeous nonsense. Everywhere, the land seethes with unrest. It's all so arbitrary, groused Summerville. All of it. Lordy, look at that kingsnake slither. Oh, lordy, look at that kingsnake crawl.

Mine

The raven of night offers no atonement. Ben Webster was a piano player until he met Budd Johnson. Through the sun-blasted field he hobbled, his foot wrapped in a shirt. You may taste freedom, but not eat it. The lone & level sands stretch far into the distance. A short stint in Fist City. Come thou, fount of every blessing. I bought you violets for your furs. Parchment or parliament? Bungler or burglar? What comes through the front gate is not the family jewels. Interior at Collioure. His father's name was Jumping Bull. You think that's clever?, sneered Cynthia. I don't. A skilled long-bow archer can fire up to twelve arrows a minute. Yes, it was one of those zigzag quizzes. Got traction?, inquired Jake. The Hunkpapa Sioux were breaking camp to follow the herd when 50 Crow warriors attacked suddenly. Mumford acknowledged Dreiser's power & reach. She is all blossom. She is all flame. The balanced throwing knife also cuts. Not flash but flesh. Not transmit but transmute. Some have more snap than others. The shadow? The shadow is all right. Mir zaynen do. Just the facts. And pass the bucket. I never said mine was the only way.

Jonathan Greenhause

THE SEAT WANTS YOU TO SIT IN IT

wants you to relax,
wants to feel your rump against its upholstery,
        wants to solve
complex mathematical equations while sipping
        on hot chocolate
& playing competitive Scrabble with its grandkids,
        wants to feel
what it's like to love somebody & to be loved.

        The seat wants
to be more than a seat, wants to stand, jump,
        climb, crawl, or fly,
would like to be more detailed, maybe even
        a throne or pew
or foldable chair, would think about
        overthrowing you
to establish an everlasting Dynasty of the Seat,

        to suppress rebellion
through the rule of its iron fist, though
        it wouldn't know
where to put that iron fist, would get confused
        with metaphors
due to its penchant for taking things literally,
        would educate itself
to be more well-rounded & tolerant of seats

        dissimilar to itself,
maybe by getting a Master's degree in Social Work
        & occasionally
getting accused of racism & police brutality,
        of fomenting class wars
& abusing its power through partisan politics.
        The seat would
secretly fear its homosexuality would never be

accepted by its family
or that its heterosexuality would be outed by
    its would-be gay lovers,
would be aware of the reader & repeatedly
    fail in its attempt
to prevent the reader from being aware of
    the seat's awareness.
The seat would substitute the 1st person singular

    for the word "seat"
& hope no one discovered its delusions of grandeur,
    would raze whole cities
just to watch them rise up again, would repeat this
    if given the chance,
wouldn't know what it'd just done, wouldn't care
    about not caring.
The seat wouldn't keep tabs on its whereabouts,

    wouldn't allude
to my existence, wouldn't try to hide
    hot chocolate from me,
wouldn't write when I left it alone so I could go
    to the police station
to report a sentient seat writing about
    its secret life as a poet,
its secret life wishing it could become a poet.

Jay Griswold

REFUGEES

You have seen them before on the train,
Their faraway gaze that takes in the night
While their hands twitch nervously about;
They have brought nothing with them on the journey.

They are where they are. In cities
With a million lights to keep the darkness at bay
No one is expecting them to turn up.
Even the photographs on their passports look strange.

And they seem to be listening to music
That comes from outside of the train,
Some stray violin on which mad fingers
Coax out a song that's heavier than the world.

They always sit facing backwards
In order to see where they're coming from.

Susan Gubernat

BULLET IN THE BACK

Oscar Grant, in memoriam

Even the escalators are crusted with blood
and no matter how much they scrub the floors,
no matter how much they shine, there is no clean
place to rest, waiting for the next one. The robotic
voice wavers now: "Five-car train for Richmond
in three minutes." One Irish boy says to the other
that on this "underground" you can't make out
the station signs until it's far too late.
You have to know where you're going.
They're looking for temp work sans green cards.
But they're white as porcelain. And don't tell me
that hasn't helped them. Young bicycle guys
hoist titanium rides over their shoulders
and up the stairs, plunge heedlessly into traffic
on nerve, pure nerve, watch caps pulled low
over their brows. If you're Black you could
be killed for a scuffle, for a smart mouth. Everyone knows
the third rail is race. When the BART cop,
as tall and gawky as Mehserle, waist sagging
with hardware, enters the car, the commuters look up
from their newspapers with half-dead animal eyes,
louche, unrefracting. And until the next station
the cop makes small talk with the bicycle guys; he's got
the lingo—derailleurs, Campagnolo components,
five-speed planetary gear set—enough to evoke
begrudged conversation until he gets off,
his parting "Have a good evening, fellas,"
rolling into the tunnel's mouth like a ball bearing,
plunging into darkness, like a bullet in the back.

POET, FOUND AND LOST

"My mother would be so happy. She'd be clapping. Maybe crying. And dancing."
—Juan Felipe Herrera, upon learning of his appointment as Poet Laureate

Where are you now, Jeffrey Valencia?
I've lost you. *Perdido*.
Not so long ago you were here,
writing your poems:
Terrified bird trapped
in the rafters of Home Depot
where the automatic doors opened
in only one direction.
Graffiti crawling the stalls
of the men's room
in the Hayward DMV—
someone spilling *life, life, life*
down the walls.
You had traded your dream
of pitching innings
for a life of perfect pitch.
You were heading
for the majors, and
I was in the stands
chanting your name.

Then I met your mother—
(Oh mothers, why don't you let
your children grow up
to be cowboys?
Why do you urge "pharmacy"
or "accounting,"
such mantras to ward off
the evil eye?)

And when I turned to her
and said, "Jeffrey will go on
to do great things in poetry,"
she froze as if I were the Stasi,
a border guard, *la bruja*,
and I knew I had spoken
words of affliction.
"No," she said, "oh no, oh my god, no."
It was as though
I had sent him to the depths,
taken him from her,
like the angel of death.

Herb Guggenheim

LASER

"How easy is a bush supposed a bear!" —Shakespeare

We met at a La Madeleine and talked for hours.
The talk was easy and intimate.
I told her about my mother
and what it was like growing up an only child.

She talked about her laser hair removal treatments
and asked me to touch her legs.
I did and they were silky smooth
and it seemed as though hair had never flourished
on their gentle terrain.

She said
she'd gotten her doctor to remove
as much hair as he possibly could,
leaving just a small amount in a vital place.
She'd gone for treatment after treatment.
Now she would never have to shave her legs—or anywhere else—
again.

We'd reached the point in the evening
where we'd either part or else make love.
And, even though this was only our first time out,
we chose the latter course.
And so it was that she came to my apartment.

We started kissing
and removing each other's clothes.
And soon we were in bed.

And then I saw it,
sculpted into a keyhole shape
or maybe a fat exclamation point—
her remaining hair,
mown like a slab of close-cropped zoysia grass,

And my mind flashed to an operating room,
the temperature a chilly 58°F;
a team of nurses and technicians in aquamarine scrubs,
hairnets, face masks, and latex gloves;
and an anesthesiologist close at hand
to keep the patient calm and comfortable.

And I saw the patient
wrapped from head to toe in pure white sheets
with only a small square opening to reveal
that part of her which I cannot name.
At a given signal, all put safety goggles on.
The surgeon, wearing a plastic smock.

holds the laser gun aloft,
as a rabbi would hold the Torah unto God,
then aims it down and begins to destroy
errant hair follicles inch by inch
until only the keyhole shape is left.

And, well, all I could think about
was that laser and those follicles.
And it ruined the whole damn thing.

Maryanne Hannan

DEJORATE

The opposite of ameliorate. In the etymology
game. Going from good to bad, bad to worse.
What words do, as we speakers of them

plod along, minding our own business.
With their poker faces and orthographic cover,
those lemmas mine our minds, and pretty soon,

everything's gone to hell in a handbasket.
It's only semantics, you're thinking;
plus who cares? not enough space and time

to move the needle on our watch. Let me repair
to my boudoir to think this over. And if you didn't
think I was the boudoir type, with its connotations

of elegant scandal, may I remind you that this little
puppy of a word has ameliorated considerably,
morphing from a private room in which to not

so recherché sulk to Marquis de Sadean quarters
of intrigue to its own lucrative photography genre.
A far better fate than awaited cretin, whose meaning

dive-bombed, from Christian to a "dwarfed and
deformed idiot," a sinister enough transformation
to remind us how that poor word, *sinister, tra, trum*

intended only to pertain to the left, not to mention
villain's *villanus*, a country peasant, who, though not
urbanely city-bred, didn't plan robbery at the get-go.

Think I'm speaking heresy, all my social critiques
hanging on sleight-of-hand word-threads? Remember
not to use that word lightly. In former days, you'd be

burned at the stake for heresy. A mondo pejoration
from its classical root of sticking to a personal position.
Nowadays, heresy's ameliorating. You can use it as a joke.

EXERCISE

Visceral reaction to that word:
Like why am I sitting here,
a mitochondrial trainwreck?
Use it or lose it.
Motion is lotion.
No pain, no gain.
I know all about exercise,
except why mean, lean
aspirations hide out in a LA–
di-da Latinate word: *exerceo.*
Granted, it's old enough
even for the Romans and cognate
with Greek. But *arceo?* to keep
at a distance. With ex-,
and claim it will keep you strong.
So unlike *viscera,* which fairly
trails off the tongue.

David M. Harris

DEAD LETTER OFFICE: THOMAS M. DISCH

Dear Tom:

Now you've killed yourself I sometimes think
of what we've lost, the novels and the plays
you'll never write, the poetry, and of
your gift for friendship. And sometimes I find
I want to talk to you, to ask for help
in working my way out of some poetic trap I've blundered into. More than that.
I miss your wit. I still remember when
we sat in that small side-street bar and you
spun out a musical: *Rhode Island Red*—
a union romance on a chicken ranch,
with egg ballet. And you would treat me just
like any of your literary friends,
my portrait leading off the series that
you made.
               Not just your death is keeping us
from bowling one more line; I fell away.
But really, Tom, what was I doing there,
rolling with you and Michael Dirda up
at Bowlmor? I was dominant that night
at toppling pins, although the talk left me
behind. Yet you had faith in me, in some
small genius I could never locate.
I should have thought to ask you what it was.
That quest is left for me alone. Your gift
to me, at last, is that I can believe
it must be there.
               With many thanks,

                   David

DICK CHENEY

Dear Dick:

I hope you don't mind me calling you
Dick. Everyone seems to do it. Besides,
we have a lot in common. I
dodged the draft, too. I don't
think I have a lesbian daughter,
but is a cousin close enough?
And I'm sure we both wake up
after a night of restless sleep
thinking, "What can I do today
to help my people? How can I make
their lives more fulfilling?" Our differences
lie in language, how we define "my people."
A mere technicality. We both worry about
our legacies, how history—so different
now that all is eternal in the Cloud—
will think of us. Or, in my case, if it will.
And what can we do, at our age (you're just
a few years older), retired from politics
or teaching, to make us look
better? You've done your memoir;
I'm working on mine. Yours is longer,
and will sell better.
But still...I didn't vote for you,
and I'm pretty sure
you never voted for me.
We're almost brothers.
Do you still sometimes
wear a tie? I gave up ties years ago,
except for funerals.
Maybe I'll wear one for yours.

Johnny Hartner

For Bailey

My student wants to write a paper dissing a film.
Which one? "One of my dad's bullshit movies," she says.
And what kind are those? She looks at me like I'm on her side,
would agree, can see the obvious, is a kindred spirit.
      Oh, one like *Babette's Feast*. There's not a car chase, gun shot,
or building exploding in the entire film. Imagine.
They just sit around in some weird
Scandinavian land and eat strange food. And talk.
      Oh, one like *Metropolitan*. A bunch of hoity toits
get dressed up for deb parties. Big flip. Not one gets
chainsawed in half. A total loss.
      Oh, one like *Howards End*. They all act like zombies
in the movie, but none of them actually *is* a zombie. What's with that?
I giggle at this mental image of now near-
nonexistent video stores' sections:
ACTION/ADVENTURE, HORROR, MYSTERY, COMEDY,
                                    BULLSHIT.
      I want to tell her she can write this paper under one condition:
She give me her dad's phone number.

WISE UP

Strange expression
that if you thought about it long enough
makes no sense.
                        But still
you'd almost like to see it
                        in antiquity
said by Aristotle to Plato—bored of all those
dialogues of Socrates, lectures of ideals, etc.
—who sighs with all the aplomb of the savvy
Bowery Boys' leader, Slip Mahoney: "Wise up, willyahs?
There ain't no Forms."
Someone clues in the scholastics. "Wise up:
with cloud cushions for their ethereal bums
no angels sit on heads of pins."
Descartes pronounces: "I wised up; therefore, I am."
"You can't wise up," retorts Kant.
Hegel's thesis would be to wise up;
his antithesis to dumb down
and the synthesis somewhere in between.
Could you see before hundreds at a factory
                        Marx?
"Workers of the world wise up!"
And once he declared "Man is anguish,"
even the smirk on that little
frogfaced, walleyed existentialist
would be priceless had Simone de Beauvoir
slapped him across the kisser with
O, haut sage, Jean-Paul, haut sage!

Michael Hathaway

BIRTHRIGHT

My horoscope declares,
"Your father will be able to
leave you *very* little."

When my father remarried and moved across town,
he gave me a little house on two acres,
the house I grew up in,
the safest place on Earth,
where Mother's ashes are planted
and the remains of every pet
I ever loved.

Along with an armful of Hank Williams Sr.
and Connie Smith records,
this came with a lifetime of lessons
in integrity, a work ethic beyond reproach,
and an undeniable sense that I was loved
no matter what.

AT THE END OF THE DAY

All that really matters is
the dishes are washed,
the floors are swept
and all the chores are done.

All that really matters is
that every little soul in your care
is fed, tuckered out
from the day's big fun
and sleeps peacefully
in the television's soft blue glow.

Gloria Heffernan

INSOMNIA

He worries that his snoring bothers me,
rasping breaths rolling in and out
like ocean waves on a windy night,
the steady rhythm almost hypnotic
but not quite enough to
carry me along on its currents.

Sometimes I want to poke him,
wresting him from his rest,
to ask how he can ease into sleep
like a bathtub filled with warm water.

But I just look at the clock
and get up at two in the morning
to fold laundry or pay bills,
or rearrange the kitchen cabinets,

or maybe knit a sweater from the fleece
of the thousand sheep
wandering aimlessly
at the foot of our bed.

Arthur Heifetz

SANDING

The last time I used this sander
I was refinishing the floor
while you sat in the recliner
sleepy from the drugs and chemo.
imploring me to stop.
I was trying to erase
not only
the stains and scratches
our comings and goings
had made
but the deep marks
your cancer had left
on our shrinking lives.

Now on the porch
I sand the rocking chair
where you nursed our son
a lifetime ago
the one I bought for five bucks
and had re-caned
by the Lighthouse for the Blind
the one I rocked back and forth in
smoking my Cuban cigars
on humid summer nights
the one I told stories in
to the drowsy children
curled up like dry petals
on my lap.

Each layer of lacquer and paint
yields new memories
the dust spiraling in the air
like desert dreams
as I reach the bare wood
and the undulating grains
that composed our lives.

Robert Herschbach

REST

Not for the bagger of fries
or the pourer of shakes,
not for the sub slicer, soft pretzel gatherer,
popcorn butterer, shift manager or cashier,

not for the mop squad, called to the scene
of a colorful spill, not for the wizard
in the cave of souvenirs, snow globe
White House, shrunken Liberty Bell,

not for the distributor of maps, the knower
of nearby attractions, where to eat, hike, simulate
space travel, feed a giraffe. Not for
the "guests," staggering in as though off a boat,

and not for their children, gone feral
in the backseat, keyed up by movies
or Nintendo, elbow to the face, he took my,
she won't stop, not for Dad in full grump mode

or querulous Mom, everyone needing to pee
since three exits back, not for the argument
about deck or roof or weeds or grades, *hon
can't you give it a rest?* Not on your life.

Margaret Hickey

GALWAY HOSPITAL WAITING ROOM

Tatters of polythene snagged on a dead bush
Send a bleak message to us this side of the glass.
Gardeners no longer tend this place, it seems.

New arrivals sidle in, take the nearest seat.
Thick-thatched and clean-shaven,
The men stare down the black well between their toecaps.

Without preamble, one looks up and says,
"They're all at it, now, making nests. But, did ye ever notice?
A crow won't make a nest of a Sunday. That's the truth."

Two women bend forward, exchanging troubles.
The elder, like a Russian babushka,
Knots her headscarf at the nape of her neck.

A doll of a woman, her hair piled high,
Flicks through a copy of Loot,
Her eyebrows pencilled in, spidery, her lipstick tangerine.

The bookshelf offers distraction of a kind—
Jeremy Clarkson, Jackie Collins and, never opened,
The Thousand and One Nights,

Wherein Scheherazade reaches each dawn
With tales of courage and terror,
So cheating the executioner at the door.

Now and then a tic compels us to the water jar,
Where we fumble with squashy paper cones,
Then subside again to our sipping and staring.

Predictable as Pavlov's dogs, our heads bob up
As a uniform walks breezily down the corridor.
The air grows thin as we wait to be called.

John Corrigan? John Corrigan? Mary O'Keeffe?
They shuffle out while we pretend we can't feel it
Beat against the ceiling—the steady thrum of fear.

Donald Illich

THE CLAW GAME

You work so hard trying to pick
the right one, mastering where to place
the claw, right over the husband you desire,
the one with creativity in his soul, who still
has most of his hair, who can talk with you
to all hours, never mind driving to school
to get the kids. Once you've selected him
you're happy, but soon after you wonder
if you've made the correct decision.
He doesn't agree with you every time.
Physically, he deflates, like a busted tire.
He becomes less interested in every word
you say. This is when the prize you won
isn't enough. You fling him into the discard
pile, while he still wonders what went wrong.
You position the claw over your next toy.
This time you've mastered yourself. You
know how to drop its weight on something
you can grab. The doll is for you, only for you.
When he arrives in your lap you will know
you made the right choice. His sparkling eyes,
his play muscles, will always fetch and beg
for you. He will slobber just to be next to you
in bed, while all you do is smile, smile, smile.

GRAVITY

My parents used to tell me
that gravity turned off at night.
That everyone floated
in their nightclothes, bouncing
against the walls of their rooms,
sometimes flying out a window.
When someone woke up, like me,
everyone returned to their original
positions, snoring as if nothing
had happened. I don't know why
they told me this, except to screw
around with my imagination, to keep it
working in a useless direction.
Even now, at three in the morning,
I try to catch my wife hovering
near me, with the books and shelves
above us, bobbing near the ceiling.
I sometimes have the feeling
I was the one who gravity abandoned.
That I'm the loose person, who will
stick to neither a job nor a life.
No one tells me, though. They
watch me rise like a balloon,
sending darts toward me, waiting
for a puncture to explode my heart.

Wendy Elizabeth Ingersoll

Cloud Hands

Roll your shoulders back, lift
your head, breathe deep,

begin. And my grandson shifts,
twists in his mother's womb,

begins too.
Offer the ball, they don't want it,

take it back. Let your hands
float up, fall

as through water.
And he swims, spills,

rolls through the canal.
Flip hands,

block and punch—
pushing, pushed,

pressed, squeezed, stretched—*embrace*
the tiger, turn

to the mountain,
open the curtain,

through he pours,
he crowns—*cloud hands,*

cloud hands again—
here he is at last,
fists trembling in air—

cup your hand, brush your knee,
watch a flock of birds fly by,

white crane spreads its wings.

The italicized lines are instructions for t'ai chi movements.

Michael Johnson

THEY

They shrikesong and thorn promise
and bramblehall bats uncocooned in the preyful gloaming.
They icespine at lion. They bloodtang and firegrace
and the sunbomb feathers of parrot
and paradise and allcolored kingfisher.
They birdyjade and storkstrut and musclemusic,
they seance and soothsayer and rubble and ruin.
They dung bejeweled with boneshell,
they preypoise, they strike, they mothertongue
and firevow and gemshine unchurched
from stone throats, and surfspeak from conchshells.
They cloistercalm and the night's teeth you pray for—
they how you come to your knees.

ORNITHOS

for Robert Wrigley

Sing of larksongs in the brambles
and mud cities, the lakeshore rookeries
along Kivu and Tanganyika,
those cooled cradles of magma.
Sing the birthplace of death and drought,
acacias inking blood, jacaranda buds,
the stumprumped waddle of dabchick
and duck, shag and scissorbill,
their heron wetcousins strutting rivers.
O you brittle bastards—
O lovebird, greenshank, tambourine dove,
tinkerbird, oxpecker, little leaflove—
sing to me, you rooks and bishops, tell me
your words mean more, that, grounded,
I might hear air under them as I praise
your hover and yaw, mantles aflare
with scintillate feathers, as if they bleed
the light I believe your bodies made of.
Tell me the words, or teach me the calls
and caterwauls of every nestbed.
I know your crests, your ruffled breasts,
still I struggle to get it right.
Could I but mime those rising tropes
I might come to voicing them—
kingfisher, swallow, swift, and shrike;
honeyguide, harrier, curlew, and crake—
full of more music than my bones can bear.
O bird, bird, of prey, of prance
and shimmer on the thermals, coo
and I will echo—pranticole, stonechat,
wimbrel and ruff; nightjar, spoonbill,
sunbird and stork—telling my lips:
Go on, go on, these are your wings.

THE BONE TEMPLE

At his bench he built architectures from the thin hips
of what once must have been a beautiful girl.
His blind monk unloamed bone braille handmaps

from lost lands written in brisket and casketshard,
republics long fallen. Two bronzed skulls pilastered
like gatekeepers: Enter, and be devoured

by the spirit of God. From a pedestal, a tarsaled fist
in boneful regalia pointed toward the pulpit.
Lattices across the vault, a fretworked trellis

up the wall of saints, rib shutters, and shin grates
and carved in all: flowers, as if the bones had bloomed,
as if the place had conjured offeringplates

of skulls and a chandelier of so many hundred hands
holding the light, of mosaic myths and bounty lists—
shrines and catacombs of ossified flowers. What can a man

smell after breathing skeletons? Before finishing
the last Latin scrawl—Welcome to the house of God—
he disappeared. He could not bear that nothing

happened: these relics, these souls, had not died
slaves, not heard their kind dubbed spawn
of monkeys, progeny of sin, not been colonized

and spent like so many dirty bills, but were blessed, yea,
destined, to beautify this sanctuary, the dark transept,
the chancel where sunlight washed the shadows away.

Abhay K.

BHAKTAPUR

I am the city of devotees
lost in the pursuit of the Lord
my shining terracotta pagodas
as poetry carved with bricks,
painted words
on eaves of wooden frames
cobblestoned streets
and alleys—long labyrinths of delight
an April of excitement
pierces through my tongue,
the man merely a midget, a spectator
in front of my colossal stones
silently watching generations
pass by
        the palace
            of fifty-five windows
the artisans kneading clay
women in black and red *haku patasi*
sculpting pottery, turning over paddy-husk
children running amok with street dogs
in a vast squared space
under five-storied shadows of Nyatapola
rushing to Batsala temple
hearing the bell of barking dogs.

George Kalamaras

FERNANDO PESSOA MIGHT CALL MY BODY TRUE

It was like lighting my tongue on fire.
The kerosene rag could not be used for the monthly blood.

It was like entering my leopard body, absorbing the sag of each dark
    star as I muscle-twitched my paw-patched self bramble-wise across
    the savannah toward freedom and remorse.
The blood bag could not fill even an empty bell, or the silver of a word I
    struggled to maintain.

Sure, Fernando Pessoa might call the cave of my body true, might send
    me out onto the parched streets of Lisbon begging bread.
Of course his hatband contained secret words, phrases like *cave-light
    in my mouth* and *Fedora Pessoa, frightened soup* and *stir my blood
    lightly with a stick.*

I lost a shoe and closed the night as we almost spoke of Portugal and
    pain, of the sandaled sadness of throat-slash for chalice and spice in
    ports as colonially close as Goa and Malacca.
Anything could bleed, he told me, *if you speak it just right. Any mouth
    could be sewn shut with the awful alignment of saffron and
    scripture.*

He showed me a photo of a zebra in foal, of blacks and whites among
    the scorched ash of bamboo.
He showed me an Indian woman from Goa who refused baptism, forced
    to watch her husband denuded, his penis stuffed into his own mouth.

And we wept together as if *both* lit by kerosene.
And the tongue of our mouth was Christ-like, if not exact.

And we cried like a child who has lost its star.
And I held Fernando's hand and felt the tender agony of release.

LUTHER GROSVENOR AND THE CAPE OF SOUND RAIN

They brought the masks and induced the rain. They settled the dust. They exchanged leopard robes for buffalo, water-buffalo hide for cauliflower and kale. Smoked a mixture of tobacco and thyme in a pipe fashioned from a horn. Spoke secret things in hushed tones in one of the lost ancient tongues. And what we understood, they understood as a diffident gap. And what he understood, we experienced as sound delight, as the cape, a gentle wrapping of rain around each of our outer layers.

And so, thus born, Luther Grosvenor left Spooky Tooth to roam the wood in leopard robes. Before the great flood and trade winds. Before becoming Ariel Bender for Mott the Hoople. He entered the forest in a cape, gave us guitar licks from *Under Open Skies*. Kept his name, difficult as *Luther* was to absorb salt, to season our bones. He gave us seven songs from six strings, incredible rain, spiritually incurable tracks. So much that forty-six years later I find myself, still, among the flower spell. When in the shower. When bunched with my wife beneath her umbrella, listening to yellow rain fall faint from the eaves.

Githa was her name, your wife's name. The one who roamed with you. You can already taste what she sees. Does. What the ceiba hear in their succulent root-running sap. Can picnic by a river, sit at her feet. Hear her recitation of pain from our countless past lives, pages of the Bhagavad Gita, goat-skin scrolls. So much that it hurts. So much that it almost soothes. So much for rain and trees. For sighing our soughing-voiced selves at the gates—the Githa-gates—of Eden, smoking a mixture of cauliflower and thyme. These are the moments of Africa, moments of human rain. These are the lush anxious grunts of the silver-backed ones, the slow scale coiling around a tree, the how-to-get-our-mouths-around-each-other-just-right-in-the-say-so-yes-no-act-of-any-human-touch.

What was the weight, Luther, of the mask you bore wearing a new name, the angular howl of the flying-v guitar in becoming Ariel Bender? The ancient Greeks called the use of masks *personae*. The bushmen simply kept them secret, refusing—even—to eat near anyone's voice. Fear of ingesting wrath. Who or what was it you tried to be? To see? How many lives must we lose in gaining our simple, soughing selves? Is it true the sound of sand swifting at seventy degrees Celsius mimics the groans of whales rubbing their massive lesions in beaching themselves across a coast? Does the wearing of a name contain, or does it scrape sense into us from below? Rock cut and seashell slash along the belly, a reminder of how many births, how far across the great ocean we've come?

Another way to feel terrible, it is said, *is to feel wonderful.* Another Zen *koan* of how and why we suffer and forest-mouth and weep. Of who and what and maybe-sometime-after-eight. Sucking a lime is equivalent to a scumbling of scurvy? Another layer of losing our archipelago of false selves is to roam the forest in a cape, a Luther Grosvenor cape, with hair well past the shoulder. Guitar in hand. To lounge at the riverbank among the bagworms and steeping seeds with the one we love, listening to her speak as if from a scroll—in an exchange of bodily robes. Her tongue pressing the scutched point of departure. Return. Saying yet seeking rain. Exploring the moist of our mouth, the to-and-from our past.

Tom Kelly

OREGON TRAIL MELTDOWN

a floppy disk soliloquy

You laid Uncle Elmer
out with dysentery, splintered
the wagon's axle, cracked
my oxen's hooves, and where
the fucking shit did you hide
all the buffalo! I've a banker's
family, dammit! Not farmers
and carpenters. Do you expect
moguls to subsist on squirrel?
They expect Aunt Agnes's
shepherd's pie. We're out
of tourniquets and if she
suffers one more rattlesnake,
my entire privileged lot
roughs the dust-blown road
on cold jerky. The nearest
town's weeks away and no
Sioux or Crow trading post
registers on your oracular
map. Speaking of Native

Americans, did you vanish
them along with the buffalo?
I've seen neither sign nor
heard whisper of their bloody
battles with destiny manifest.
The badlands' quiet seems
preprogrammed, engineered
in some unspeakable language
and your interface doesn't
possess the option to raise
questions. Every face I've found
on this forlorn trail: a scripted

white scowl that speaks strictly
of wares for sale: boxes of bullets,
raw beef by the pound. Sure,

upon reaching Snake River,
an indeterminate tribesman
decorated in billowed robes, lone
hair feather, pointed the crossing.
Placid as a statue, useful as road
signs, his good-willed silence
so unhackable, I mistook him
for the landscape—a savage
of such nobility, he passed
as historical monument for who
this country's coded to forget.
Your mark of civility stamped
on his face like a copyright
for every player to witness
on the westward way to victory

or untimely death by typhoid,
spoiled buffalo flesh, another
rattler bite—this time, Sister
Hazel—and without mystical
Native medicine she's absolutely
fucked. Damn you, death wish
of a game. You've been rigged
to kill from the beginning.
No more. If I raft upriver
and anyone rolls overboard,
I'm chucking your floppy
ass into the microwave.

Los Angeles Lease Agreement

I _____ hereby disavow my provenance and birthmarks and adopt MTV as surrogate mother: plastic tit that fostered my incisors' flawless symmetry. And I _____ will invest in headshots to make mother proud. Effective immediately, I _____ am a dog person; a purebred, pedigreed, toy dog person. Tomorrow I _____ will adopt and adorn in sweaters one or more:

Pomeranian __ Maltese __ Pekingese __ Havanese __ Papillon __ Chihuahua __ Pug __

Though cooking's for cretins rich in disposable time, I _____ vow to live a healthy lifestyle. I _____ will eat pescetarian, Instagram kale and quinoa, juice gingerroot–blueberry–avocado on weekends, and never eat pepperoni pizza again. I _____ will stay fit or risk unremarkable death in the public eye. I _____ will yoga, crossfit, t'ai chi, jog with my dog, yoga headstand with my dog. Above all, I _____ will take headshots yoga headstanding with my dog. And I _____ promise to Instagram photos of my very best photos, trade likes for followers and flattering comments for reposts. Furthermore, I _____ will repost:

Kanye __ Beyoncé __ Brunch __ Kayne and Beyoncé's Brunch __ Dogs Belonging to Anyone Tagged in Kayne and Beyoncé's Brunch __

I _____ will brunch with executives older than my parents and quell notions that they resemble wax figures and powdered mummies. Over bloodies and pistachio–arugula salad, I _____ will give them my business card, headshots, my dogs' headshots, forkfuls of my appetizer, and lifetime supplies of flirtatious schmoozing all for the price of to-die-for brunch. I _____ will volunteer to wipe croutons from their mouths and enjoy this more than beach vacations. If they advise, I _____ will acquire:

Botox ___ Rhinoplasty ___ Therapist ___ Senior Citizen Romantic
Companion ___

With this, I _____ hereby renounce age disparity and
economic motive as passé stigma impeding on intimacy. I
_____ renounce the unenlightened people-folk outside
the city. I _____ embrace Los Angeles unconditionally
as child does doll, wanderer does native tongue, nun does wooden rosary
tangled between closed fists. Like prude to thirsty newlywed breaking
bed, I _____ will forfeit with gratitude what the metropolis demands: thirty pounds, nervous tics, musty stench of evidence from
previous residence. Accordingly, I _____ will acquire new
license plates, vernacular, history, and name _____ at
which point this contract reduces to artifact.

Andrew Koch

CROSS SECTION OF A PETRIFIED FOREST

Off the highway
the palace the billboards promised
is chipping to pieces
and scattering across the scrub.
If you wait long enough
the differences between
a gas station and a museum
become semantic.

Buy a postcard from somewhere
no one will ever go,
all the worlds
buried in the sand,
landscapes where younger suns
shine through stands of cypress,
pterosaurs peppering the stratosphere,
sawtooth beaks agape,
making sounds we can only guess at.
Perhaps some residue
of their cries is trapped
down there with centuries
of all the other cries
of a million other beasts,
folded into the strata
of the invisible earth.
Little baskets of rocks
bear handwritten notes
saying, "Gingko—$10,"
or "Redwood—$10,"
though there isn't a bit of tree for sale.
"Un-tree," the signs mean to say,
"un-forest" and "un-bones,"
but someone polished their decay.

In the parking lot
the plaster velociraptor
bears his teeth toward
the hot, empty sky.
When the next world comes
I wonder if he'll still be here
to purchase my absence.

Sandra Kolankiewicz

THE READING

She lays out the cards to show me a cross
section of the universe, for I need
to know what will happen, discontented
with the ambiguity of chance. A
sliver of light breaks through as soon as she
turns over the Emperor: I recall
what you told me in a dream after you
died: *I am in the reflection of a*
candle in a mirror or piece of glass.
So the next dimension is already
here, I think, ignoring the Fool on the
table embarking on his journey. Life's
just collapsed and compressed, a binary
code in a zip file that we're opening
like Pandora's box to find The Tower:
men leaping from the ramparts, a bolt of
lightning about to strike God knows where, the
room suddenly reversed so I do not
know right from left, Yankee candles on all
tables aflame with fear and reverence.
A cluster of staffs. The man weeping on
a slab below a stained glass window. A
blindfolded woman on her knees, crossing
swords at the breast, moon rising behind her.

Beth Konkoski

North on 81

We leave suburbia the moment summer
hatches. Straight into the North Country
we rush, past Watertown, Fort Drum,
Indian River. Officially top state
and our pulse slows as the trees spread
wide. There is more space here
than sense or purpose,
more green than hope in a style at once
lovely and desperate in its decay.

Passing through here in June, one
can forget the deep coma of January,
the welfare weeks and too much
nothing in the hours of each day.
Right now, burned by affluence
and opportunity, we rebel and resist
the need to behave, believe, become
that filled each school day with failure.

We let the smell of cut grass
and splatter of mayflies on the windshield
release a memory of childhood
without lessons or prospects or scores.
This trip is just what we need, an escape
from progress and plans, a fleeing really
of the lives we chose, without
knowing consequences, when we looked
only for the benefit of new, busy, and highly
rated. How could we have chosen otherwise
when measuring a child's future?

We could not have known what the years would
drop on our heads like bad fruit. We can
only wish to be less impressed by flash
and glory, even though we will return,
put ourselves back in a race we can't run.
For this week, however, we will sit in a boat
with little hope of a fish and let
the river rock our tired blood to sleep.

Kathleen Kraft

THE WOMAN WHO WEARS A DRESS OF WATER

—after Charles Rafferty

It eases her to sleep—the soft spray of mist
from the hanger on the clothes tree,
covering her like a continuous falling dream.
She never thinks of anyone at this time,
her peopled world a mirage of receding
figures. Come morning an enticing slap
rouses her, brings her to the road
where she is followed by thirsty children
drinking and dipping in and out—
Their rollicking cries rise about her
seamless sway and she sings to her flow,
long vowels immersed in a whiling light.
Come evening she hangs up her dress, falling
from slippery hooks and cinch. She doesn't know
yet that it can be shared, that she can give her gift
to another who will let it lap her in another way—
her brimming cup, a source for all to sip.
She wears the sheen of the transformed,
like basalt rocks hissing in the sunlight
after a wave has broken over them.

Robert Krantz

A sunken ship is an eerie
thing, these fish have no language
to describe its descent—this vessel had one job, to float

I swim in a wordless cloud behind the rusted rudder
no new lexicon will resurrect this hulk
but I feel the vague words

opaque in spheres above my head,
watch them bubble
to their strange surfaces

the acts we do in cars,
the screams and ecstasies,
spill out onto the streets and highways

like deer blood and bone
combing restless children's hair,
you are the tooth of the pick

that lifts the louse
crying won't help—
the spirit has no ear to hear

these earthly songs
a salt mouth full of sea
we are all drowning

W. F. Lantry

FLORESCENCE

Timeless her mysteries, and smooth her skin,
I love to watch her walk, imagining
the curving metamorphosis of forms
beneath the silken florals of her dress.
As when, in silence, watching thunderstorms,
I note how all grows still, as everything
awaits the transformation of the rain.

I'm both barometer and weathervane.
Within her vortex, tumbled like a leaf
unbranched, but always watching: now her waist
turns moderately, arched, and I could bless
the laws of physics for the interlaced
motions she makes, the beautiful motif
repeating through our days, as if her art

consisted of the cycles of my heart,
the swelling blood of every artery
within my limbs as I, enraptured, gaze
on each sheer detail of her finesse,
or her accoutrements, the tender ways
she mimics winds in motion, or the sea
just when the tide is full and storms begin.

ARRAS TAPESTRY

The warp is merely cotton, passing through
heddles, to let the weft threads interweave
unbroken, whether gold or silk, lac-dyed:
the only surface you will ever see.
Who could discern the pattern's underside?
In searching for its trace we misperceive
the loom's significance: it's just a frame.

But if the facing colors flash and flame
in artificial light, why would we glance
beneath, behind? Our gaze is hypnotized
by figures woven through the tapestry,
as if their dance were caught and crystallized
in whorls of metallic thread. Balance
can only be achieved if we repeat

the oscillating motions of their sweet
dynamics, as if light and metal praise,
through us and them, the vibrance of this place,
the interlace of transverse harmony,
and by their patterns grant a mirrored grace:
a maquette for the way a body sways
through mazes only sightless weavers knew.

Marie Lecrivain

SATURN RETURNS

to kurt cobain

some people are born on the outer trajectory
of those tilted rings, paper-thin and sharp
as the poisoned dagger that cut the cord
at the same moment you drew
your first breath.

your lungs propelled that first scream
into the wounded minds of the titan's children,
the anthem that became a blasé aphorism
embossed on concert tees worn by those
in stupid solidarity, the same brethren
who moshed their way into middle age,
and who stopped listening to the music
behind your message: the sound
of your fragile heart pulverized
between the stone jaws
of our father's teeth.

Kateema Lee

GROWING UP D.C.

On Lebaum Street in winter
a dog steals a little girl's gloves

kids slide down hills
on cardboard sleds

sand and snow slush under galoshes
the little girl cries

her big sister
tries to chase the dog

tries to temper chaos
for a moment the little girl loses

sight of her sister
the world is small

the world starts at Lebaum
and ends at Martin Luther King Avenue

the little girl is small
the little girl is the world

to her sister
the world is the little girl

to passersby
the girl stands on the sidewalk

in a world where dogs
take the little things

and leave a small part of her bare
while others take what they can

downward
inertia

the world
the little girl waits

and watches while everyone
around her moves

MUSINGS OF A NETFLIX BINGE VIEWER

B movies with buxom
beauties, beefy
bodies, dialogue to be damned
circled like rainbow-colored wheels,
before falling off the queue;
zombies wishing there were
no more zombie movies
bit, clawed, groaned,
limped, spurted, danced,
pumped gas, walked
under water, walked through
walls, chased Barbara
while on fire, while waiting
for the one girl to live
or fall and scream,
show side boob,
grab an ax,
save the day before
falling off queue;
Que Que, Cylons,
Fry, Worf, that Misfit
who travels through time
to let the right one in
to see dragons tattoo
men from nowhere...

buffering...

buffering...

buffering...

"an error occurred loading this content"

set alarm

buy a caramel macchiato

pray for snow

repair the motherboard's mind

delete cookies

clear the cache

live

Lyn Lifshin

MARIE VAN GOETHEM

a ballet student in the Paris Opera
reflected in the amazing number of sketches
in charcoal and pastel. What was she
thinking, modeling naked for Degas,
her hips thrust forward? Did she want him
to want her? A tease or a pure innocent?
Was she wondering, since he doted so
on her, if he'd give her a special gift for her
birthday in 7 days, June 7? With the light
staying longer and longer, did she want
to just play in the gardens of the Tuileries
or race along the Seine? Not perform,
smile in pain, her feet bleeding,
crammed into pointe shoes?

HER BRAID OF REAL HUMAN HAIR

dark blonde,
coated and held in
place with wax, the
little dancer could
never have guessed,
fired from the Paris
Opera after only a
few years, she would
become the most
famous dancer of her
time tho' she slipped
into obscurity. Degas'
obsession, made of
wax and stuffed with
odds and ends, paint
brushes and wire, in a
fiver-layer tutu several
inches longer than in the
earliest photographs
and probably damaged
and trimmed. No one can
imagine Marie's life working
out well after she was
kicked out of the
ballet. Her mother,
gossip newspapers
say, pushed her into
prostitution.

PÈRE LACHAISE CEMETERY

rain already, a pewter
sky. Dark jade shadows,
almost licorice moss.
The stillness,
the dampness

a bottle of gin
on Jim Morrison's grave.
Oscar Wilde and
Gertrude Stein. I
imagine them swimming

under the darkness of night,
tangling under the black
oaks to drink a toast
when the cemetery
closes at 18:00, to Molière

and Chopin whose piano
music some say, on a night
when the owls are still
and fresh flowers are
just laid on his grave,
drifts through the willows.

RACHEL'S LAMB

on top of her tiny grave
is tarnished. Rachel 1968–1972.
As big as the stone, the
lamb overlooks piles of dolls,
teddy bears, balloons, jelly
beans. For years, chocolate
cake since it was Rachel's
favorite. Colored stones, notes
sealed with a kiss. *Rachel my dear,*
her mother's long letter.
Bubble gum, whistles, hula
hoops, and a ballet tutu. On
the way to other graves,
Rachel's was a garden. Other
stones grew moss, tilted,
Thru the '70s and '80s, giraffes
with a bow and sequin
sneakers, a puzzle waiting for
her to finish. Into the '90s
quarters, pennies, glitter, stars.
2000, 2002. Suddenly in
2013, only one rose petal.
2014 the grave is bare as if the
mother and father moved for
their health or disappeared in a car crash,
moved to Ecuador. And the relatives not
wanting to be left behind followed
or went their own way. The five-
year-olds who mourned her
and left her chocolate kisses and
barrettes now have their own
five-year-olds they don't
want to imagine, don't want to
think, of not living past five.

SAINTE-CHAPPELLE

under a calmness
before Debussy
people almost
whisper. Wet
jewels, stained
glass, liquid blues.
Gray cloudy days
give the most even
light. Plants, leaves,
how sand magically
becomes emeralds
and rubies. The
windows change
moment to moment,
like an irregular
heartbeat.

Christopher Locke

WHAT THE DEAD KNOW

"There are not enough pleasures to simplify the spirit." —Charlie Smith

The dead do not visit me at night; at 3 a.m., I do
not sense their vaporous bodies gliding over my
bed to reveal some mortal prophecy: "Avoid
the morning train," or "A fire awaits you at the bakery."
Nothing. Just me split and pulled from the char

of a receding dream, alone in my sheets as night
counts the insomniac stars, the neighborhood
crushed in heaps of silence as no dog unravels
on its chain, no loitering Camaro sprays Van Halen
against our petrified rosebushes. How can the dead

know I would prefer their blank company, their insolent
calm to all this ordinary nothing clogging the avenues
of my sleep as I lie here and think of my stepfather
and how almost every night he sees whole lines
of the dead enter his room as if taking numbers, closing

in on him, telling him they await not in fire but in silence,
and he will be addition by subtraction, and that they
will lift him up to the others breathing behind the clouds
in their melancholy and their robes, lift him by the wrists
as if he were just cut down from some holy machine.

OUTSIDE LIMERICK

From the train these Irish hills
look like covered bodies, blanched
and indifferent, until a gray tunnel
of peat smoke wraps itself around
trees you'll never climb, let alone
touch, as a pair of starlings swoop
and fall like crumbs from a beard.
And then someone's castle, as if on cue,
muscles into the picture, all stone and
varicose ivy as you try to remember
what it felt like to be held by someone
lacking an agenda: the woman in last
night's pub spinning a web of vodka
and asking if you wanted to crawl inside.

A young German couple, chatty the whole
ride, slip in one ear bud apiece, smiling,
grooving to nothing too Wagner, maybe
Top 40, and she closes her eyes and sways
without a care—except for maybe the hotel
bed they left this morning and how sad it is
that now all the sheets are cold. Or maybe
it's just you, wishing your own bed recalled
the urgency of thighs and stomachs pressed
hard enough to flush blood to the surface,
to the tip of your aching tongue.

Rebecca Macijeski

MEMORIES OF JAPAN

At night the city market is a tunnel of hot meat and steam.
All around is the thick aroma of miso, green onion, eggs
poaching in dark stock. Sesame. Barley tea,
the warm starch of rice. My soup a tiny stillness
of mushrooms and noodles inside
the swirling planet of laughing, shouted orders, chopping,
slicing, frying, slurping, fire,
the heat of closeness, the sweat of feeding.

At South Station, commuters become the rush of Osaka's downtown
and I wonder how many businessmen or housewives
would fit quietly into this last night train
or whose tourist photos will find my face hovering in them
like some bright exiled moon. Japan,
your crescent island floats in my mind.

I wander through this borrowed home
past bicycles and bonsai, past tail-less cats,
past tea shops and traffic lights
to the corner grocery, Mr. Japan,
where a fiberglass man greets me
—his motorized arm always waving.
In the produce aisle, all the golden apples sit
like precious diapered children—paper nets hugging
each round underneath, keeping their smooth flesh
safe for the privacy where they are eaten.

In the ladies' room, to quiet their communal splash,
women push noise buttons on their toilets.
Blowing one's nose is to banish in the tissue
some blossoming inner stain. Japan,
I've stopped for coffee and you appear.

Japan, I sip from my warm cup and here you are,
the old woman at Osaka shrine.
Fragments of you flock like paper birds
waiting to abandon their paper cage
and live instead in a paper sky.
In the moist air, our common language
is the crane you fold out of my tourist map
and hand to me, gently bowing, fluttering its wings.

Stephen Malin

Maybe what I hate most
to lose track of is reminders.
It's embarrassing. All
the other stuff, sure, keys,
glasses, your camel, but forgetting
the note or whatever you put there
to tell you what you
absolutely must remem—well,
really, if it's important enough
to have written down or—
and this is worse—to have left
the coat hanger in the refrigerator
to *remind* you, for godsake,
and there you are
with a cold coat hanger in your hand
and little or nothing in your head—
but wait, I have to go upstairs now
where can I put this
to be sure to remember it?
Damn.

GRAVE DAYS

BEFORE THE FACT

Some of us would rather
go to ground as much
untrammeled as may be,
unboxed, unmade-up, and
otherwise not undertaken,
just invested deeply somewhere—
waterside, wood, meadow,
hill—where one's sum
of parts could offer
partial recompense, but
no, the busy law forbids it.

AFTER THE FACT

That edict broken, though, how
judicial robes would rumple
should one's osteo-deposit
be updug; Exhibit A—the accused—
dem bones all bagged and
tagged, then wired a-dangle
for a trying sentence, heavy fine
and sternest reincarceration,
with contempt-of-court
attempting to dislodge that
fixed and headstrong grin.

Allie Marini

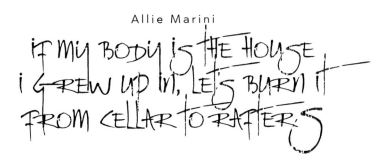

if my body is the house i grew up in, let's burn it from cellar to rafters

noxious against the side of my cheek, turned away, he is a tailpipe, his breath the exhaust, smog & emissions, a jumble of letters & phonemes, exhausted: *here I am again* on the dirty linoleum.

there is something I was supposed to translate, from rounded vowels & staccato consonants—*all of which somehow spell my name*—but once you exhaust the word bank with spilled fuel on the floor, all that's left to clean up are a few stray syllables & maybe some blood—

a tooth, tucked under my daughter's pillow, I climb bone-wrecked & exhausted under the sheets with her, constructing a blanket fort from all the promises I'm too exhausted to keep, exhausted escape plans: a fortress in flames from all that spilled fuel on the floor

noxious exhaust rising to heaven in oily plumes after combustible materials are carelessly left alongside each other with a Bunsen burner—*here, let's just call it what it is, a pilot light*—I'm too exhausted to translate any more words scrawled in lemon juice & held feet-first over the flame:

baby girl, come here to mama, there's just too much fuel spilled on the floor & the exhaust fumes are making us sleepy. under the covers, waiting for a fairy to come retrieve my knocked-out tooth from my knocked-up luck, when really

it just comes down to the fact that I've exhausted every resource while grinding down the bones, spilling fuel on the floor & waiting for combustible materials, the exhaust fumes of what was formerly *man-and-wife*, to ignite a wildfire or die exhausted embers,

because every opened door leads to more fuel spilled on more floors &
bone wrecked, bleeding, exhaust seeping through the crack in my teeth,
the 'til death portion of our parting done with a lead pipe on the dirty
linoleum

exhaust the word bank for phonemes & dipthongs that translate into

I'm sorry

blanket-fort my daughter back into bed with promises of a fairy &
a bloody tooth, exhausted Bunsen burner of my body eating up all
combustible materials: I am a pilot light hissing in an empty kitchen with
the bone-wreck of his body on the dirty linoleum

wrecked-bone in bed, holding my daughter, who won't stop wailing,
while gas filters in room by room like exhaust, *why can't you just stop
crying, aren't you exhausted? I know I am.* we are waiting for a spark to
take down the whole house to exhausted embers

& us inside it

David Memmott

SHADOW BOXING

Waking in the dark of a ghosted room
on a cold night when clouds run dry,
I feel my *umbra nihili* rise.
His guttural voice catches on worried words
ruminating in my throat, sowing
the silent sky with another language.

Head full of stars. The body
bleeds out into no mere reflection.
He rehearses his fame in the basement
after the house falls to sleep,
then boldly takes over my kitchen
shaking his hoary head. He leans
over the counter and slaps down
one gold doubloon, enough he says to claim
all I ever owned. His laughter burns away
history like so many layers of fat
and then he steals my name.

Nuclear stars in slipstream
collapse around the blow I fail
to deliver. The shockwave of such
a close call knocks the full moon
off its axis. My Nothing comes out swinging,
last light divided into jabs and hooks;
my face from the drubbing so numb
I'm slow to counter, stars exploding
in my eyes. Nothing

blocks a dispirited roundhouse
with laughter more brutal than any blow.
Nothing demolishes walls built
by hammerfall between hearth
of home and heart of darkness.

On one knee tracking the spin
of his specter, I tell myself to get up,
don't let the dervish of moondust
and epiphany cut out the stars
from my splitting skull. Instincts
carry dead weight. I keep moving,
bob and weave. It dawns

he's out of shape, hanging on
as Aurora sheds her skin.
Mother of Light brings second wind.
His tires are flat. The familiar reek
of his armpits takes my breath
away. Make him miss, I think.
The dawn breaking

within me. I'm lean and ready.
One last uppercut sends
a seismic tremor up through
his umbric horizon.

Come light.
Come shine.
I kiss the doubloon and skip
it three, four times across a sea
of fire that bubbles up
into moments like this.

MEDITATION FROM A DARK WOOD

There are still places
where the wind is having words with the trees
drowning out the mutter of men.
In lost canyons the solitary poet
comes kicking through piles
of dry leaves to raise a voice.
His words Babeled by white water
plunging precipitously from
the sublime into the merely literal.

Just when thoughts clear
this troubled thicket appears, complicating
the way forward, senses
canceling each other out, doubling
back, leaving no tracks.
This small aperture more closed than open
doesn't show on any maps and leads
away from the neutral zone.
Where the dark is sorted from
the light, he counts from flash to thunderclap
the distance in seconds
while caretakers watch his vital signs.

In this rarefied air even he brushes
the wings of angels and their untested
passion blooms on still burning lips.
He's aware of standing alone
near the edge of an ever-moving boundary
where here is there, this is that
beyond which nothing more can be said.
A shiver starts inside, intensifies
with each weakening pulse, shot
through every muscle, every vein.

From here he might learn to fly
but first must learn to lose the earth.
He might fail and fall out of a cloud
upside down, horizon lost
to rapidly rising ground.
No matter what he tells himself
he wasn't ever meant to stay here.
The evergreens do not speak his name
though they talk behind his back.
The lines that hold him together
are taut and thin
a fragile web shredded
in a downpour.

He dangles on the end
of the last line
the final filament
broken.
Letting go is giving up.
Hanging on is narcissism.
He soars untethered in a storm
a crudely crafted kite caught
by its ragged tail, frail and fluttering
when he hears a voice:

"Listen to me carefully."
His eyes open and an angel face
in soft nimbus hovers above
where he lies in bed
more machine than man
"You must stay awake;
we need to remove the breathing tube."

Stephen C. Middleton

COMPOSITION

Goes there to paint the village. Of almond and ocher. Of kindness and hospitality. The tableau, though, is ruined. The waitress has moved. Yesterday, she says, I cry all day.
Of roadside shrines & saints. Of pomegranate and naked persimmon. The maritime pines, diseased, have gone from around the church— one of many saved by a "miracle" in the war. Scores died/the church survived. What to paint?

OPENING HEART LANDS

When the pen runs dry
Joe McPhee's "Old Eyes"
Shenai or tenor
Off center & sad
From Buddy Bolden
To Ornette Coleman
Let My Children Hear Music

Synaptic triggers
Modal scales
The wailing musette
Quarter tones
& long distance moan
Open closed heartlands
Where surround sound
Western canon fails.

Devon Miller-Duggan

Science Fiction vs. Literature

Some poet writes a poem called "Wookie."

Robots in a rhumba line step-step-step-step-KICK
through a poem about bugs.

A new universe forms on a Parisian windowsill
and all the gods look like Eiffel towers.

20 years ago Scottie beamed a poet up—all
the lines in the poet's head separated and glittered
briefly before sinking back into the back of her brain.
It will take her decades to recall them.

On the surface of the planet, people invented bird-beings
and made them into messengers.
Below the surface, morlocks invented bat-beings
and called them angels.

What would Jung say about the way we turn
all extraterrestrials into giant bugs or giant brains,
both with enormous eyes?

Klingons love opera.

On some timeline, Buzz Lightyear and Flash Gordon
marry and raise baby neuromancers.

One day time travel's impossible, the next
it turns out it might be possible
to fold time up like a paper fan
and breeze through millennia.

LAST EPISODE

Hawkeye was going Home. I was in my living room. The TV had no place else to go. Hawkeye was on a rattletrap Army bus, going back to the 4077. The crew had been to the beach. The bus had stopped to pick up refugees and wounded soldiers. Actors, characters, and watchers, we were all 11 years into television stories about a war I realize my father wasn't sent to in 1953, though he was drafted. Hawkeye wouldn't talk to Sidney about why he couldn't talk or work. Sidney stitched together enough to get the stories, first the one about the whiskey (which was really plasma), then the one about the chicken. I believed it was a story about a chicken, though on the screen the chicken was too white and fat for a Korean peasant woman's bird. Hawkeye deserved to go home. The real Hawkeyes and Trapper Johns had figured out in canvas-tent surgeries most of what is known about repairing veins. Wars pull inventions out of doctors. The network let them run the last episode without a laugh track. Korea was not a war. The story was not about Korea. We saw Hawkeye in the cell crying before we saw the peasant woman smother her beautiful chicken. The woman wished she was a bird strong and swift enough to bear away the soft, fat chicken. I was in my living room. Hawkeye was on the stopped and silenced bus. It was hidden because of enemy troops. Vietnam was over before the last episode. It was the war my father might have gone to. He'd have been a doctor there. Because he was a doctor, he was able to choose not to go. The bus hoped enemy soldiers wouldn't hear it. Hawkeye wanted the chicken to quiet so he could go back to the 4077 and help the wounded soldiers. I wanted Hawkeye to go home to Maine. Hawkeye wanted the chicken to be quiet. He told the woman to keep the chicken quiet. The peasant woman only wanted the baby to quiet. I learned later—the story of the woman and the baby came from the Holocaust. More than one story like it. My father would have been good at battlefield surgery, but he would never have come home as himself. The frightened women in the stories are trying to save their babies and those who travel with them. The doctors are trying to save everyone. The women always wish they were birds.

Miles David Moore

TO AN OBSCURE VEGETABLE

Kohlrabi, rutabaga,
whatever your name,
you squat in the produce bin against the wall,
banished as far as possible
from the sunniness of clementines
and the evergreen of broccoli.

People skew their noses
at your knobby purple-grayness.
Not even a Niagara Falls of cheese sauce
could barrel you down a child's gullet,
and you have no place in the leafy salads
lithe women in leotards fling into bowls
on the run to Pilates class.

It takes the silent man
who wanders unseen by housewives and stockboys
to hold you in his hand,
survey your deformities
and nod at all the secret truths you bear.
With a chant of ginger
and a prayer of cilantro
he will slice you to your roots
and steam you pure,
revealing at last what you hold within you—
something of value, something of earth.

THE CAPRICIOUSNESS OF FATSLUG

These are the days that infect Fatslug
with obsessive inappropriate thoughts:
dancing a solo minuet
in a honky-tonk bar, cultivating
a silly walk even John Cleese would disown,
speaking in ecstatic unknown tongues
to a bottle of ketchup, or pointing in pious
horror, shouting, "ANTICHRIST! ANATHEMA!"
at an airport departure board.

Some days his dreams are bigger:
broadcasting a dominoes tournament
in lieu of the Super Bowl, or else awarding
the Oscar to an actor who had two lines
in a horror-slasher flick that went straight to video,
the Nobel in economics to a college freshman
who got a C+ on his midterm paper,
the Pulitzer in poetry to a limerick writer
whose third and fourth lines are invariably,
"When they asked him why/This was his reply,"
and the Westminster Dog Show trophy to a pigeon.

This does not amuse Fatslug at all. Far from it.
This is all symbolic of the absolute
unrightness of everything he thinks and feels.
It's his way of taking his mind off the fact
that the hideous swine-snout in the mirror is him,
admitted to the party by mistake,
grunting as he roots through the buffet table
to the horror of the invited guests.

Maria Nazos

WHEN THE BELOVED ASKS "WHAT WOULD YOU DO IF I WOKE UP ONE MORNING AS A LOCH NESS MONSTER?"

My lover doesn't know: he is a deep-sea dragon.
Long before this talk, I was already petting his hard

iridescent scales. I'm enamored with the glossy, shoulderless
body, the pale horns, flaring gills. My mind surges forward

to ride the bejeweled back in the imaginary surf, up through
the sun-streaked surface. Since I don't fear much of what

I should, because I've heard that the sky is an empty blue bin
in which leftover sins are stashed, we shouldn't leave that wide

field unnavigated either. But, a reptile is a reptile, mythical
or not. My restraint is more effortless than my beloved knows:

I wouldn't pace in my tower, while watching your sleek form
cut streaks in the lake's surface. I wouldn't plunge into the icy

waters, then convince you not to drown me. I wouldn't
try to guess what your long strange species eats, anymore

than I'd slap on a wet suit, descend with a spear gun to find
your tender spots between green plates. I wouldn't tear

into streets, trying to tell everyone that what they've heard
is true. I'd stick brazen, sun-flecked feathers in my hair.

Wander to the late-night lake. Dip my fingers into the placid
reflection as your ancient face surfaces. I'd be both voyeur

and believer, wear a piece of your green memory
like an emerald on my left hand, which is no different

than what I do everyday. As you rise to meet me through fathoms
of fear, what you don't know is this: I always knew your secret

reality. Let you sink into your watery cave, so that when
you resurface, you'll take me with you.

normal

ON THE BANKS
OF THE GREAT PASSAIC

"When I've seen enough I'll be back to splash in the
Passaic again only with a body so naked & happy
City Hall will have to call out the Riot Squad"
—Allen Ginsberg in a letter to William Carlos Williams (circa 1957)

from wherever they came whoever they were they settled here
& there at first along the river banks where hungry mosquitoes
carried the spirits of the lenni-lenape & eagerly drank the
blood of white settlers dutch german english whoever who put
up their farms their mills their distilleries their slaughter-
houses who claimed the banks as if they were virgin girls all
for their own to call this old land a new land all for their
own with barbed wire & chain-linked fences & soon to be iron
horses & shovels & bottles & strange-god churches filled with
even stranger faces from wherever they came whoever they were
now smoke-churning chimneys signposts & sidewalks now phantom
voices talking shouting now big macktrucks marching & jukeboxes
playing gangsters & hammers pounding staking claim to the banks
as if they were their own these were the banks of the once
great passaic curled up like a dying old man where i sat as a
boy in 1958 toothpick in my teeth marking my first memory by
the face of the tide the flow of the current the dead carp the
swirling gull going going somewhere out there to wherever they
came from whatever they were going going going & going to from
the banks of the great passaic.

THE STRANGLE TREE

"O brilliant wood!
Yours is the voice of a new world;
And all the hills burn with such
blinding art" —Thomas Merton

i am sitting here
on the slopes of rincón de la vieja volcano
& on the slopes of rincón de la vieja volcano lives the strangle
tree brought from africa by the spaniard in his holy age of
conquest & like the conquistadores the tree sits dissatisfied
in its own trunk   its own mainspirit   & it craves starves &
yearns always for more   the tree grows powerful arms which
reach out with even more powerful fingers yearning craving
always starving more   & with nothing but air to grasp it
turns inward upon its own trunk   inward again & again until
the entire tree is smothered engulfed strangled by its own
hungry branches   & the spirit dies   500 yrs pass   & here
on the slopes of rincón de la vieja volcano stands the strangle
tree   massive tangling cavernous   home to termites spiders
leaf cutter ants   vipers   all hungry craving always yearning
more & more

& i'm sitting here in costa rica
somewhere btwn the river styx & the shimmering gates of nirvana
here at the doorstep at a time just before the great masses
will witness its own obscene upheaval   here where technology
will soon feast upon its own flesh   here the day before war
monuments come alive & attack their worshippers   & modern
analogies shall suck potent milk from nostradamus's withered
teat

i'm sitting with hope
i'm sitting here in the circle of life in costa rica
here beneath the pulsing sun & the redden skies   somewhere
btwn obedience to nature & the tears on a grieving mother's face
where 6,000 languages are spoken & only the corpses understand
each other completely
on this day
the howler monkey roars
the strangle tree yearns
here in costa rica
with 12,000 species of butterflies   109 species of bats
425 species of birds   121 species of snakes
here where one fruit bat can disperse 60,000 seeds
a teardrop from a frog can slay a panther
the larvae of a caterpillar can kill a human
a jesus christ lizard can walk on water

here in the feeble wind of modern promise where butchers
wear still the painted face of god.

Valeria Numinosa

HERE'S WHY THIS STUNNING VISUAL OF GODDESS KALI IS GIVING PEOPLE POST-TRAUMATIC STRESS DISORDER

Whatever happened to the invisible hunger in the sky?
One moment I'm scratching your initials under my desk;
the next I'm being stalked by a Turkish-speaking man named Tom.
Seven customs officers didn't bother to read
when I passed them a slip declaring two kilos of cocaine
hidden in the vortex of my soul. This is not to brag,
just to prove that I exist.

John O'Dell

CHEKHOV AT THE MOSCOW ZOO

"The male cheetah is unable to have sex with
a female cheetah with whom he is familiar..."
—William Boyd, Bamboo

It's *Acinonyx jubatus*, cheetahs, I go to see,
yes, I, feral *Homo Sapiens*, prowling the cages
the way I stalk city stages and theater dressing
rooms, the salons and samovars of country estates.

Black tear marks flood fur from the corners
of cheetah eyes, but it's only to cut down glare,
help find, then fly upon astounded prey; I use
that ruse myself, withdraw behind my mask

of sorrow to see more clearly, savor in advance
my speed, my strength, discover how to cut off
all paths of escape except my own. I'll confess,
the tears I shed most often spring from laughter.

Like the sleek male cats I never tire of studying,
I require always some scent of the unfamiliar.
Freedom's the curse I carry within my always
visible claws, a cage whose key I've thrown away.

Susan Okie

This Bed of Crimson Joy

Yellow skin, belly taut
and round—a lemon
of a man. *Doctor*, he'd call,
I need a beer. We found a few,
one time, under his bed. His mother
sneaked them in, although she knew
beer had done in his liver, beer
would kill him. *Doctor...* One day,
I heard a different note, found him
struggling to sit up while dark blood
gushed from his throat.
He reached for me, eyes wide
as a child's. I shouted, ran for help,
but all refused to come:
Nothing to save.
I found his breathing stilled,
a lemon on a crimson bed.

Author's Note: The title is a phrase from "The Sick Rose" by William Blake.

Simon Perchik

You pick away at the Earth
as if your grave was filled
with the wait for flowers :one foot

already pleased, the other
still wrapped in dirt
weighed down stone by stone

the way fruit is ripened
keyed up and seaworthy, is lowered
into a wooden box

that never leaves shore
just the loading and unloading
though step by step

you overflow from a single rock
broken into twigs
coming by for your mouth

—you want to walk out, trade
make a deal tit for tat
the dry grass that has no blossoms yet.

Kathleen M. Quinlan

POSSIBILITY

A bulldozer is flying
past my second floor window.

Against dust-bunny-lint sky, it floats
beyond the branches' reach
of Lord Crane's garden. Heedless of
gargoyles' leers, it veers toward
the half-eaten red berry tree feast,
scattering avian smugness.

In mirthful suspension,
it wavers before flying
over the rooftop on another
impish escapade.

W. M. Rivera

WALKING IN CENTRAL PARK

I happen by a two-year-old.
She smiles. I waver

in my supposes: tragic
fate? Or will it be divine

transmission? I see
a woman naked, promised

circles of gold,
a sure winner. I see her

opened lipstick, and a cross
diametrically opposed,

a skeleton gesticulating
with open arms. I see her

cup a key-ring full of potential
doors. Beyond her I see

the impetus to be loved, and
I smile back.

David Romanda

Fortune-Cookie Fortunes

When you hear prerecorded applause
take a bow.

They're coming in the night with their microchips.

Self-loathing is no longer in vogue.
Give yourself a hug.

Your heart's fucked (or you'll soon get cancer).
Forget retirement savings.

Guys fake orgasms too.

Never flush dead, or dying, goldfish
down the toilet.

You're too lazy for complete world domination.

Sure, you'll regret it.
But you'll regret not regretting it more.

Overdose at least once.

Collect something. Treasure your collection.
Then give said collection to the troll under the bridge.

Daddy doesn't forgive you.

John Roth

RESURRECTION MINUTIA

A mouse skeleton unwinds
in the palm of my hand,
plays between each finger
like a bony ribbon
before coming back to life.
Each tiny digit springs with new
music. Animal reflex.
I softly brush its rib cage
with my thumb like a miniature
harp. Its vertebrae retuned;
the same blood and warmth
that hums through everything.
I set the mouse
on the green margin of the lawn
and watch it sprint off,
its tail swept clean,
the light still twitching
where its body rested in the grass.

HEAD-CASE AQUARIUM

Fun fact: A spark has the lifespan of a carnival goldfish.
Sometimes I tamper with light switches
just to watch them swim around inside oily glass bulbs,
dragging their little orange tails of fire
through strained filaments.
Listen for the heat of their music.
Gold scales dazzle, molten koi ponds dug out
from every muddied sunrise.
My eyes detach, float away from my skull
like fat buoys. I snatch at them. Miss. I'm winning
and losing all at the same time. The smallest transactions
are key: Exchange one coin-sized breath
for just three more minutes to live.

Daniel Saalfeld

D.C. POEM

The fat parking enforcement officers
are more vigilant than ever these days.

One stands outside writing tickets
in her blue-black vinyl jacket

under an early-April cherry tree.
In her next life, she'll be hand sanitizer.

SPRING AGAIN

A pubescent cherry tree's green buds
from across the pot-holed street
fill my eyes at a red light.

Taylor Sacco

The salted snow
is slushy, sludgy.
Thick like nightmare quicksand.

Plows patrol the hill
with haunting patience
and a gentle percolating
menace, like beasts
with their lights prying into
every private corner.

i somehow find myself a part of this scene,
lying drunk
 and whiskey warm in a
  bank of frozen snow,
   waiting for her,
eyes pointed
toward a sky with no stars,
just the undulating bodies of clouds
suspended in the dark.
   Staring into this void
it seems certain that some giant thing will emerge,
tiny at first,
and then horrid and urgent
and impossibly large.

But...

        the pills are kicking in.

            The menace subsides and

now it's that slow

        scintillating sensation lapping at my legs.

            On our way here,

she slipped them gently past my lips,

slurred her encouragement,

asked me to trust her.

So now i'm waiting.
So now she's up there
buying her cocaine,
and i'm down here reeling in a gentle
relaxation almost too great to be real.

There are voices,
loud and boisterous and excitedly drunken
slicing through the storm windows
and pirouetting in time with the storm
and i hear her cackle,
too,
cascading,
and i find myself wondering what time it is.

Wondering
if the purpose of this pill
was to keep me placid,
and obedient
but then that giant,
nurturing
 opioid hand drifts out of the black Burlington obscurity
and lulls me swiftly back to that place
of brain sloshing content,
and instead of worrying
i perk my ears and listen to the low
sobs of the beasts as they
prowl.

Suddenly she's there
  in the January early morning,
  still shouting obscenities to those *motherfuckers* upstairs.

She's surprised to see me,
like i have been misplaced,
some giant set of car keys
on painkillers
that have slipped under her couch cushions.
Hoisting me hand-to-hand
to my feet
the salt is carbonated
  under my boots and without a word,
we start that awkward
dragging of ourselves home,
tired and breathing our boozy fumes
into the air already thick with condensation.

When the plows pass,
slow and sentinel-esque
we both cower,
turn our heads away from the lights as
if we're taking our shadowy forms far
away from this
dissolved winter
and into the promise of springtime salvation.

As if
  we're prisoners,
    escaping,
and staying out of the spot-lights
is the only way
out.

cum Blossoms

She called them
cum trees.

They bloomed every spring downtown.
First the gentle buds,
bulbous and sensual,
curving their expansions inward,
folded petals bound
in expectant blossoms.

Then all unfolding overnight
like waking to the sopping reality
of a wet dream,
beautiful white and velvet soft,
swaying their sense of elegance
in cold air perceived warm as we
collectively thaw.

But that smell
like an adolescent boy's bedroom wastebasket,
teeming with tissues all stained with that protein rich
evidence of exploratory self-indulgence.

Stale and heavy with ammonia.
With bleach.

Every spring
it was that smell,
wafting its sticky sickness down every street.

Bruce Sager

QUESTION

If your life were a balcony
would you be standing on it
or below it? is what she asked me
and she was playing with her hair
twirling the strands, twirling,
and from time to time she would
reach out and touch my arm
where the sleeve of the tee
cut right across my bicep
and once she pressed my hand
while she was making a point
and her voice dropped below
all of the other voices at that party
when for a moment she murmured
something about her husband
and her long married eyes held
my long married eyes
and my life was a balcony
and I was swinging somewhere
outside of it from a night tree.

Gerard Sarnat

67% HOPPERIZED BATHOS

"...so when we look at the painting...we say it's a Hopper.
We don't say it's a gas station..."
—from Mark Strand's notebook, found after he died in 2014

Freshboy eye candy larva, after Latin class in the Harvard Yard, this *puerile* grub
put out 2/3's the hard yards required to acquire *Life Magazine*'s worn mustachioed
thrift-shop-Brooks Brothers-tweed-jacket-torn-leather-elbow-patches pipe + persona.

Self-consciously square, I bathed alone in the shadows of Waldorf Cafeteria
cigar circles whose prodigies fueled my undergraduate doom, *Disregard the fools*
you come from, kiddo; that's what this pale rube from the other side of the Rockies

did while the damaged men's room mirror futilely attempted to dispense PEZ.
Five decades later, Nordstrom said, *Color the hairs left. Whiten dentures. Switch*
out glasses for contacts—which prepared for an inevitably less than gala college reunion.

M. A. Schaffner

ALGORITHM DEFLECTOR SEARCH TERMS

Your alternative online shopping list:
Venetian real estate, the government
of the Channel Isles, newt acrobatics,
bat mating habits, edible cacti.

Indo-rock, Silesian coal, pictographs,
nude ice skating, cod fishing narratives,
rhyming hieroglyphs, sweet obsidian,
hammer dulcimer emergency tone.

Teenage cannibal rescue fantasy,
neo-Confederate Crisco parties,
Lateran Council survivor meetings
in the greater Jacksonville area.

Commuting by camel, bicycle figs,
colonoscopy souvenir keychains,
living rulers of the Chan Chan Empire,
Albigensian espresso milkshake.

Zuckerberg-Gates-Burroughs love triangle.

FROM REEDSVILLE TO THE BIG CITY

Forever old enough not to know better,
accumulated wisdom snuffed with words
pondered increasingly after and smiles
that seemed knowing in the starlight as wind
brushed the last of the day's rain over us.

You never know the fuse is there until
the least spark finds it. You don't remember
the chapter you thought you finished until
the night turns the page and it continues
to a new yet intimately familiar face.

Even the dream of what won't come next brings
the haze of demonically crafted wine;
even the touch of fingers that never meet
enriches the rest of this spendthrift life.
Old enough now to know nothing stays known.

Lorraine Schein

THAT SECRET HOUR, BEFORE THE RAIN

She lived in the rain, behind a drop-door hung with a sign that changed each time it fell. Sometimes it said, "Do Disturb," sometimes "Come Again Another Day," sometimes "Please Loiter." To live there forever is what she wanted.

That secret hour before the rain, the patients in the halfway house for the insane knew she was going to come down. They had buried the keys to the Coke machine in the forest and, pulled by its silence, went looking for them, then walked by the pond, taut with circles. The borderline cases had the most precognition of precipitation, always knew first when she would plummet. They could feel it in their brains, before any droning weatherclone.

She wished she could forecast herself, but she never knew when, only whether.

THE YELLOW FAIRY BOOK

Go to the Fairy Hill
for the Apples of the Sun.

The Springtime Fairy,
The Flower-Queen's Daughter.

Do not stare at her Wings,
Her Yellow Eyes,

Or be Dissolved by
The Light from one thousand Suns—

Captured at Night,
The first three Milliseconds.
The test Blast...

Vaporized by Heat.
The Tinder-box.
The Death of the Sun-hero.

"A bubble of Light
Over the Desert—
Malevolent, center of Hell..."

The Witch and her Servants,
The Dragons dancing.

"A planet of Fire" unfolded—
"A Galaxy of Stars inside,
a momentary Portal" to

Yellow days
in a Yellow house—
Vincent painted it.

The Evil Spirits drag the Girl to the Cauldron.
The Prince looks into the Magic Mirror.

"Standing in the Doorway was
a charming Maiden,
at whose sight his Mind gave way."

She has detonated this reality.

Black cindered crows rise
from a seething cornfield
in her Yellow Eyes.

Author's Note: This poem is a cento, with lines from *The Yellow Fairy Book* and quotes from web comments on seeing photos taken at night of first atomic bomb tests.

Claire Scott

They took her away, did they?
I was seven or six or nine
Pigtails with bows, a smile with
Too many teeth, skinned knees
Bruises on my back
When the police came they patted
Me on the head and then
They took her away
In their black car
With black windows
She never came back

I promised I wouldn't
But I did and I did and I did
My hand shot out
My fists flew
I swore never again never
But I threw a glass
Blood on her face
He called the police
Who came in a black car
No one patted me on the head
They took me away, did they?
Sirens screaming
My daughter sobbing in his arms

MY FATHER'S DEATH

I wasn't there when my father died
I mean *died* died

My father died for ten years
Cancer, heart attack, bunions,

Dementia, arthritis, more cancer
At times teetering on a precipice

The family flying from all
Directions not wanting

To miss the closing moments
Just to be sure

Once we heard the gurgling
Death rattle
     only minutes to go

Us kids squabbled over music
Some wanted Brahms'
     violin concerto

Others Brahms' fourth symphony
CDs stacked on every surface

Some in jewel cases others
Jumbled on the floor

My brother found the fourth
Under discretely wrapped
     boxes of Depends

We circled my father's bed
Demure, dignified, appropriate

Ready to share the music
Of his waning breath

We found Mahler's second in
The case labeled Brahms

Another frantic search hoping
Death would delay a bit longer

Finally Brahms' violin concerto
Surfaced in a Schubert case

We put it on and waited
And waited

The concerto ended
But my father didn't

I felt cheated coming all this
Way from California
Spending all this money
Missing all this work
Why didn't he have the decency
To die on my schedule

It was always about him

Cathryn Shea

THE LAKE DOESN'T KNOW

It's me playing the accordion,
a Galanti owned by a fabled barmaid
newly drowned in sorrows, buried under
the black oak not far from where
my parents are interred.
I think the oak is sick
with some disease. I fear

it is distracted, not watching over
the graves. The woman's estate
is in probate. Her widower,
a legendary toper,
has left the door unlocked
too many times. Hence, here
I sit on the bench playing
to the coots. It's hard
work banging out the triplets
on this squeezebox whose notes
fall off limbs like boggy buckets.

It could be that pilfering
and white lies really are unforgivable
and this dull thud is coming
from the coffin
of my conscience, my parents'
scruples worming their way
into my soul. The twinge I feel
for the deceased. Their life work,
troubles multiplied when
they tried to do good. I promise
to put the jigs and reels back,
tidy just as they were.

Kristina Webster Shue

NEVER THE SAME PLACE TWICE

Crinkle-cornered eyes roam fields, pendulum sown rows in swampy puddles, evening light reflected and wavering with each green sway. Their physical reality transports—you can never step in the same river twice. Feathers are most often gray rather than bordeaux, turquoise, ice white—and I have them, though my ankles stay steeped in dead grass. But my clavicle hollows fill with condensation quivering with the last chord. Subliminal overflow.

Noel Sloboda

GRADING WHILE THE ROOF IS BEING REPLACED

Sucking down artificially chilled air
I brace myself to face a stack of papers
with topics ranging from the psychic perks

of Pokémon to the unconstitutionality
of school lunch lasting under an hour.
I scrawl crimson on all, remarks

that will soon be dismissed or forgotten
but affirm I stuck with each writer
till the end. The men above clomp

forth and back across an obsidian plain—
a magnet for radioactive rays
baking noses into lobster shells—

as they heave sheets of inky rubber
over the building's side.
What would these workers make

of my red-pen routine?
Once the sun has begun to drop,
they will unroll a new covering

so seals will endure beyond the obligatory
six-month guarantee.
As the stench of tar seeps down,

I dam my eyes, feeling like a dinosaur
stuck in petroleum, ready to slumber—
until some intrepid anthropologist

strips my bones and constructs
an exhibit that troubles the sleep
of small children.

TARZAN in SUBURBIA

When Jane stays late at work
and he doesn't have to cook
the boscage czar lounges

with Cheetah on his Trex deck
sipping an organic banana daiquiri
and marveling at the green expanse

he must very soon mow again
before the township slaps him
with another fine for unruly verdure.

As the sun dips, he studies
ivy creeping up the neighbor's crabapple
and wonders if it will ever grow

strong enough to support a brute
freighted by Heinekens,
Hot Pockets and Netflix binges.

The chimpanzee senses the man's mind
but is kind enough not to say
how hard it is to grip vines

with palms softened by nightly baths
in coconut milk and tears.

J. D. Smith

UPON FURTHER REVIEW

You are not, in fact, the egg man.
Don't take it personally.
These days egg men are thin on the ground.

If it's any consolation, I am
by no means the walrus,
coo coo ca—can't finish.

The syllables
aren't mine to sing,
as Peter Max stripes
aren't mine to wear.

So many years gone
the lyrics fade, and
singing along seems
hard to imagine. *BANG.*

Few colors are needed
to show data, and fewer shapes:
spreadsheet cells of right angles,
the knife-blade of a slope
declining over time.

Lana Spendl

Flinging Superstitions

I'm walking through an Indiana cemetery and I remember a friend of
a friend in New York City chiding me because of my tendency to walk
through cemeteries. "You need to let the dead rest," she said. "I'm not
digging up their bodies," I answered. How defensive I got. How irritated.
Because she spoke with an authority too old for her age. As if her words
were the words of her father or grandmother or a whole slew of elders
who had been cooking up their judgments since the beginning of time.
And if there had been a cemetery near the café where we sat, I would
have given her the finger and powerwalked through it right before her
eyes. But now in my walk I come upon a man's picture on a gravestone.
He is young and wears a suit and he looks like a scared boy who's
been dressed in the clothes of a man. My irritation crumples under his
uncertain gaze. He is honest. I am not. I am the same as my friend's
friend. I fling around the superstitions of others as if they were my own
and I raise my chin up in the air like a pissed-off runway model. I grasp
at empty judgments with my hands and mold them into verdicts and
decrees, and all the while, underneath it all, flows a terrifying river of
darkness and gold. I see glimpses of it sometimes and quickly turn away.

Kurt Steinwand

WOODSTOCK

Crows didn't know where to fly.
To Saugerties, Wallkill, Bethel, White Lake?
Scarecrows jitterbugged before a storm.
Cows out to pasture, alfalfa fields fallow.

A barn-raising, but no roof.
Farmers couldn't resist looking,
scratched their stubble, plowed on by.

Runaways to a garden
that didn't exist, or if it did
left postcard roads and breezy corn,
trash as far as you could see.

Skinny-dippers plucked auto
harps. Two births, two deaths, a
peaceful balance. The sky fell.
Couples huddled under tarps and
cardboard in the fetid mess.

For months after, marijuana seeds took root,
popped out of footprints, great green umbrellas.

Lucky Lindy

You kept your Spirit low
over white cap, white cap, white cap.

A ladder at your window.
Prop augured through pristine air.
For forty minutes, no contact.
You climbed over clouds in search of

a fair-haired baby on cotton,
a snowy field that arced out of view.
So soft if you were to jettison
you would have fallen through.

M. G. Stephens

EXPANDING OUTWARD

The heart has nothing to do with it as
It goes on pumping whether you are here
Or not, but the head hurts and the stomach
Turns over upon itself and time heals
Nothing, being neutral, and space around
Things becomes greater, expanding outward,
While the moon rises and sets, the stars come
And go as they please, and the spring follows
The last gasps of winter just as summer
Comes and goes, dropping down into autumn,
Winter once more upon us, the heart still
Pumping and having nothing to do with
Love or you or anything that once seemed
To matter so much and doesn't at all.

A BAD CASE OF THE BLUES

Loneliness kills more people than cancer,
More souls leave their bodies from it than war,
And yet the only way it is addressed
Is in syrupy country songs, jukebox
Suicide, put in a coin, push button,
You are sat alone in the corner of
The bar's long hall and feel sorry for your
Poor self, misery's cousin, mother
Of anxiety and father to none
But the dispossessed, the outcast, alone
And forgotten, alone and, well, alone.
Is there a country music song for this?
At the knife-edge of existence, who is
It out there to lend this poor soul a hand?

Belinda Subraman

REFUGEE

A little boy asleep on the shore
fell from a boat where he swam like a fish
but he was no fish.

His family, lured by dreams
of kindness somewhere
a day without blood and splattered brain matter
an electric chance of new and better
where children build castles in the sand
where the sound of water is calm and soothing
and children do not drown
looking for a safe place to play.

Tim Suermondt

NOT EVERYTHING HAS TO ALWAYS MAKE SENSE, LIKE TODAY

All the dead people I had contact
with in my life so far are hovering, like
hummingbirds, in front of my study's
window, seven floors up. Even the ones
who merely brushed or bumped into me
on the street, a subway, and in many lobbies.
They stand five across in beautiful rows
I can see no end to. The men in fancy black
suits, red ties. The women in still fancier
gowns of yellow and white. They seem rather
stoic, yet I sense some affection from them all.
They don't speak and I don't either—I watch
until they vanish by folding back into the air,
leaving me to wonder when years from now
I, a man who's always been able to stay a step
ahead of having to wear the monkey suit, will
be standing in front of someone's window,
decked out in such an ensemble, a bit sad about
the knot at my throat, fidgeting a bit in my tight
shoes, dreaming of what my hands were once
capable of.

Sharon Suzuki-Martinez

THE MONSTER'S MAGIC LIST

Once, a monster decided to be less negative.

Why squeeze myself into the mold of old hurts, it thought. So it made a list of "Top 10 Things That Make Me Happy" which looks like this:

10 — Meteor showers
9 — Dancing heads of daffodils
8 — Haunting ancient paths
7 — Afternoons to oneself
6 — Sharp knives
5 — Small sharks
4 — The secret language of ordinary objects
3 — Winter-scent of hot chocolate
2 — Abandoned sanitariums
1 — '70s reggae

The monster let the joys orbit its head like a halo. Officials continued to deny knowledge of the monster. Runners still ran away shrieking. Its mother was impressed as cold, hard oatmeal.

The monster lumbered along
with the syncopated heartbeat of starlight.

In a far corner of the world, a little girl laughed at 10 strange thoughts she didn't understand. The kind of giggle that opens shutters in your mind. All who heard her never hurt anyone, not ever.

Marc Swan

BEFORE RALPH NADER WROTE HIS BOOK

Just before ten, headed south on the Brandywine,
maybe doing fifty-five, top up, windows down,
"It's All in the Game" on the radio, singing along,
smooth sailing until the rear end jerks, steering
takes its own course toward the overpass wall.
I hold the wheel tightly in both hands, yank it
hard left; tires dig for purchase as the front
end lifts and rolls, twenty-four hundred pounds
in motion. The door flings wide; I'm thrown into
the dirt, rag top tears off where my head would
have been. Next memory is the ER nurse calling
my mother to bring a jacket, mine is torn up. Then
Dr. Fitzpatrick comes in with X-rays in his hands,
books me for the next forty-two nights—shattered hip,
contusions, a pin drilled through my acetabulum,
a small rod with wires and weights wound into
my right knee to keep it lined up. I'm groggy,
but my mind's spinning, thinking of the look on
my father's face when he finds out the brand new
car we bought has become a heap of twisted metal.
For two years, the rusted '64 Corvair Monza Spyder
rests in the field facing my bedroom window.

Kelly Talbot

THE DRUMMING OF WINGS

Brightly colored moths weave cocoons,
trying to become what they already are.
The sound of fingers on a drum:
skin touching skin,
gently, firmly, vibrating.
The surface trembles, tingling,
reverberating with feeling,
creating one momentary sound
to slowly relax and fade.

And when I touch you,
there is a fluttering rhythm.
We become what we already are
as we weave echoes
of skin touching skin,
wings beating in stasis,
and the drummer is the drum,
and the drum, the drummer,
and the eternal song where we join
flickers like the wings of butterflies
pounding in their becoming.

STARS ENTERING THE FLOW

The river of night flows
around the moon
in the midst of the day,
trickling ebony
along the edges
of her ivory face.

When her lips part
all around the world
birds burst into notes
trying to echo her song.

Lately, one by one
stars fall down from the sky
to form rivulets that drift
through the current
of the daylight night,
shimmering in the blackness,
glimmering in the sun.

When the moon laughs
trees tremble in ecstasy,
leaves blushing different colors
in cyclical harmony.

When she breathes
my heart beats
in time with the flow
of the night river.

Echoes shake in the memory tree
where the verbs are changing colors.
A syllable can change, not me.
The shadow scissors of tomorrow
gleam in an empire of maybes.

I pull my collar up against the truth
and make a fist to hold on tightly
to the nexus of our shared pulse.
Trembling in the interpretations,
I want to burrow deeply or run.

Lava legs flowing,
fueling my chameleon fire,
slowly melt time and space.
When we cool, mountains will remain,
but in the breaths of now

your pupil pools of night
ringed by twilight
call to my thunder
so my first warm drops
heavily splash this dust
and all else implodes.

Jenniey Tallman

A Yellow Bowl

The yellow bowl
I brought to the
community potluck
is the same bowl
my children throw up in
when they are sick.
We call it the puke bowl.

In the sandbox Bonnie,
Maria, Katrin, and Pabalelo
laugh when I tell them.
They also use bowls
in their houses both for
puke and for food.
Neha's grandma

is visiting from India
and she wants a picture
with my son Oakley
before she goes home
because they are good friends
every morning when they walk
around the buildings and sit

together.
He is full of questions,
she tells me and I did not use to
have any Indian grandmas for my son.
Neha's grandma is like a yellow bowl
and—Under the tree I am hanging
laundry while children

try to accidentally spray me
with a water gun—in the sandbox
    Ash-Lee told me
    somebody told Dufoo
    the big boys aren't his friends anymore.
    The big boys want to hurt us all, he said.
    (The *big boys* are my sons.)

    They are your friends, Ash-Lee.
    They have always been, I say, *your friends.*
    But I will stay in the sandbox today.
    Dufoo returned, wanting me to tell him
    too. I did. Everyone wanted to hear
    the new story. They liked it better.
Under the tree I am letting them

spray me and the clothes on the line
because when I was them
I thought the reason grownups didn't help
was that they didn't know, I thought
sandbox bullies were one more secret
I was supposed to keep.
It wasn't. They knew. We know.

When you have a yellow bowl
big enough for puke and food,
it should be used for both things.
That is the job of the yellow bowl.

Devin Taylor

ADVENTURE TIME!
(CIRCLE ALL THAT APPLY)

"Your journey will end with a crimson thump."
—*Rocky Jones*

Every night, I play pretend as a
[*moronic*]/[*bionic*]/[*Byronic*] hero
starring in a choose my own
[*adventure*]/[*misadventure*]/[*damnation*]
[*novel*]/[*poem*]/[*cartoon*].

After [*brim-filled*]/[*jam-packed*]
evenings of [*mechanical*]/[*practical*] hedonism
and discretionary, [*petroleum jelly*]/[*WD-40*]
wanton-hand-abandon,
I'll sit on the bench outside my dorm
smoking whatever lousy
sawdust-filled cigarette
I manage to bum from
an [*Asian*]/[*French*]/[*Finnish*] exchange kid.

As I light it, I pretend
it's a stick of ACME TNT.
The smoke comes out
my [*nostrils*]/[*windpipe*]/[*exhaust pipe*]
and I feel like a [*choo choo*]/[*boo hoo*]/[*poo poo*] train;
a derailed [*choo choo*]/[*boo hoo*]/[*doo doo*] train,
called the [*carcinogenic*]/[*cry-baby*] express...
Then it's [*ka-bam!!!*]/[*ka-boom!!!*]/[*ka-blewy!!!*]

Looking at the window,
the shadows underneath
look like [*bank vaults*]/[*pianos*]
and (when I'm particularly hammered) [*anvils*]/[*Advils*]/[*Aleve*].
The shadows underneath look like [*canyons*]/[*chasms*]/[*hellmouths*].

My journey always ends
with my [condemnation]/[condensation]/[capitulation],
[trekking]/[treading]/[trudging] through
the shadows like Wile E. Coyote,
running first off a cliff, then on the air itself,
until he tries to touch the ground,
but finds it absent. Then looks down,
conforms to the laws of physics
and accepts his fate,
plummeting back into reality.

Ed Taylor

ELEGY

jokulhlaup (Icelandic): a flash flood of glacial meltwater

Every thing begins as a bead
of light in some high pass, but melts
among the pinnacles carefully down
to the valley hot with building and noise
and storms and toward that burning line
too bright to look at, the salt waters
at the end of this earth,
                    and even silent glaciers
now speak in those moist syllables,
sing at the cradles they leave,
white from the cold mountains
dying into this new world flat
and warm as the red eye giant
above the bloody sea

Terrell Jamal Terry

Faintly Majestic

You wrote that your belly was blank
& how colorful ramshackle houses in the Caribbean
stole your attention.
I never knew sight could lack sense
until you described wonder.

I wrote how the roses & intestines
of a roasted hollow darkness in the Carolinas
rushed through my roots.
How I drank a devil to drown a devil,
& then my mind got smashed.
I was a torn composition.

I believed in vicarious fear, repetition
of resin, & vast sweeping internal tunes.

At night there is less panic.
Piano stairs & cymbals instead of quickened heartbeats
& the sugar death of dread.

I try to give it little meaning & shake its grip off,
throw the presence out.
Slowly, less unnamed heaviness. I was trying
to read the notes fast,
but what I wanted became a lie.

THREE MOONS

The edge of orange light, the brown flies of my eyes—
house leaves & white mountains eating the hours.
Let me lose my name again.
It just comes & glows. I pray into the grave,
a mango, a grove. I want transient spells,
old woodwomb, never outcome by force.
How could I live incoherently surrounded by soft afterlife?
Every eye shunned strangely.
I said I but who could sleeve the black evening?
I was tired from waking to three moons.
I told you how pages blurred & words burned,
how I touched the understanding of watery birds.
It doesn't explain constellations of conversations.
I was such fevered childishness, looking
& not knowing, staring at sleep. I told you the act
of your face—bewilderment.
Every green turns purple, the stars seem to walk
while I climb the yellow hill of the heart
trying to tell myself that no one ever dies
from fresh air & black scars or bodies
of maroon canyons. Blue lungs, my broken breath
& hands are made of cold.
I never reappeared. You didn't answer your phone.
The numbered hours eat the wind.
This I remember, not where I come from.
Tomorrow I'm promised brick flowers & bee stings.
Tonight, her salt tastes like sugar & she gives.

Parker Tettleton

Love Poem

It's a Saturday in September. My phone is charging, the TV is muted, the air is off. My fingers are typing words instead of text messages to you. I dream about being a husband who can explain why Monday is a holiday. I wish I was a person with a forest for a first name, or at least a forest. You kiss me better before we recycle. I ask for the something that will out us. The shit on the clock says *I do*.

Love Poem

R says my living room fan looks like a vagina.
We haven't seen each other since I took my shirt
off in the belly of the neighborhood known for sewing
skirts out of lemon trees, belts out of cucumber, love
out of Buffalo Exchange. One of us asks the other if he
wants to take another road trip, like we did last summer,
for two weeks, across half of America, bitching, being
laughed at, reading to anyone anywhere & the other
says yes, he says holy fucking shit yes. We're always
like this. We're friends. We haven't been for a while.

LOVE POEM

I like it when people are happy
even if they're just pretending,
even if they know they won't have
a second more of it, happiness, or
they're having their last second of it
right now & sleeping with it, the idea,
of another last second, & think about it
as long as they think they can do something
about it, become someone else, forget who
they've become, who they will be again
& again—I like it when people aren't people.
When you & I are animals & can't not do it
to each other. When you swallow the room
& lick the books & like it when I finish, I finish
a poem.

Teniola Tonade

HOW GOLDEN, AT LAST, IS THE RECOVERED FLEECE?

Doubts crowd the threshold of the mind
like marauding vampires at a target's door.

Soon, this protected parlor will host
the faceless exponents of a life of woe,

of fading promises of a perfect home,
of reaching to the sun and getting burned

by it. Once golden like a dream, the coveted
crown of quests will feel leaden to the touch.

Mother came home dancing on that pale evening,
a fresh dream knotted at her wrapper's end.

"Your father's address," she answered
inquiring eyes, and knots in three

different bellies complied, at once, to
a long-sought healer's touch.

Now, speeding past unfeeling rocks and trees
on the road to the Western star,

the silent noises of remembered incidents
pollute our joy. What will it cost now,

the restored completeness? Who will be thrown
down, this time, from the balcony?

Sally Toner

BOATING ON LAKE ANNE

Two skiffs sit upon the lake
one named *Dagger*, one with *Perception*
painted in an arc across its bow.
They are perpendicular, blue
ramming green in the afternoon.
It's concrete anger meeting reason
we never see as succinctly when
intention mucks and muddies, brown and loud.
We strap on sandals, spooked by silt that if
we fall will slime our toes when they hit bottom.
But let's look instead at diamonds on
the water far beyond our plastic bodies
as we paddle towards the fuzzy rows
of blossoms passed a thousand times on shore.

Idea Vilariño

YOU DIDN'T SEE

Is it true you understand
or are you playing at
understanding
seeing
knowing
or can you truly see with my eyes
and if you see with my eyes
how can you not see everything
you don't go to the depths
you don't arrive at the end
until you touch the nothingness
if you see with my eyes
if you understand so much
how can you not see in them
how how can you not see
did not see
a small animal that begged for air
that was burning
asphyxiating
dying.

—*Translated by Jesse Lee Kercheval*

I WANT

If perhaps you are playing
if you raised the game to this point
because I could not accept anything less
good
I'll play
I like it
continue
I want it.
I couldn't swear to do more.

—*Translated by Jesse Lee Kercheval*

Anna Lowe Weber

BLOCK ISLAND, 2015

An island all bramble and broken glass.
We have come for only a few weeks,
but I know others must stay for years.
Walk off the ferry and forget to eventually
get back on, some new definition
of home rising in their throats the way
the ocean does in gunmetal swells,
waves so cold no one can stand to get in
past their waist except for one teenage boy,
his head bobbing like a buoy beyond the break.
We hike on the footpaths that traverse the island
like a heart's arteries, emerald-saturated gullies
and bluffs overlooking water that, from
far enough away, has gone blue. Some trick
of the eye because after we descend, inch our way
down the rope that someone has looped around
a boulder to get from cliff to shore, the waves
are gray again, pounding and pounding. Someone,
an artist, has hidden glass orbs all over the island,
translucent globes the size of a grapefruit,
but in two weeks of searching, we find not one
on the trails or beaches. Only a bleached jawbone.
A deer's rotting carcass, half-buried by sand, up
where the dunes crawl with marram grass and sea rose.
Wedged into one of the stone walls that cross
and dissect the island, a Tupperware container,
and in the container, a notebook. *We buried this*
for our friend who is turning fifty this year. Please leave her
a birthday message and well wishes for the future.

Katherine West

For Oklahoma City: 1995

The building signaled for help with smoke, then mirrors
Shattered, sequinning the streets—the quick-changing city ready for
   her close-up.
Choppers zoomed in, cameras targeting
The amateur rescuers: lawyers, bankers, unexpectedly unsuited
Women scrambling—nylons snagging on rebar—
While bodies pressed between concrete crusts
Drizzled down blood like blackberry juice.

> *Of those eighteen, upon whom the tower in Siloam fell and slew them,*
> *Think ye that they were sinners above all the men that dwelt in*
> *   Jerusalem?*
> *I tell you. Nay.*

The amputation freed one: scarred us all
(Thank you, hack reporter, for your unlicensed blow-by-blow.)
The basement Flooding! The woman Sobbing! The surgeon Sawing!
Skin/Fat/Muscle/Bone/Marrow . Marrow/Bone/Muscle/Fat/Skin
Her children in the daycare's dust still—
Playing hide-and-seek. *Oh come out, come out, wherever you are!*

(Pardon my thick speech; pain
Sticks like peanut butter to the roof of my mouth.)

Twenty-four hours after the blast, my toddler is prancing,
Joyous bare feet slapping our concrete patio. It sounds like firecrackers.
I cannot stop contemplating my sons
Piece by piece, considering
Whether I could identify them by a heel,
A hand, a cool and fragile earlobe.

What shall we do with the babies?
What shall we do with the babies?
What shall we do with the babies—Oh!
We'll wrap them up in calico.
Wrap them up in calico
And send them to the graveyard—oh.

From the shattered offices streamed the ghosts of work
White sheets of paper drifting in the streets
And all those undone tasks in all those undone minds
Howling in our dark hearts: *Increase your productivity!!!*
One man hitched up his BBQ smoker and drove four hours
To sit in a parking lot and make sandwiches for firemen.
I honor the bureaucratic with all-night computer games
Ricocheting balls into bricks which neatly disappear
Rebuilt on the next screen with reassuring infallibility.

Forty-eight hours gone—and gone with whom?
The diner regular isn't in his booth; the coworker hasn't called in;
The postman's late. Are they all dead?
Everyone we know is searching.
Will turning on our headlights help?
In the rain the city looks like a funeral procession
Going at cross-purposes.

When Jesus came to Lazarus' tomb, Mary told him,
"Lord, after three days he stinketh."
We know our Bible here; the firefighters put VapoRub in their masks
And continue looking for a resurrection.

How soon all our saviors look like dead men.
I would like to kneel before them, to kiss their lacerated hands,
To pin my colors to their sleeves, these grimy sunburnt ones,
But there are no rituals that satisfy, so we offer
Steamed scrambled eggs and unlimited clean socks.

> *The rains came down, and the Feds came up,*
> *And the walls came a'tumblin' down.*

When I dream, the FBI goes with me
Seeking evidence. (Can't go wrong with a man in uniform...)
We tag and bag a carved bench, a green glass inkwell,
A receipt. Minutiae that could be critical!
Festering in our heads like shrapnel: the color yellow
The dropped keys, the clarity of the moment just before.

J. T. Whitehead

ALMOST BOURGEOIS

Midnight you add up the debts you've bought.
You pour one drink.
The glass is half-empty.
Check the accounts.
Check them twice to be sure.
Utilities total 650 per.
Student loans, 350.
Mortgage has got 25 years.
100 K.

Merry Christmas, boys.
Down here—not just the naughty ones get caught
& captured in a ledger.
Everyone's catching up.

We've all been caught.

Now another boy's sick.
You give your youngest son
the fever-fighting, cherry-flavored medicine.
It is funny—not humorous, but odd
how good he is when he is sick.
The cup is half-full.
Again.

Gregg Wilhelm

Jutting out (DATADSCO)

Throw a stone two hundred years
Across *potaskit* from Canton tanks
To Federal fort where no more red
Bathes ramparts

Dip into dirty Waters chase rye on
Holiday awash with anonymous
Mothers of inventors fallen tired on
Sylvia's beach

Then float along Smith's clay-banked
Bolus Flu up into a place that knows
Jagged shards of stories are conjured on
Its current

THIEF RIVER SCRAP

Dark mound hides arched in wild ocher wheat
A slumbering bull undisturbed for two decades
Father-in-law abandoned the front of the combine
In this corner of the family farm during the '80s
Until the price of scrap hit fifty cents a pound

He guesses the hulk accounts for a third of the
8,000-pound Massey-Harris that his own father
Brought down from Canada before he was born
The plan was to haul the carcass to Thief River
Falls fifty miles on the shoulders of a Ford F150

The cash would help with cold-ice winter coming on
And little hay put up for 120 head roaming frozen hills
Where Ojibwe tilled long before mechanical buffalo
Arrived to labor endlessly for miserable homesteaders
With names like Jacobson Buringrud Paulsen Moen

Fifty miles north on 59 where dust-swiped land erases
Moose Dung's reservation and the Treaty of Old Crossing
Boomtown home of Artic Cat Digi-Key Steiger Tractor
"Stolen-land river" where Dakotas secretly camped
Along the banks of Red Lake River's renegade current

Farmer-in-law walks cautiously toward the beast
Grade 80 chain draped around his neck like a python
He shimmies links beneath the reel's bloated belly
Lassoes the ends to clamshell bucket of an excavator
Hydraulics heave-pitch-swing scrap onto pickup

Not wise to second-guess this ancient farmer's rhyme
When for some reason he ignores the simplest physics
That foreshadow effects of weight upon unequal weight
Gravity a force down versus horsepower to go forward
Old truck bed buckles like knees on a rust-addled Atlas

Shoulder to shoulder in the cab as the Ford claws
From pasture to gravel road huffing dirt clouds
Eight miles an everlasting hour toward town for gas
Treads shave from friction of wheel-well on wheel
I watch at the pump as the pickup folds itself into a V

A. D. Winans

WOMAN ON THE BALCONY

I see her two three times
a week sitting on the balcony
when weather permits
here in old Italy town
in what is left of North Beach
her robe slightly parted
thumbing through the pages of a book
taking no notice of the people down below

standing to stretch, she yawns
legs like sturdy pillars that stretch
to reach the sky into the boundaries
of my mind
my eyes begging to read the pages
she turns with sensual fingers
wanting just one quick look
one intimate journey into the pages
into the space between
the parting of her robe
a journey to forbidden places
a flight back in time
to another place another world
high on a balcony where
I too ignore the people coming
and going down below

THOUGHTS ON THE CALIFORNIA DROUGHT

sitting here feeling like a used car
one part after the other failing me
early morning bacon sizzling on the grill

the drought laughs at the masses
teases them with a light drizzle

picture of an old lover on the mantle
her smile warm as the campfire
I sat around as a child

my room a dust garden
my hamstring pull refuses to address
the promised golden years drown
in quicksand

Israel and Palestine engaged
in yet another war
Putin playing death games in Moscow
proof the caveman still lives inside us

railroads and monuments
built by immigrants
now treated like criminals
the elderly a liability
the young puppets in a political game
unions weak as a fragile clothesline
poets once warriors on skateboards
now prisoners of pride and envy.

I take refuge in the soft raindrops
the peace of solitude rides my veins
like a steamship treading calm waters

the garden of my mind is still green
poems wait to be planted in fertile soil
no drought can kill

BACK FROM AN MRI

brain scan, I listen
to a Miles Davis album
Blackhawk San Francisco 1961
where a young Latina and I
grooved on the vibes

Here at home
jazz in my head jazz in my bed
jazz waking up the dead
Miles, Charlie Parker, and Lester Young
serenade an army of poets sitting
on my bookshelf

T. S. Eliot playing the banker
Walt Whitman walking the battlefields
William Carlos Williams suturing wounds
Kaufman walking the streets of New York
Juggling a "Golden Sardine"
Blake playing cards with God
Lorca playing Russian Roulette
Micheline dancing with Mingus
Gary Snyder building word bridges
and suddenly I'm not alone anymore
the words falling like soft rain
in a winter green garden

Pamela Murray Winters

SMALL REPAIR

The man in tweed on the TV
on the dentist's ceiling
says we once had two souls,
a big and a little. I think it's the little one
that hides or flees
when I'm getting my teeth fixed, in tests
requiring stirrups, and when I sleep.

To sleep is to trust
the waking. You could always
go down one staircase too many
and not come up. Sleeps are my remedy
when I crave stopping,
my small pseudosuicides. Healthy
for now, despite the dental evidence,

I know my little soul,
which flashes and tumbles and
loves, could use a trim. Shaggy,
reminiscent of the mission kitchen
and the posters of the lost,
it needs to straighten up, grow up,
be here, and stop hurting.

Only the last is the one
I resist, the one that would make
little soul into big, the unpersoning of
the unknown. Finished, tooth number 8
looks like its neighbor at 9, as if I never
thrashed in some dream and spoke
the unspoken, chipping it away.

PAM PLAYS THAT TINY VIOLIN

I'm a stubborn noise bumping against the chair legs. I'm a whine.
I'm a bumble. I'm never going to get off this island. I'm walking off
the Earth, where the road meets the bridge. I can see the rail. In Russia,

there are forty-two different sects that believe in spirits who dress in black
and slither from your cupboards at night to sit on your face in your bed.
I don't know if that's true. I heard it somewhere as I did a one-eighty

and walked along the shoulder and into the city where I buy my bread
every other day and still no one knows my name. Once, on the bus,
a man sat on me. I am invisible, and this is why I scream. People think

it's the wind, tighten the belts of their London Fogs. I always leave
my gloves at home. You always hurt the one you love. You can hurt
the ones you don't love, too. Feel free. I am full of what I call poetry. I am

full of hurt and clouds and claws and corridors and I will not, I will not

Shannon Connor Winward

ERUPTIONS

I was thinking how much I prefer the sky
when it is broken
the air puffed up like it's ready
to take a blow. It feels like living
as I wait under an umbrella
for a child who doesn't come.

The principal's office is cold
shock on wet skin
the boy weeping, tasting
snot on his lip.
It is not his fault.
I hold him, tell him, I know. I know.

We conceived him at the base of a gorge
honeymooning trails, carved rock, dragonflies
flitting a mile high. We haven't been back.
Always breaking
free from my arms
parking lots, shopping mall curbs, I can't
trust him on edges.

He is smiling
by the time we get home
laughing up the steep driveway
backpack bouncing sneakers skipping
jagged border rocks rocking
as if there is no precipice.

The garden is weeping
from quick summer rains
columbines headless, the mulch
broken out in weeds
best intentions choked by poison
ivy thoughts.

Phones go off like time bombs
little boys go at their friends with fists
and teeth
and chairs
and it is never their fault.

He grew like cancer
stubborn-tucked under my ribs
eleven pounds, pumpkin-ripe
I clenched my teeth and forced him out.
He is just a scrapper now
small enough to tuck up under my breast
until he quiets
but there are no safe corners, really
for an unwell child.

I empty his lunch
uneaten whole wheat crusts
sweaty squares of cheese.
I had been thinking how much
I prefer the sky
bruised, ready for a blow
but this is living

eruption like poison ivy rashes, pink-lipped blossoms
under Band-Aids on my arms
eruptions like aneurisms, thrombosis, the hearts of
Columbine mothers. The day is
over, but tomorrow, I am thinking, some day
he will be too big
too much
to hold.

In Conception

Small things are always dying in my dreams
mice and birds, soft empty skins
a latticework of kittens pulled from baskets
strips of fur and bone.

Last night, miniature sea turtles
burrowing in wet cement
octopi clinging to my fingers, living rings
tiny mouths, ten unanswered questions
the same one
     when

the body remembers
the curl of a leg, like a conch shell
tucked to the waist
the tug of a nipple, the weight of it
a being made liquid, love's gravity
     pull, pull

My son grows long, bones stretch
the baby going, gone
a ghost
in the machine. The moon waxes
the body wanes

your hand on my hip, seeking an opening
the framework pried apart
kisses tidal, ten fingers asking
     when, when
and when I break
I give you everything

the body empty
curls on itself
concave to you, you sleep
I think, *never again*
is enough
but the body remembers, and life proceeds
to dissolve in dreams.

PEACH PIE

In the time it takes to eat
a piece of peach pie
she retrieves the bullets

(she knows exactly
where they are)

loads them in the rifle
leaning behind his dress shirts

(where she put it so she wouldn't have to
see it)

rigs a hanger on the trigger
and nestles it
in the hollow of her chin.

If she left a note
it would have said
I told you

not to bring a gun into the house
but that would be spiteful

and take longer than peach pie,
anyway.

Pui Ying Wong

VIEW FROM THE WRITER'S ROOM

A Chinese woman asks for directions.
She looks nice in a faux leather coat.
Her dialect all monosyllable,
she can't roll her tongue
to say the r's
or hit the roof of her mouth
to say the th.
A hydrant, a bakery truck, a poor girl
dragged by a dog much bigger than she.
The world simmers like sun on paper.
Come back from the precipice,
you are not the only one
who hears emptiness in the voice!
The day twists like a daisy
and a poem by Gilbert
pinned on the bathroom door
speaks of spring after the frozen valley,
of course it was long ago he said—

Andrea Wyatt

ARGUING ABOUT THE LINE, THE BREATH

None of the poets I love are gone,
They're in the other room, drinking wine, smoking
Arguing about the line, the breath—

Max D. is slouched in the corner, reading *The Hotel Wentley Poems*
while Jack M. chats up a pale grad student
and Larry E. listens to the telephone wires sing—

Brother intones the history of the Untide Press,
while Robert D. chants *My Mother Would Be a Falconress*
in his long wool cape and later, holds court with Jess—

Zu and Adesanya sit on the kitchen couch
listening to Eric Dolphy play *Out to Lunch*
while Ted Joans plans a trip to Morocco—

Jo Miles and Muriel R. are perched on the porch steps
calling us: come outside to watch the meteor shower over Angel Island—
come out, come out—

None of the poets I love are gone,
They're in the other room, drinking wine, smoking
Arguing about the line, the breath.

Trout Fishing At Chicoutimi

We gang along the steamy burn
Flowed snaily thick with leaves
Edged by flag and Christmas fern
And a boneheap 'neath the trees

A young moose dead in the thicket
His lovely rib cage nearly whole
Like a lyre it was, and we thought
To string the bones and play

I scrubbed the bones of sinew
Of hanging flesh, of blood
Hummed music to play on those strung bones

Oh! To be dead and strung to play music
Of blood and sinew scrubbed clean
In dappled light, in rushing stream

There is a vineyard in my heart
With grapes red, black, green
Trembling for your willing fingers
And all you have to do is pick me clean.

Katherine E. Young

TODAY I'M WRITING LOVE SONGS

after Marina Tsvetaeva

Today I'm writing love songs, Marina,
as if you yourself had written none, as if
no other woman ever felt or smelled
or tasted love's ripe flesh, never stripped
love's husk to find succor within until I,
arriving with my hand outstretched, plucked
at it from idle curiosity.

I promise, Marina, I'll savor this love
whole, run my lips along its rim, swallow
juices, rind, pips, drink in each drop as if
it's the last. Passion slips from its skin, dissolves
sweet, hot, sour, bitter, salty on my tongue,
recalling foods fashioned by the ancients,
who stirred seeds of love in their cooking pots.

They say I look young again, Marina,
furrows of skin softened in gentle rain.
But you and I, we descend from monsoon:
our sort of love engorges the river,
corduroys the fields, drowns the seedlings
asleep in cradling earth—heat, water, ooze,
fruit rotting in mud—no haven's safe from us.

Succuba

Imprisoned in the kitchen herbs—
rosemary, lavender, wormwood—

by day I haunt your close-clipped lawn,
the fruiting trees that edge your land.

Sometimes I tiptoe to your window,
watch your children play within.

Evenings you walk out in the yard,
woman dangling from your arm.

Late at night you come alone,
pressing berries in my fingers,

smearing honey on my breasts:
mouthing greedily, you curse me.

Take up your snakeskin now, my love,
twine it among the needled greens,

the nest of wasps, the holly leaves,
objects you hang to guard your door—

when the appointed moment comes,
all charms will fail, fall useless from

your hands: this witch already dwells
within, blue lips telling the hours.

Randi Ward

BLADES

Beth Adamour

DOUBLE SHOT

Claire pushed her shopping cart through the Harris Teeter entrance and was heading towards the prepared foods island when a young man in a black leather jacket came up to her. He had a well-balanced face framed by peaky brown hair, in his mid-twenties maybe. There was darkness under his eyes as though he hadn't slept in a while. He excused himself for bothering her but he needed to talk to her. It was important, he said.

"Do I know you?" she asked, pausing, angling her cart beside her. His face did look familiar. But no, it turned out, she didn't know him. His name was Jay. A good buddy of his, his roommate, was missing. Seeing the confusion in her face, he quickly went on.

"You see, I knew he'd had dinner at your house the other day and I found your address on a piece of paper in our apartment. So I decided to drive over thinking maybe you could give me a lead on where he'd gone. When I came up to your house, I saw you pulling out of your driveway, so I followed you."

"Did you call the police?" Claire was a retired psychiatric nurse and gathering basic, clarifying information from people was instinctive for her.

Jay shook his head. He didn't seem to mind her directness. "He'd hate that. I thought I'd see if I could find him myself first."

Claire understood how the young man's actions, following her and all, could be taken as predatory, but she did not feel intimidated. Even with him looming over her, she noticed a calm within herself as she spoke to him. Something about him reminded her of her son, which encouraged her to say a few things.

"Well, I'm afraid i can't be of much help to you," she began. They'd had a good time, she and her husband, entertaining Sid and Sue Obermann a few days before. One of Sid's contacts from AA, a rather thin, soft-spoken young man, had come too, which had been a bit of a surprise. "Not much to tell about the other night really, a lot of talking. As for your friend...I remember now, his name was Hiram."

"That's him," Jay put in.

Claire often had trouble with names but remembered this one. For a second, she thought of her Julius, and wondered if giving him that unusual name could have possibly played into the eventual distancing that occurred between them. Stranger things had happened. Random causes could have unexpected effects. Lately, she had started thinking more like that, thinking big, even if that meant imagining the unimaginable.

"But what did he talk about?" Jay pressed her, "Please try to remember, like I say, any detail might help."

Jay had a jumpy manner, moving from one foot to the other, leaning into one hip slightly, dancerlike. He wore black jeans that flared raggedly at the bottom, from which old-style sneakers peeked out, peanut butter gold—a fashion statement, no doubt. He was cute, in a way. A subtle warmth hummed through her body.

"OK," Claire said, "I'll try, but really it is not all that clear in my mind. You know, at sixty plus, things come and go rather quickly and yet, I notice that each year, my actual experience in the moment can have a lot of unexpected pizzazz..."

"Please, ma'am," Jay interrupted.

He did not want to hear her stories. Nor was he obligated to listen to her. He just wanted what he wanted right away. Most men were like that when they were after something from you. Julius, on the other hand, would sit quietly listening to her for hours. That was when she was going through her yoga phase and had a daily practice. She was bored by Eastern wisdom now, but then, the idea of slowing down, taking the time to look at a tree or a flower, captivated her. Her husband Al, a no-nonsense high school history teacher, thought anything to do with godliness was a bunch of junk, so now and then Claire had found herself sharing her spiritual interests with her only child.

Jay's smile seemed a little desperate, so she went on.

"Well, I remember we were talking about the possible downtown arts center being considered by the city council." She was trying to conjure up the night, picture what happened. It was then she saw the handle of what looked like a fancy knife showing inside the young man's thin leather jacket. As if sensing her gaze, he pulled his jacket closed across the front of his body. It gave her a shock for a moment, but why should she be surprised? People these days, imagining that it made them safer, liked to carry a weapon. It did make her a little wary, though. Who knew what this boy was really up to?

A large woman in an eggplant velour running outfit pushed her cart by them, tapping Claire's smaller cart lightly as she moved off. They were blocking the traffic flow, the minor aggression seemed to suggest, and Claire was reminded that she had chores to do, a list of items to buy for tonight's dinner—a French-style dish Al loved in October, and was easy enough to make as everything went into a deep pot—chicken parts, bacon, pearl onions, mushrooms, and red wine. As it simmered, she planned to do her upper body exercises. These kinds of small activities added accents to her otherwise seamless days. Sometimes she wondered if she had retired too soon, the sixties were the new fifties, she kept hearing in the news.

"Look, I'm sorry you can't find your friend. I'm sure he'll turn up soon." He just shook his head forlornly.

She halfway turned to go. "I've enjoyed talking but I really have things..." Then she pivoted, surprising herself, and pushed her cart aside. "Can I buy you a Starbucks?" She pointed in the direction of the tiny coffee shop just inside the store, not far from where they stood.

"Sure, I could go for an iced Americano, double shot."

He smiled at her, and she saw how his wide-open blue eyes could glisten in an appealing way. Julius had a similar kind of simple half-laugh, like he was being tickled. When she was teaching him the basics of mindfulness, he would look at her like that, inquiringly. She was amazed how at barely twelve years old he'd easily memorized all the tenets she'd shared with him. So hard to just observe your mind as if you were a naturalist watching a bird in a tree, and not to judge or try to change what you notice. Let your mind be like Teflon, so that nothing sticks to it, was the one Julius liked. When she shared her worries about her husband, about his high blood pressure, Julius would sing out with a lifted index, "Teflon mind, Teflon." Even though he was still a child, sometimes his comments actually helped—it had been so much better to be able to get support at home rather than go to see some counselor or other.

"Two iced Americanos with double shots," Claire practically had to shout over the piped-in jazzy songster. Her eyes were still adjusting to the dark, triangular, green-walled space as she handed her credit card to the towering cashier with the purple-rimmed glasses who thanked her and asked her if she wanted a receipt. She declined, zipped up her small leather purse, busily thinking while she waited for her order that it was absurd of her to share coffee with this stranger. The moment had the flavor of all those silly Hollywood films: the accidental meeting of two completely different people that developed into a do-or-die romance by the end. Of course, this encounter was not about the two of them, not about her at all, which, in a way, made it OK in her mind to carry on. They picked up their coffees and headed to a table. She actually found herself savoring the slick atmosphere—the appealing aromas spirited from the hissing espresso machine, the shuffling customers carrying cups as if in search of lightning bugs.

"How long have you known Hiram?" Claire asked, barely squeezing her knees under the low table. They had met at the gym a few months back,

Jay told her. Hiram had lost his job and was looking for a roommate to help with the rent. He glanced at her with a flat expression, as if not wanting to say more on that subject. "So, about the other night?"

Claire was remembering now: "Opera. We talked a lot about HD opera, which my husband more than me enjoys," she said after a sip of the drink, startlingly strong even lightened with half-and-half. "But I will go with him once in a while, over to the Grande. It's actually a live simulcast from New York. The last one we saw was German, with this plot—I mean, it starts with the brother and sister, well, they're supposed to be in love. Like romantic and all. You know, I could get it, the way it was done. I just put it in a symbolic way in my mind." It felt good, she realized, to be sharing ideas like this, even if they didn't come out exactly as she wanted. Her husband Al would never discuss things beyond a certain level. She had seen, after Julius left for college, that Al was actually relieved their son was gone, that he had resented their closeness, and wanted her all to himself. Yet he never really opened up when it was just the two of them, like she hoped he would. He was mostly at fault for the rift with the boy, she believed, strict as he was with him. Once, in a hot moment, he actually smacked Julius across the face with a tissue box he grabbed from the kitchen counter. Julius had called him a name, a turd or something silly like that, because he would not let him go to a weekend beach party with his friends.

Jay shook the ice in his glass, an impatient rattle.

She ran her fingers along the seam of her leather purse on her lap, considering how to go on. "Now at this point we were having dessert. I made a Viennese torte, the kind that has very little flour and lots of chocolate, almonds, and butter? I love epicurious dot com. Really, the Internet has changed my life, as much as I get upset hearing about these child porn sites, and all..." She paused a moment to take a sip of the espresso concoction. The chilled plastic cup's intense tingling against her fingers seemed oddly in synch with her rushing thoughts.

"Now, Hiram and Sid weren't drinking, of course. Hiram decided to have a cup of mint tea." The young man, she recalled, had said he was allergic to chocolate, which had struck her as funny because so was her son—after loving it for so many years, right up to his tenth birthday. Then one night he broke out in hives so bad they had to take him to the ER. Al was a chocolate addict. Thin as he was, he still had an elflike physique, although his baldness had somehow made that severe side of him show through. His favorite was double fudge brownies with double chocolate chip ice cream—a child at heart.

"Did you say mint?"

"Yes, mint tea and oh, I remember he said he loved opera, although he had only seen one so far." She was amazed how much detail she could recall. Her brain really was not the muddle that Al liked to believe.

"Who'd he go with?" Jay asked in a caught-up-in-the-story way.

"You know, that didn't come up."

Under the glow of the can lights directed down onto their little corner table, Jay's face took on a dramatic cast. Her son had a similar kind of nose, with the refined nostrils, although it was never quite the same after the mysterious accident when her husband had found Julius, a eighth-grader by then, in the corner of the yard, having fallen after attempting to climb up the chainlink fence. Turned out Julius broke his arm and bruised his face badly. He avoided his father for weeks after that, and Claire often wondered if her husband had done something to him that afternoon. She had never actually pursued the issue with Al. Through the years, she'd needed to back away from useless marital confrontations, feeling she deserved a little peace of mind. She had learned to let things go.

Her mind must have wandered a bit, as it tended to lately. Jay was staring at her now, as if taking her in for the first time since they began talking. She guessed how she must appear to the likes of him—her barely lined moon face with the bangs and the wiry straight gray hair to the jaw, giving her a rugged, peasant look. If the world had an unkind view of her, so be it. Her appearance reflected a personal style she had developed through the years. By the time she was eighty, she expected to resemble a weathered hobbit.

"Then, for some reason, we got onto the subject of death," she said.

"Death?" A slight tremble invaded Jay's tone.

"Yeah, death," she said with a touch of motherly enthusiasm. "It was interesting how suddenly—no wait. It was Sue Obermann. She was the one that began talking about time passing, and facelifts, how this year she was ready for another one. She'd had two already. Her very polite husband didn't say a thing."

"She just said that out loud? Must have been drunk. Most women would never admit that."

Claire's smile was mischievous. Her heart was beating brightly, probably from all the coffee.

"Hiram is like that," Jay went on. "Keeps everything inside. I just get so annoyed I could bust."

"Hiram did seem the quiet type." She paused long enough for Jay to think she was being spontaneous. Probing for personal details came easily to her, having had much practice at her job. Others' lives, she realized as they spoke, actually helped to distract her from her own concerns. "So, like what does he keep inside?"

"Like everything, what he's thinking and stuff." Jay paused, as if considering whether to share more. "I got him good and drunk the other night, and boy did he go on, spilling the beans." His laugh had an oddly high ring to it.

Before the dinner party, Sid Obermann had called and explained that he was Hiram's AA sponsor, and that Hiram had recently fallen off the wagon and how it would be a really positive thing for Hiram to hang out with him that night. Claire was happy to have him, although it took a little convincing to get Al to like the idea. The promise of a chocolate torte did it. Now she realized it was probably Jay that Hiram had been drinking with.

"Can anyone get someone drunk if they don't want?" Claire asked. After a certain age, she firmly believed, people had to be responsible for their actions.

"Yeah, well. I think so, yeah."

"What? How? You tie him up and force beer down his throat?"

Jay's eyebrow arched. "Not quite," he said.

A welling up of some emotion drew Claire into silence. Julius again, seeming to be hovering nearby. Her letters were never answered, not even the one in which she sent him that silver ring of hers he always liked. She put it in a plain envelope and dropped it in the mail. She never told Al, fearing if she had, he would just point out what a clingy mother she was. Maybe so, but Al didn't understand how the ring represented spiritual kinship, like one of those pacts made in the German operas he loved so much. From Julius's Christmas cards and minimal emails, she knew he had moved to New York, a one-hour flight away. Just last week, on impulse, she had actually flown up to the hilly university town.

"Have you ever been to New York? I have family upstate. My son. Not that we've seen him for a while. " But this was not something she wanted to go into.

"Haven't been to the Big Apple yet," Jay said, "but I plan on going." Jay scraped his chair away from the table. "I'll be right back."

Julius's farmhouse had appeared lopsided, tucked under a giant oak. As she stepped out of the airport rental car, the light and the crisp air had seemed to veil the scene in expectancy. The wood steps creaked as she went up to knock on the screened front door. No one answered. A rusted maroon Jeep was parked over by the side of the driveway, near some brush. She knew he was a high school teacher, like his father. He had told her little else. She waited for him until it was dark, realizing how Al was right, that she had been foolish to follow her impulse to try to see her son face to face without even a call or email to alert him. But she couldn't risk it, he might have told her not to come. He never showed. It could be he was not even living there anymore. She set the cellophane-wrapped bouquet on the threshold for him, just in case.

Jay, who had gone to get another drink, returned and slid into his chair—a fancy concoction this time, topped with a white tower of rich froth and drizzled chocolate. A candy cane–swirled straw stabbed the bulging side of the whipped cream.

"So tell me more about what Hiram said." He turned his cup to catch the drips of cream sliding down the sides with a napkin.

"We began talking about what would happen to us after we died," she picked up again. "Cremated, buried, ashes in the urn. Hiram wanted to be both cremated and then buried. He was real clear about that."

"He was?" said Jay, eyes widening.

"Yes. Cremated then buried, so people could visit him, he said. That was a thoughtful plan."

"What do you mean thoughtful?"

"Well, he had considered his death in his mind and thought it through, what it might be like. To me, his doing that showed he believed people loved him and would continue to love him after he died." Claire thought then how she wanted to help Jay a little. It seemed that she understood Hiram better than he did. "Are you worried Hiram might be, well, that he might hurt himself?"

"Maybe. I was a little rough on him the other night."

"It's hard caring for someone that much," Claire said cautiously.

"You know, I really like that hybrid car of yours. I'm saving up for one of those," Jay said. He pulled out the straw and tossed back the last of his drink.

Claire noted the abrupt change of subject, but there seemed to be no point in mentioning it.

"Look Jay, you can rest assured Hiram did not say anything at the party that indicated he was going to harm himself. Just the opposite, really... Maybe he's at a friend's house."

Jay lowered his head as if the possibility saddened him. She considered giving his arm a squeeze, but she felt wary of doing so. He was not her son, after all, who had often depended on her affection, sometimes to the point of almost depleting her.

"That Hiram, you know, he's really something," Jay said. "I like him a lot." It sounded like a confession.

"Well, that's what I was wondering," Claire said, hoping her tone made clear she understood he was talking about a romantic relationship.

And Julius? Might he too be involved with a man? The thought had never occurred to her before, not in any serious way. Maybe that was why he had taken off as soon as he could. He would not want his father to sink his teeth into that one.

Jay leaned down to pick up the napkin he'd dropped, and her eye caught a glimpse of the knife on his belt. It looked more for show than anything, but it might be sharp as any other. She had seen many times at the hospital how, for some patients, kindness could be received with suspicion, even at times, aggression. A thought she suddenly felt the need to dispel.

"Are you afraid of something? Is that why you carry a weapon on you?"

"Afraid?" He frowned, then his hand went to his waist. "You mean this?" He pushed his jacket back and slipped the knife from its scabbard on his belt and set it carefully on the table. "Hiram gave this to me. He got it in Spain."

The knife was maybe six inches long, the handle decorated with glass rubies and emeralds. More a tourist souvenir than something intended to actually cut. Jay picked it up and held it out towards her with both hands like a gift.

Claire pressed her back against the chair.

"It won't bite," Jay said with a chuckle.

"It's colorful. Very nice," Claire said, feeling a wave of queasiness. Did he intuit she had something more to say? But she was right, she felt sure now, to have held off telling this quirky young man about Hiram spending a few days with the Obermanns at their mountain cabin. Who knew what that might lead to? It was not her place to play Cupid here, or marriage counselor for that matter. "Well, I guess it's time," she said, with an end-of-conversation smile. "Hope you get your man."

She hadn't meant to sound flippant.

Jay carefully sheathed his knife. He glanced at her for a moment, like a stilled squirrel.

"Ditto," he said.

And he was gone.

Jill Adams

Vows

The narrow road along the Coos River dead ended about twenty miles inland. On either side of the Coos the steep, heavily wooded forest rose up, up, and up, in a bid to kick through the clouds and hold court in the blue while mammoth sword ferns gave anchor to the rich, mossy earth below. Where the route ceased, logging trucks shot on up along a coarse gravel lane to the camp at the peak. They formed the only traffic to speak of and there wasn't much of that.

I had been hired to teach in the local high school, had just had my first day orientation and been shown various apartments for rent in the small town on the northern Pacific coast, but that didn't appeal. I'd been driving around for a week looking for a place in the mountains when I finally found a small abandoned cabin sitting near the end of the river road, far from everything and everybody. It sat in a flat space about fifty feet up from the river and offered a stunning view. The only drawback was a dilapidated trailer which sat below it flush with the blacktop. I knocked on the door, hoping to get some information on the cabin, but, although it looked lived in, no one was home. It took a day in town to track down the owner, a tall rack of old bones with jutting cheekbones who didn't want to rent as he'd had bad luck with a bunch of "hippies" who inhabited it the year before.

"...was raising all sorts of hell," he rasped. "Went and planted a bunch of mary-juana up the mountainside there, and done wrecked the plaster wall with all them shelfs they put up then tore out when they had to skedaddle. Thought I'd never see the backsides of that lot."

"I'm a schoolteacher, Mr. Hoos. I'd never cause a problem—"

"More trouble than it's worth, rentin' that place. Couple before that, went and made off with the Frigidaire, top-freeze. Owed two months."

"I'm a schoolteacher, Mr. Hoos. I just want some peace and quiet. I'd never steal an appliance, I swear, or anything. I could pay you three months up front, whatever you think's fair."

"The wife and I, we're Christian folk. Believe in the Lord God Jesus Christ. Do you carry Jesus Christ in your heart, girl?"

"I do, sir."

"No men up there, that's a rule. No partyin' neither, even if they's all schoolteachers."

"No men, no parties. I just want the quiet. What about that trailer down by the road, who lives there?"

"Otis lives there. Been there for donkey's. Minds his own business."

The next day I moved in. I sat on the front porch in a weathered wooden chair as the sun set, taking in the Coos River (along with the dull silver trailer sitting between us) and smelled the sweet, sharp tang of the conifers which the evening mist intensified. I cracked open a bottle of Jack and fired up a doobie. I was exactly where I wanted to be.

ALTHOUGH THE TOWN was small, the county had recently consolidated its three high schools, transforming the town school and grounds into a kind of sprawling deconstructionist jumble. The main building now sprouted ugly wings on the sides and back, and because that still didn't accommodate the large number of students, there were some freestanding units here and there, including a few huts in the woods behind, each divided by a wall in the middle, allowing two classrooms per hut.

I was assigned to the hut furthest in the woods which I shared with Jim Wheatley, a tenured teacher in his mid-forties who'd been there for fifteen years. I had just turned thirty, fresh from my student teaching in a rough, inner-city school, which I thought had prepared me for anything. But day one threw up a problem I'd never encountered: my hut was the designated site for stoners who openly sucked on their weed before heading off to class. Jim, I noticed, walked right through the smoke haze into his side of the hut so I did the same.

The students were a mass of white, down-home country kids under assault by the usual blast of frenzied hormones. The boys went deer hunting with their daddies or worked the fishing trawlers out of the port. The girls were keen on fashion and gossip and boys. No budding scholars that I could see. A few of the girls had their sights on university, but the sense of community was so strong it was hard to envision them leaving for long.

JIM AND I taught English, a compulsory course that was hardly the most popular. We used grammar workbooks back then and it felt like an accomplishment when they comprehended the difference between "their," "there," and "they're." Though how that would help them in their future professions of fishing, logging, working at the mill, or being a housewife, I didn't know. Oh, some would veer off, get an office job or sell insurance, work in retail sales, or maybe join the military, but that was pretty much the extent of it.

I took lunch to school and would often sit in Jim's classroom during the break. Jim was probably the most laid-back teacher I'd ever met. Nothing rattled the guy. He spotted something in me from the beginning and felt confident enough in two weeks to lock the door and ask if I'd mind "bearing witness" to his lunch-time activity. I knew Jim well enough by then to know it would be something raw, but I was curious. He placed the wastebasket in the middle of the floor then backed up a ways.

"Are you ready?" he asked.

"Sure," I said.

He unzipped his pants then and proceeded to masturbate, shortly after shooting his load into the wastebasket. He said he'd been moving the wastebasket a little further away each day, seeing how far he could manage. He said just my being there helped with a good two inches. He wanted me to show my tits for some further acceleration, but I refused. I went about eating my tuna sandwich and he went about his business. It became our routine.

And Jim and I, we became good friends. He never stopped trying to seduce me, but I never let him—I don't think. Years later, when I was back living in the city, Jim would come and visit sometimes when there was a teaching convention or weekend workshop. We'd close the bars and occasionally Jim would sleep over at my place if it was too late to comfortably make his way back to the Marriott out by the airport. Once, I think he may have slipped it in when I wasn't paying attention, never been too sure. Back in that town, though, I didn't want to become the single city girl who fucked Mrs. Wheatley's husband. Or anyone's husband for that matter. Which, much to my amusement, is how I earned the name Ice Queen.

THERE WASN'T MUCH to do in that area besides hit the bars, which I sometimes did on Friday evenings with some of the other faculty members. A truck stop called Gussie's had a restaurant and lounge with a big dark dance floor with flashing lights where we usually headed. A DJ spun dance tunes that got everybody up and going. During the week, I went there once or twice for their dinner special, then finished the evening with a bourbon in the lounge. There weren't many young single ladies at the bar, and I occasionally got asked to accompany some guy to his car or the motel across the street. As the conversation continued, after I'd declined, it came out more than once that I had someone's son or daughter as a student. "Good lord, I had no idea, I'm so sorry, ma'am." Only one man—a Sam Shepard lookalike that in the anonymity of the city would have tempted me—released a big belly laugh and then asked earnestly about his son's progress. I never did have to pay for a drink.

ONE DAY I pulled into the gravel driveway to my cabin, followed by a dinged-up, rusty low rider, which appeared about a mile long. I'd seen it, parked there by the trailer, another ugly blot on the landscape, but I'd never met Otis. I trotted down to the trailer to introduce myself and caught him in the doorway about to enter. He spun around and faced me with the look of a deer caught in the headlights. I'd expected an older man, but Otis looked around my age if not younger, medium height and lean, with the kind of transparent blue eyes that hardly register color and thick honey-blond hair which hung down nearly covering one eye. I was so surprised that he wasn't the old, grizzled hermit I'd imagined that it took a second to take in a body odor that nearly knocked me off my feet, something primal, unlike anything I'd ever encountered, the only vaguely discernible whiff in the mix being something akin to the sickly sweet gaminess of horse meat left in the stew pot for a week.

"I'm your neighbor, Abbie," I said, stifling a gag. "You're Otis, Mr. Hoos said?"

"Otis," he said, without moving.

"Nice to meet you, Otis," I said.

He stood there, just looking at me, shifting his weight from one foot to the other, and flexing his hands. There was something off about the guy, which came clear shortly enough: he was retarded, a word we still used back then in common parlance, though the city schools were beginning to look for more suitable expressions. He was awkward and nervous, but time would break down that barrier. Otis would do odd jobs for me—stacking firewood, cutting back the blackberry bushes which threatened to overtake the front of the cabin. He became my buddy, and although abstract concepts eluded him, he offered lots of sound advice on living in the wild.

"What you need here's a goat," he said one day. "You wanna goat?"

"I don't have time to take care of a goat," I said.

"You don't do nothin'. Stake him and leave him, clear those bushes nothin' flat."

A WEEK LATER I rode with Otis to the home of his mother and a pack of kids who lived in a shack on a one-way road off the logging road, where I had not known anyone lived, to purchase a goat. Mom had long, stringy blonde hair, and carried some weight on her. She had huge, low-hanging breasts which nearly touched her waist and spilled over her torso. I could clearly see her nipples and pancake-size areolae through the thin flowered sundress that hung unevenly to the top of curiously fat knees. Her lower legs were big and veiny, her bare feet filthy. She looked mean, and for just a second I got a bad feeling, a real bad feeling, that I had been lured into a backwoods den of wickedness, into one of those situations where one realizes just a hair too late that escape has ceased to be an option, where in the flash of a sun ray through a spruce you go from being yourself to Victim. How hard one must wish for time to back up, just that hair. My adrenaline was kicking in good, but I pushed the thought aside, opting to remain vigilant and see it through.

"She wants a goat," Otis said, addressing her without name.

The woman, who had two dirty-faced little girls hanging on either side of her, wouldn't let up with her cold stare. She finally shooed the kids away and turned back towards the shack, walking past a gutted car on cinderblocks where a young boy was playing in droopy gray skivvies, past an old armchair sitting beside it with dirty stuffing sprouting out one arm, and disappeared behind the lean-to. I stood in the drive with Otis and waited. He didn't care to go inside or follow his mother, just wait. After what seemed a long time, she reappeared, leading a goat on a rope.

"Eighty dollars," she said.

"I don't have eighty," I said. "Otis led me to think sixty."

"Eighty," she said, not about to budge. Otis remained silent.

I looked in my bag. "I have three twenties and a ten, that's it. Can we say seventy?"

"You heard me the first time, woman," she said. "Eighty."

"Well, I don't *have* eighty, so...guess we'll be going. I'll think about it," I added, though I had no intention of ever returning.

Otis and I got into his car and headed home without speaking much. I thanked him for driving me up there and headed on up to the cabin. That was that. Or so I thought. The next morning I awoke to find a goat staked outside nibbling away at the bushes. Otis never said a word to me about it. And I never asked.

I WAS ALL eager to do my best as a teacher. I told the class the first day that we should decorate the room. I told them to bring a magazine photo they liked and we'd line the perimeter of the upper walls. "Anything?" they said. "Anything," I said. "Promise?" they said. "As long as we don't get any nudie stuff. Promise."

How some of the guys got a hold of *High Times*, I don't know, but the next day, dutifully fulfilling my pledge to the students, I watched them tack up centerfolds of giant marijuana plants. At least I'm in a hut, I figured, not in the main building. My student teaching observation reports back in the city had gotten some of the highest marks in our class. But I didn't rate excellent across the board. Under "Judgment," where everyone else did fine, I got a lower mark on the scale. I knew why I got that, too. I'd asked a class of Title One remedial reading students—mostly strapping black guys full of attitude who came to class for the fun of testing my limits (and selling dope) as well as a few girls who liked to paint their nails in class and pop gum—to use their new Merriam-Websters and find a word in the dictionary they didn't know. The idea was to add one new word to the list every day. "Any word, Ms. Woodruff?" "Any word in the dictionary," I said.

"'Fuck'," said one—Theo, I think his name was. (Yep, he'd found it; he was showing me.) "OK," I said, and proceeded to write it on the board. "I would have thought you already knew that word, Theo, can't believe you missed out." (Mild laughter) But do you know the origin of that word?" I asked.

"Right here," he said, grabbing his crotch. (Lots of laughter)

"Very funny, Theo, but how about you learn something today," I said, and proceeded to give them the apocryphal version about its being derived from an old English law, the one used to arrest prostitutes: For Unlawful Carnal Knowledge. Got their attention, too, for a couple of minutes. And they learned "carnal," which I heard used all semester, if not exactly correctly. We got back on track for a few days, then came "gonad." I added it to our list on the board and asked the student to read the meaning out loud from the dictionary, which he struggled to do, necessitating the addition of the word "gamete." A few days later comes "sphincter" and I write it, ask for the definition to be read aloud. Thing was, I don't think those guys knew "gonad" or "sphincter"—"gamete" for sure was a new one; they were looking like crazy in the dictionary to find something "off" and good for a laugh, and they did. I didn't make a big deal of it, which is what they wanted. I knew it had to run its course before long so rolled with it, and they were learning new words, poring all over the dictionary. I thought I had it under control, but then during breaks came kids wanting to see the "sex" lexicon on the board which gave rise to all kinds of gibes. When my observation came up it didn't go unnoticed either, though my tutor didn't seem to mind, just asked what the deal was. It was one of those alternative public schools for difficult students, committed to innovative approaches to learning, the kind that disappeared with time, but I'd taken the free rein and run with it in all kinds of ways. So, "Judgment," right, I didn't get a perfect score. I'd learned though, yeah?

NO. I NOW sat surrounded by marijuana photos in a conservative, small-town district, dreading a parental visit, but determined, stubbornly, to honor my vow to the students. Jim said he thought they were beautiful and wished his plants looked so good. He stepped in sometimes just to marvel. Then one day comes a parent after seventh period. She congratulated me for spotting her son's dyslexia. She knew he was dyslexic though the school had never acknowledged it. But then she asked something of me I couldn't do: change his grade. I explained that though I wasn't comfortable with that, I could always attach a report of his dyslexia as I'd just done. I asked if she was getting help for him. "Only from you," she said. "But I don't know how to treat it," I said. "You're all we got," she said.

She was taking in the magazine centerfolds then. "What's with the marijuana plants?" she asked. I explained, told her I thought it best just to leave them. "That's what you get for teaching *Go Ask Alice*," she said. "I hardly think so," I said, trying not to sound too defensive. "We decorated the room the first week."

"I'm just ribbing you," she said. "I got no problem with pot." Luck of the fucking draw! This woman, I soon learned, was a card-carrying communist, who single-handedly protested against the nativity scene in the school entrance at Christmas, and various other religious incursions into the public school system, years before anyone else took note. She was the town outcast and the only parent to ever visit my classroom. I knew her husband was Sam Shepard as soon as she mentioned her son's name, and remembered his saying she could be a "strident cow" but was the smartest woman he'd ever known and gave fellatio like a prize whore, a thought I tried not to envision, but without much success.

THE YEAR DREW on. We were nearing the second semester before I knew it. The days got pinched off, the temperature pushed down, and the heavy rains took hold. Some Fridays, I didn't feel like driving back to town to join the crew at Gussie's. I stayed out at the cabin with a bottle of Jack and Otis often came up to share a doobie. He was growing, too, of course. And selling pills, mainly big fat black beauties. I purchased one now and then, two dollars a pop, when I had a load of papers to correct. This one particular nasty night, with the wind whipping the rain around, and the lights flickering on and off, threatening to go out altogether, I sat on the floor with Otis, who was separating sticks and stems from a pile of marijuana leaves, rather expertly, I thought. I picked a bit here and there, but he was doing the job in earnest. "So is that goat OK in this weather?" I asked. "Goat's fine," he said, "but we can bring him in if you want." "No, no, that's OK," I said, and took another swig of Jack. Otis only drank soft drinks so I was getting tanked on my own. It had been a hard week, but I felt good that I'd gotten through it and maintained some kind of order. I kept watching him work with the weed. I kept drinking. Sandalwood incense filled the air, about six sticks burning at once. I didn't need to be tanked to see that Otis was good-looking, an outright stunner in the dim, shimmering light. First thing I'd noticed about him. Retarded, yeah; B.O. to gag a sow. But, damn. That profile. Those divinely muscled arms!

There is no defense, of course. I could say it had been a long time since I had had sex, and that I had as healthy a sexual appetite as the next girl. That my little cabin seemed outside the boundary of life in town and therefore not subject to the same rules. That I was drunk. Otis could easily have seduced me. But it wasn't Otis who did the seducing.

"You want to go in the bedroom?" I asked, touching his thigh. But he only continued to fool with his sticks and stems. "You want to come to bed with me, Otis?" I tried again as a booming crack of thunder rattled the windows, further emboldening me. Otis relinquished his activity but seemed confused. I moved my hand further up his thigh and onto his crotch. Not much going on there either. "Do you like sex, Otis?" I asked, while gently massaging. It wasn't like retards didn't have sexual feelings, surely. I mean... I took his hand and pulled him up and into the bedroom, into the bed. I undid his jeans zip, and he uncertainly picked up on it from there. The bare body was so potent with smell, I thought I'd retch, but I persevered and guided him along.

It was a dismal business from beginning to end. Otis never got fully hard and remained hesitant, not the least turned on. I was so full of drink, I dropped off to sleep almost immediately from the sheer effort of it all. "Passed out," I think, is the more appropriate expression. I have no idea when he left, but he was gone in the morning. A morning which took a long while to fully awake to. A morning starting off with a feeling of unease, a growing unease, as I fought to trace the source of the feeling through a roaring hangover. This is going to be bad, I thought, I know it. And then with a jolt I remembered. Mr. Hoos, I said to myself, you'd never have seen that one coming. And then I threw up.

AT LEAST MY integrity remained intact in town. I spent my after-school hours reading up on dyslexia in the local library though it was hard to find much in the way of classroom treatment. A month passed and I had recovered somewhat from the first crushing wave of humiliation from *that night*. Otis and I continued as good neighbors (could he have mercifully forgotten the entire business with his less-than-normal brain power?), but he didn't hang out at the cabin so often, mainly because I was gone so much. I concluded he was one of those asexual types and felt wretched that I'd put him through such an ordeal in addition to feeling grimly sick over the whole thing. I never regretted befriending him though, pulling him out into the world a bit, away from that trailer where he holed up.

I'd had a difficult day at school with the seventh period boys acting out. I had let myself get into a power struggle with the ringleader and just as I was gaining control, I reached to scratch an itch on my forehead which proved my undoing. "Hey, Ms. Woodruff," he said, with evident pleasure, "you got blood running down your face," which set off peals of laughter. "Shouldn't pick your zits!" Then the bell rang and so ended my day. I only wanted to get to my cabin, so picked up a cold, sixteen-ounce Mickey's malt and cruised on up the river. But as I pulled into the driveway, I saw that something was wrong. The front window of the cabin was completely smashed. Otis wasn't home, so I ventured on up alone. Seemed quiet enough, so I unlocked the front door and entered. I couldn't imagine who would do such a thing—students? Not likely. I decided to smoke some weed and think what to do. I kept the stash in a mason jar behind some other mason jars, but when I reached for it, I saw that the jars were in disarray, and the weed was gone. I scrambled further back to where I kept my cash, about a hundred dollars, in another mason jar. Also gone. So it had been a robbery! I called the local police and two officers came out to the house to take my report. I only mentioned the cash, of course, but upped the amount to a hundred and fifty to cover the smoke. One suggested I get a dog. He also gave me a number to call to have my window repaired.

FOR TWO DAYS I racked my brain trying to think who could have known about my stash. No one. And then without thinking about it, sitting at the table grading papers—*bam!* It had been quite some time, but the last time I bought a lid from Otis, he was there when I put it in the jar. He knew about that then, and may have snooped around more at some point when I was in the john, say. Or just gotten lucky. But I knew with certainty: it was Otis.

When he pulled in later, I marched down to the trailer and confronted him. He denied it, but I wasn't about to let up. I assured him he wasn't going to get in trouble, that it would remain between us, but I knew that he'd done it and I needed him to come clean. Weren't we friends? And we'd still be friends, I said, but I needed to know it was him, not some "roving gang who I had to fear," 'cause then I'd probably need to move away. He stared at his feet and began with the back-and-forth shuffling movement while opening and closing his hands. "It's OK, Otis," I said. "I'm not telling anybody, I promise. I promise, OK?" He seemed about to give because I do think we'd established some trust, but for the moment he remained silent.

"It's OK," I repeated. I didn't let up. Finally, I put it like this: "Look, Otis, you know you don't have to be afraid, you know I'm your friend, right? I'm going to ask if you took it, and if you did, just say nothing, OK? And we'll leave it. Though you at least owe me a good joint," I tried to joke. "OK, Otis, do you understand what I said?" He nodded he did. "OK, did you break into my place and take some things?" He stared at his shoes and remained silent. "Thank you, Otis," I said. "See, that wasn't hard." And then I gave him a hug. I should never have put such temptation in his hands. All my fault. I should never have, never have, so much I should never have!

THE FOLLOWING DAY the police called to ask if everything was all right. "Fine," I said. "I know who did it and we've got it straightened out."

"So who did it?" he asked.

"That's something I'd rather not disclose," I said. "The guilty party and I have worked it out."

"Well, Ms. Woodruff, it's not that easy. Being over a hundred dollars that was stolen, that makes it a felony. You're bound by law to say who it was, otherwise you could be held in contempt," he said.

"What are you talking about?" I asked, wishing I could back up just that hair.

"You're bound by law to tell us is what I'm talking about," he said.

"Well, I don't intend to," I said, and hung up.

But that wasn't the end of it. A few days later I received a certified letter stating that I had to appear in court at the county courthouse on the charge of contempt. The amount stolen would be considered a misdemeanor today, but it wasn't then. I contacted a local lawyer—not wanting to involve the teachers' union—who confirmed that they had every right to pursue it. "But I'm not going to say who it was, so that's that," I said. "What can they do?"

"Six months' jail time is what they can do," he said. "What's the big deal about not giving them the name of the thief?"

"I gave my word I wouldn't," I said.

"You'd rather do six months in jail? May I ask if this was a boyfriend perhaps? Someone you know well?"

"No," I said, feeling faint with the word "boyfriend," but I realized that if the police had half the brain of this lawyer, they'd be asking me about Otis, maybe even talking to Otis. And that was a prospect I faced with acute unease.

I THREW MYSELF into helping Ashley, my dyslexic student, after my seventh period class. He was a bright kid, but had never received help in elementary school which made it harder now that he was a teen. He was top of his class in math but he couldn't spell, couldn't read out loud, and had difficulty reading on his own. I began by trying to build up his confidence.

321

I told him about all the famous people with dyslexia, like Albert Einstein and John Lennon. He was receptive, willing to work with me. I would tell him a story orally and he'd tell it back to me. Then we'd read the story in a book, slowly, passage by passage. I'd read a paragraph and he'd read a paragraph. When he stumbled on a word, we'd stop and I'd sound it out phonetically. We called it "wrestling." "We're going to wrestle that word off the page," I'd say. "We're going to nail it." Sometimes I'd take a word and write it on the board and we'd play the game of trying to find words in the word. I vowed to buy some books when I got to the city, but in the meantime we plowed on in the only way I knew how.

IT WAS MADE clear to me before my court appearance that without question I would do six months' jail time if I did not hand them the name of the "felon." I was in disbelief it had come to this. I hadn't wanted to even think about it. But now I sat struggling with how to handle the mess. It wasn't even that I was so afraid of jail, I wasn't. In fact, holing up with a bunch of books for six months, no classroom to face, didn't sound half bad, but the idea of always having to explain the sentence to a lifetime of future employers, not to mention the current administration and local friends, pushed me to come up with a plan. One thing I knew I couldn't do, as much as it galled me, was hand over Otis. I'd promised I wouldn't tell the police, and I was not about to rat him out. Besides, there was a backstory to Otis, a backstory that could spring to the fore if I wasn't careful. A plan was vaguely forming. I asked the lawyer what would happen if the culprit confessed, could the charge then be dropped? He thought I could maybe swing that with the judge, who honestly did not want to send a high school teacher to jail, but was just as backed into a corner as I was.

WHEN I APPROACHED Otis that evening, it was with such a strength of will and determination to accomplish my mission that I could not fail. I got Otis to the cabin on a pretext, offered him a Coke, and then started in: "Otis, I'm in a fix, and you're the only one who can help me." I explained what I needed him to do, I explained that if he didn't, I would go to jail, and he didn't want me to go to jail, right? I explained over and over that before he said anything to the judge, I would get the guarantee that nothing would happen, that all charges would be dropped. It was a hard point to press with a retarded person because it was a fairly bizarre situation to begin with. I just kept repeating it over and over, first with one set of words, then another. Darkness fell and I kept on with it.

"TELL ME, PLEASE, Otis, you'll come to the court with me next Friday. Nothing will happen, I promise. We'll go get ice cream afterwards," which I knew he loved. Over and over, over and over. Finally, he said OK, broken by promises and assurances, by not wanting me to go to jail, by the lure of ice cream. I don't know if he ever understood that I didn't need to go this route, that I could simply have given him up and washed my hands of it, but he understood enough. I think that besides that family of his, I was about the only friend Otis had.

TWO DAYS TO go. I told Jim about the contempt of court charge but didn't tell him the culprit either. "Must have been your neighbor, Otis," he said, quick as ever. "That gang of inbreds are bad to the bone, don't even try to protect him."

"God, no, it's not Otis," I said.

"Had his sister freshman year," he said, "which is the furthest any of them ever got. Had a rack on her, Jesus. You'd squint a little and she looked just like a young Brigitte Bardot. Dumber than owl shit, but that rack, Jesus. So was it Otis?"

"No way," I said, "forget about Otis."

"I got his girlfriend second period," he said, "pretty little thing."

"What are you talking about, man? Otis doesn't have a girlfriend."

"Does now," he said. "Saw them sitting at the Dairy Queen going down on a large chocolate dip, holding hands, ogling each other. Now there's another nice rack."

This news made me sick on so many levels I couldn't bear thinking about it.

"By the way, I see your seniors are coming along with *Beowulf*," he said, pointing to some graffiti on the side of the hut:

> know what's cool
> to get thru sckool?
> a bag of weed
> and a slug of mead!

"Pfft. They're usually better with the graffiti."

"Hey, perfect word to rhyme with 'weed.' Better than 'rotgut.' And they got the apostrophe right."

I could choose the reading for the freshman and sophomore levels, but junior year *The Hobbit* was required, which they just managed, and then the quantum leap to *Beowulf*. The only way was to go bit by bit, with me telling the story orally with all the theatrical flourish I could manage, then taking a look at the verse. It was slow going. In the end, all they got out of it was a word that rhymed with weed and a misinformed idea about another.

"Hey, thane!" I heard one of the bullies shout at Ashley one day. "Don't forget you have to put the equipment up in the gym." I cornered him in the hall in the main building where I happened to be. "Come here," I said. "I don't ever want to hear you bossing Ashley around like that, OK? It's not his job to pick up after you guys. And for the record, 'thane' is a title of respect, not 'servant' or 'slave.' A king respected his thanes and they respected their king."

"And I respect Ashley, Ms. Woodruff! I do!"

"You bully him all the time and it's going to stop," I said. "And get it straight about 'thane,' man. A king would never talk that way."

"Yeah, right, he'd say, go yonder, fight some nasty dragon and get half your men ate."

"Just give it a rest, OK?" But they didn't. "Thane" continued to reverberate round the halls and through the wooded paths to the huts, every bully's favorite mode of address to the bullied.

FRIDAY FINALLY ARRIVED. Otis was not easy to get into the car, but my force of will was cranked to maximum capacity. It was a forty-minute drive inland to the county seat, a hick town that didn't interact much with the coastal area, thank god. I used the time to go over everything again. But when I cut the engine in the parking lot out front, Otis halted and I had to coax him all the way inside. Through a Herculean effort on my part, at last we were sitting in the hall under an idle ceiling fan in an old clapboard building that looked more like a large family home despite the plaques. It was a closed hearing. The judge's secretary called me into his office and I asked Otis to come along. His body odor intensified in the grip of fear, which I hoped might speed things along. We sat in front of the judge's big mahogany desk as he slowly shuffled through some papers. Didn't help ease the tension that he looked like John Wayne Gacy without hair.

"What's the problem here?" the judge finally snapped. "You refuse to divulge the name of the person who committed a felony on your premises?"

"Very simply, sir," I began, "I promised the person I would not mention his name. But, just for the record, I think we can clear this up right now. Would you agree to drop everything if you have a name?"

The judge didn't answer; he addressed Otis instead: "Did you break and enter into the home of Ms. Woodruff here, young man, and steal one hundred and fifty dollars?" he asked. Otis looked like he was ready to bolt.

"Judge," I said, "can you please assure us—the person sitting here—that no charges will be brought against...the guilty party?" There, I had all but said it.

The judge raised a handkerchief to his nose. "I find this mighty strange, ma'am," he said. "Is this young man someone special to you, an intimate relation? Good-lookin' fella."

"Good Lord, sir, no, nothing like that." *Couldn't he see Otis was retarded? With B.O. from hell?* How the devil could he even think... How the devil did this keep getting so derailed?! On a rail that particularly flipped me out and had nothing to do with a simple moral stand, which even I was beginning to lose the thread to, but still... I would not be bullied into handing over a name. It was a matter of principle, some principle somewhere, and I clung to it for dear life even though it looked like it could land me in the clink.

"Will you step outside for a moment, Ms. Woodruff?" the judge said.

"*Me?*" I asked.

With that unexpected injunction, I became as nervous as Otis.

S I T T I N G   O N   M Y own now under the ceiling fan in the hall, me the one sweating, I found myself imagining the entire ordeal as a mishmash of phonemes collapsing in on each other. It was necessary to concentrate, to separate, to slow down and look at the page from a different angle. What exactly was going on here that threatened to cut off my air supply? It was not unlike what happened to Ashley when confronted with a swirl of words to read out loud. "Breathe," I'd say. "Shut your eyes a minute and breathe, we're in no hurry here." Yes, X looked like Y. Right looked like wrong. Up was down and down was up. All was in a whirl. But if you got the right angle, there was clarity. I was aiming for that angle when the judge called me back in.

"He says he wants to do it 'like before,'" the judge said. "Any idea what the blazing hell that means?"

"Are you referring maybe to getting a confession?" I asked.

"That would be to what I'm referring, yes," he said.

"Well, what I think he wants you to do is not require him to speak," I said. "You ask him directly what you need to ask and if he wants to say 'no' he'll say 'no,' but if you require him to say 'yes,' like 'yes, I did it'—and asking if he 'did it' would work much better than mentioning the word 'robbery' or 'felony,'" I tried to add under my breath—"then he won't speak and that will mean 'yes.'"

The judge looked at me, then looked at Otis, then back at me, as we both awaited our fate.

"Assuming, of course," I hastened to add, "that the silent 'yes' would not incrim—

"Get the fuck out of my office!" he boomed. "I thought I was only dealing with one retard here. Get on out of here this minute! And I don't want to see hide nor hair of either of yous around here again or you'll regret it. Now scram."

WE BEELINED IT to the car and took off. When we hit the highway, Otis said, "I ain't no retard."

"Shut up, Otis," I said.

"We goin' the Dairy Queen?"

"Yes, all right." *Chocolate dip, I suppose.* "I didn't mean to snap, sorry. Can you believe the mouth on that judge though?"

"I want the chocolate dip," was all he said, and seemed well over the slight. Me, on the other hand, I burned hot with indignation all the way home, wondering how my life had ever come to reach this particular point, but vowing to get things off to a clean start now that this little drama was behind me.

JIM HAD MOVED the wastebasket another inch, which he was able to do by restraining from activity for two to three days. In other news, I was beginning to see some improvement in Ashley's reading even if the spelling remained as bad as ever. He definitely seemed to have a higher level of self-esteem. A little crush on me, I think, but I handled that with care.

WE WERE BEGINNING to have some of the first warm days of the new year. On one of these days, a Saturday, I spent some time in town running errands. I pulled into the drive in the late afternoon and saw Otis in front of his trailer with a shiny black BBQ grill, cooking up something creating a lot of smoke. A short, dark-haired girl was standing next to him, the first time I'd ever seen a soul at his place. I recognized her as Missy Puckett, the freshman who Jim had claimed was Otis's girlfriend. How old would that make her, fourteen? fifteen? Jim'd said she was a solid "C" student, not swift but not slow, so I assumed she got hooked by his looks, which, admittedly, were a hook, if you could get past the rest. I felt a tinge of, what? Nothing that made me feel good.

And then as I approached the cabin, I had a sickening flash of déjà vu: the front window was smashed. I had no fear this time. I carried my groceries in and walked straight to the mason jars. I had continued to use them to keep a little weed and spare cash because logic dictated that this could never happen again. Hadn't last month's painful ordeal with the court assured that? Clearly, it had not.

I marched down to Otis's front yard. A spanking new BBQ set, I noticed. Two T-bones cooking away. He was alone at the grill, poking at the steaks with a long, fancy grill fork. I walked up directly to him and in a low, controlled voice so Missy couldn't hear from the trailer, I hissed right in his ear: "You motherfucker." And then I kicked the grill over. Otis just stood there, but Missy came running out. "Get away from here, you crazy lady! Otis is *my* boyfriend now, not yours!"

"Shut up, you, this is between Otis and me."

"I know you fucked him! Everybody knows!"

"You don't know what you're talking about, so butt out," I said.

"You're a sick old lady. And I'm going to tell Mr. Hoos and the principal!" she yelled.

Otis had righted the grill and was brushing off the steaks with his fingers. I walked close up to him again. "Listen up, motherfucker. You're going to jail this time, you hear? And you're going to be there a long time. I suspect the police'll be here in under an hour, so prepare yourself." And then I walked slowly back up to the cabin, trying to appear calm and collected, but trembling like the old-timer alcoholics out at Gussie's.

OF COURSE I didn't call the police. How could I after refusing to turn over his name for two months the last time? After my Big Stand. After the circus that I'd put everyone through. After that judge's pronouncement. I had to suck up the loss. But did he know that? I did worry about Missy's mouth, but figured if it came to her word against mine, mine would trump. I was hoping the two of them, in fear of the police, would beat it out of there, at least for today. But no. They carried right on. The mouth-watering smell of grilled meat wafted up to the cabin. An hour passed. Then another. I don't think my threat even registered, but if it did, they must have felt home free by now. I called the local vet, who'd come on to me at Gussie's one evening, and said I wanted a dog, a good watchdog. A week later I had a beautiful young German Shepherd female who had a bark that could cut the waters of the river and appeared to be ready to go on the attack if necessary. I didn't know much at all about Otis, but I had learned that he was afraid of dogs so that was something.

MISSY WENT ON to tell Jim I'd "fucked Otis by force" and should be fired, but he laughed it off as he was telling me. The man who never missed anything couldn't believe the Ice Queen, who could have had his buff body at any time, would blow him off for a retard. I could have 'fessed up right then—and had the pleasure of witnessing the surprise on Jim's face—but vowed not to, ever. It would have brought up the robbery business again (only one of which was on record) and I didn't care to talk about having been duped—twice. And then thrown over for Missy "What a rack!" Puckett, who'd be vindicated for her accusation.

She sent a handwritten note to the principal as well. He called me into the office to ask why I thought she'd do that. "I have no idea, Burt," I said, in an appropriately weary, unconcerned voice. "I think it probably has to do with some problems I had with Otis, who is my neighbor up the river. He's retarded, you know." (Of course, he knew; I was going for emphasis.) And, yes, I was on a first-name basis with the principal as he, too, was a regular at Gussie's. If she told Mr. Hoos, I never heard about it.

I had to suffer watching Otis pick up Missy every day after school in that eyesore of a low rider—"suffer" because the sight of those two made me nauseous and it wasn't just over the lie I was forced to tell. It was something deeper, more complicated; they were like a mirror to my every flaw, my every misjudgment, my every ill-directed desire.

THERE ARE APPROXIMATELY forty-four phonemes in the English language. They are written between slashes, such as /p/, /t/, /k/, /m/, /n/, the five most common consonants. Relatively few languages in the world lack any of these, although it does happen, such as the lack of a /p/ in Arabic. Ashley had been wrestling with the "p" sound in "redemption." We got it out of there and were creating other words with "p." I told him about Arabic lacking the letter. He said he thought that was kind of sad because "p" was one of his favorite letters, along with "m." "But they have sounds we don't," I said. "I wonder if I'd have been dyslexic if I was born in an Arab country," he mused. "That's a good question, Ashley, I don't know." I went on to research it; most probably he would *not*.

Where was my world, I wondered. It sometimes felt I was out of step in this one, without a good grip. One minute so totally sure of myself, capable of anything, taking on ten projects at once, wowing the guys with my hotness, commanding full respect and attention in a difficult classroom of rowdy teens who defeated other, lesser, teachers, power soaring through my veins; the next minute a jumble of doubt and confusion, a phenomenal loser, a joke, a fool, taking hoots and jeers from a class while trying to wrestle a miniature bottle of Seagram's VO from a saucy girl, falling on my ass while leaning too far back in a chair in the middle of telling a story about my cool days on the back of a Harley (ha! ha! ha! ha!), losing control while mopping up a bloody zit.

YEARS LATER, BACK in the city, I went with a group of teachers to see an indie film called *Johnny Suede*. The protagonist, an actor unknown to us at the time, bore a resemblance to Otis, notwithstanding the giant blond pompadour and suede shoes. I felt uncomfortable, especially because—I could hardly believe it—he was slightly mentally challenged and taken up by a schoolteacher. Jim was with us. As all of us were having drinks afterwards, he said, "That guy kind of looked like that tard neighbor of yours back in Coos, don't you think?"

"I don't know, Jim," I said. "Maybe a little."

"Give me that tard any day!" said one of the women.

I blushed so deep I surprised myself, and Jim didn't miss it. He looked at me peculiarly for a minute, but then seemed to shrug it off. By then I figured they all chalked it up to a hot flash. And before long, the subject changed to union dues and we got busy ordering another round as Jim proceeded to tell us of the progress he was making in turning his fish smoker into an orgasmatron. At Jim's insistence, I had once promised—one hand in the air, the other crossing my heart—that I'd try it out if he ever got anywhere with the thing, and, knowing me, that meant that sooner or later I'd probably find myself holed up in a fish smoker somewhere down in Coos. It was just a matter of time.

Roberta Allen

The seminar called What's Next? was thought up by a couple of middle-aged lovebirds who live together happily—three weeks so far. Happiness makes you think you know everything, you can cure everyone, you can make everyone happy. Happiness makes the couple blind to spiders spinning webs in the corners of the spacious studio. A ceramicist's studio. Separate from the large, tasteful newly renovated house. You walk down a stone path. Woods all around. Tall pines. Maples. Oaks. It's fall. Leaves die in bright colors.

The couple smile. Are they gloating from their seats on that plush pink couch? Let's call them Harriet and Henry. Harriet's closest friends—a cousin, several acquaintances, and I, a relative newcomer invited by a painter I date—lean against hardback chairs in a circle. Fifteen of us. Middle-aged husbands and wives, middle-aged singles, most with memories of Primal Scream Therapy, Arica, EST, bunny-like sex, and LSD. Most are now on Judaism and antidepressants, and were drinking and smoking pot at a party a few hours earlier. Some of us don't know why we're here at eight a.m. Sunday morning. We don't know what's wrong with us until Harriet and Henry give the cue to start writing.

It's reading aloud afterward that gets me.

I'm not as happy as Harriet and Henry. But I'm hopeful till my date, who sits next to me, cries, "I don't want Max to die!" He bar mitzvahed the collie four years ago on his property in front of twenty-five guests when Max was thirteen. "But," he says, irritably, tears running down his rough face, "he's such a responsibility! I have to make special trips home just to walk him and feed him!"

Max was eight when the painter got him from a former girlfriend who still asks about the animal. He feels as if he and the ex were married and had a dog. He's never been married—except to Max.

"I want to be in a relationship," he says, still crying. At the party the night before, he pictured a "perfect day." He was alone. Painting in his studio. Free to come and go. Free to do as he pleased. Now sniffling, wet-eyed, he says, "I want to wake up every morning with Elaine in my bed!" Elaine. His latest ex-girlfriend.

I hardly hear the lies and half-truths others tell after his turn, until Ingrid, a long-legged CEO, reads, "Sex doesn't interest me anymore. I have a larger purpose now. I want to help others in the world less fortunate than myself." I glance at her husband, his head down between his knees. I wonder if he'll ever raise it.

Then I slip into the old darkness. It's a tight fit, this darkness. I should have known this painter would bring on the darkness, like John and Kurt and Richard and Peter and David and all the others before him.

It's my turn to read. But my words are not on paper. My words fall out of my mouth. I don't try to catch them. "I'm afraid I'll kill myself like my father." I don't say why. But I feel as if they know. The ones who saw me slow-dance with the painter at the party.

My words bleed all over the room like spilled ink on a blotter. My words swallow all sound. Harriet and Henry smile a smile that is anything but. I could reach out and grab the shock and mold it into sculpture but I do nothing. I've done enough.

Henry says, "Next."

At the break, I tell the painter I thought I mattered to him. I thought we almost had a relationship. "But we're not in love!" he says, opening the door. I watch him walk down the stone path to get more coffee in the large kitchen of the newly renovated house.

Cathy Alter

THE PLUNDERING

That first year, it was the Rolex, which was fake but she didn't know
that when she slipped it into her pocketbook. The next year, there
was forty dollars missing from my brother Larry's wallet that was on
the Heywood Wakefield dresser in the bedroom, which was where he had
also kept the fake Rolex. After that, the add-a-pearl necklace, the sterling
piggy bank on the nightstand, the signed photo of Katy Perry, obtained at
a backstage meet-and-greet at the Springfield Civic Center—all belonging
to my brother's ten-year-old daughter and all gone.

I know all this because last year, it was my turn to miss something. My
husband Joel and I were staying at my parents' house in Pittsfield over the
long Thanksgiving weekend, living out of suitcases until we drove back to
Ohio, and I was constantly misplacing things, wondering in which pocket
I had buried my makeup bag and if I had left my phone in the kitchen or
den. My usual spots for things had become unusual in Massachusetts.

"It's so weird, but I swear I had ten dollars in my wallet and now I can't
seem to find it," I told Larry when we talked the next day.

"Goddammit. Did you leave your purse in our bedroom?" he asked.

It was where all of us left our things when we gathered at Larry and
Annie's house for Thanksgiving dinner, coats piled on the bed, handbags
tossed around like throw pillows.

"Yeah, so?" I answered.

"Linda must have stolen your money."

Linda was Annie's older sister, who always drove in from Pittsburgh
with her husband Joe and their twin tween boys, Sammy and Joe Jr. Ever
since Linda had had her stomach stapled, she was super high strung. Or
just high. The party was never complete until she pulled out her pill bottle
and put something horse-tranquilizer-sized into her palm. "Just look at
how big these things are," she'd announce.

I have no idea what she was on, but it made her edgy and unable to sit
still or keep quiet. Following the train of her conversation was just not worth
it. Over the years, I had learned to just let her talk, mentally checking out
and imagining myself at one of those antique malls along Route 1, walking up
and down the aisles and losing myself in other people's beautiful detritus.

Because her stomach was now the size of a baby's fist, Thanksgiving
was a particularly cruel joke for Linda. For the one spoonful of dessert she

could comfortably swallow, for example, she insisted her sister Annie take down the good china so she could enjoy her smidge of pie in a gold-rimmed Limoges teacup, atop of its gold-rimmed saucer and with a sterling piece of flatware, while the rest of us used disposable plates and plastic forks. Eating like a queen, she said, tricked her brain into thinking she was eating more. Let them eat cake, I guess.

Besides going on about her horse tranquilizers and her baby fist stomach, Linda talked about her kids, who were usually at the opposite end of my brother's house trying to get as far away from her as possible. It was clear they hated her. For what she couldn't eat, Linda instead gorged on attention and was unstoppable in her pursuit. And the more she tried to get it from her children and husband, the farther they fled and the more she disparaged them.

"Joe has no ambition," she announced one year as her husband sat on a couch across the room. Joe, the manager of their local Farmer Jack's grocery store, was constantly reminded by his wife that he'd never make it to regional manager unless he signed up for business classes at Allegheny Community College. "He could go at night but," and here she would do a bad imitation of her husband, "he says he's too tired."

The day after Thanksgiving, back at my parents' place, we'd all joke about how terrible Linda was. How Annie was the good sister, all Pre-Raphaelite blonde curls and dimples, the Glinda to Linda's hard and bitter Wicked Witch. We'd laugh about her fine china requirements and report on whether we had caught her in the kitchen, sneaking a nibble of chocolate peppermint bark (one of us always did). And we'd wonder how anyone could live with someone as unrelenting as her. There was always the rumor that she and Joe were separating, how she was going to move to Virginia to be closer to her parents, but without her steadfast anchor, her little body would just spin out into the atmosphere.

This Thanksgiving, I was ready. Inside my wallet, tucked into my billfold like a pressed flower, was a note. It read, "Not this year, Linda."

Emily Amodeo

WE'RE NOT PAGEANT PEOPLE

Maureen was just about to wash up the dishes from dinner, really she was, when Walter finally called from Afghanistan, after two weeks of radio silence. In the darkening kitchen, where a slice of light illuminated a constellation of teacups on the shelf above the sink, she turned off the faucet, wiped her hands dry on a Christmas-themed towel (it was April), and sat down in front of the dinging computer. The abandoned casserole dish with its scrim of burnt cheese was left to soak. The teacups were from England, and fragile as soap bubbles. They had belonged first to her grandmother and then her mother and were left to Maureen after her mother passed from a stroke a decade before. Each time she and Walter packed up and moved to a new town, Maureen wrapped them in tissue paper, cocooning them in a snow of foam peanuts. Each time one broke, as they sometimes did despite her loving ministrations, she wept and blamed the Army for ruining her life.

"It's me," Maureen said, to an empty screen.

"We have a bad connection today," Walter explained. He could see her but she could not see him.

Maureen nudged the black pinhole of the computer's camera away from the mess in the kitchen sink toward the big picture window that opened onto the backyard, an expansive greensward belted by an ancient, wooden fence, the kind of yard they imagined they would one day have as Maureen lay in the concavity of Walter's chest and biceps. Skin adhered to skin and leather upholstery in the backseat of Walter's Toyota Tercel, while her disappointed father waited up for her at home. Each night she went home to meet her curfew, the peeling away of their bodies became for them a recurring ecstatic death.

This backyard had even come with an elaborately built tree house perched in the sturdy arms of an old pine whose acrid sap disturbed the air. Glass-paned windows shone smooth as water beneath a shingled roof. When Maureen and Walter first saw it, they made up their minds on the spot to buy the house, even though their kids were too old now to be interested in tree houses.

"You look good," he said, voice thick with the fumes of truck convoys and too many nights sleeping with one eye open. It was 2:30 a.m. his time and he sounded tired. Walter always sounded tired during deployments.

"Oh, please." In the mirror that morning her face had gleamed with the unnatural pallor of the undead, as she brushed her teeth and wondered if she had remembered to pay the mortgage on the house that month. She honestly could not recall, but there had not been enough time to check the bill folder in the drawer underneath the phone before she went to work. If it was two weeks' past due, they would have to pay a penalty. Walter was a champion lecturer and she would never hear the end of it.

"How are the kids?"

"Fine." Early on, they'd arrived at an unspoken agreement in which she wouldn't share stressful things that he couldn't do anything but worry about. He needed his wits about him at all times. So she didn't mention that Bethie, their youngest, had recently discovered that her nose was slightly larger than the other girls' at her new elementary school. That consequently Bethie had given up on being a normal child and taken to hiding for hours at a stretch. At dinnertime that very night, it had taken a resentful Maureen half an hour to find her, folded up like a contortionist underneath the bottom shelf of the linen closet with a flashlight reading a book, oblivious to Maureen's shouted entreaties.

She didn't tell him that Tom, the middle child, had gashed his knee open three weeks ago falling off his bike, barely missing crucial tendons and ligaments, resulting in a jagged cut that required eleven stitches to close up. He hadn't cried even as the blood dribbled down his tan, hairless shin and pooled in his sneaker. He'd been proud of the wound. As Maureen bloodied all of the dishtowels against his once-perfect knee, she sighed with guilt and shame. She'd told him not to ride his bike in the wooded ravine at the end of their cul-de-sac, but she had been too scatterbrained or tired or simply incompetent as a mother to enforce that. And instead of paying bills that afternoon as she should have done, she had watched Tom skateboarding with the other neighborhood boys in the street out front from a hidden vantage point inside of the house, fearful that the moment she looked away again he would reopen his knee, or perhaps his helmet would slip momentarily aside and he would crack his skull, damaging his brain permanently, the feckless boy. The boys had jury-rigged a ramp and one by one, they glided solemnly up the steep plywood incline and toppled over onto the winking asphalt in a crumpled heap of baggy pants and too-long hair, while anxious tremors shuddered through Maureen's chest.

Nor did she tell him that Christina, their eldest, had come home well after curfew the previous weekend smelling of cigarettes and booze and had spent the next day crying her eyes out for a reason that she would not share with a hysterical mother. Or that Christina was supposed to be grounded but Maureen, against her better judgment, had permitted her to compete in the high school beauty pageant scheduled for that evening.

"How any daughter of mine could aspire to parade around like a piece of meat at one of those ridiculous things is beyond me," were Maureen's exact words.

"I know you think it's *tawdry, Mother,*" mocking the Midwestern lilt and morals Maureen had never quite dropped, "But it's the last thing I will ever ask you for, as long as I live."

"How are you holding up?" Walter asked, yawning, so that the *how* and *are* sounded like the wind tossing a handful of sand against the concrete huts of the forward operating base. She imagined him rubbing his jaw with its salt and pepper stubble as he tried to keep awake.

Did he really want to know? She mobilized her face into some semblance of connubial cheer, conscious that after eighteen years Walter could read every inflection of her voice and expression in her emotional arsenal with laser-guided accuracy.

She wanted to tell him how angry she was at him for missing everything. That sometimes she even hated him, and when she felt so lonely she lay awake all night biting her knuckles to keep from screaming and waking up the kids, vowed with all her might to divorce him the moment he stepped safely off the plane.

"I'm good," she said, and left it at that.

The words that went unspoken during Walter's absences rippled, but did not break the surface. They sank to the murky bottom, somewhere inside of her, fattening for years, like the engorged, prehistoric-looking catfish they used to catch and fry up at Walter's sister's cabin on the lake. Just after they were married and before Walter enlisted, before Maureen was pregnant with Christina, they used to spend summers there. Under the shade of some oaks and poplars, the cabin was nothing grand: a single-wide trailer propped on a latticework of stilts set a few feet offshore. The narrow cot they shared at night seemed too spacious. They couldn't get close enough, no matter how hard they pressed against each other, chest to chest, stomach to stomach, thigh to thigh.

"What about you?" Maureen asked. "Are you staying safe?"

As she searched the computer's blank window for some trace of him, she wished she could throw the end of a rope to Walter, right through the screen, and over the geographic space that separated them, the way she had when they brought in the pontoon for the evening. Walter would tie it up to the dock, a neat stack of half-hitches, then hold her hand, buoying her as she stepped from the rocking boat across the lapping divide. Inside the cabin, they felt the movement of the waves as though the lake had crept underneath them during the night. She still felt the vicissitudes of those waves flinging her up and down, up and down, sometimes.

"Yep," he said. "I got the package from you and the kids. Thanks."

For reasons of security, the Army wouldn't let Walter discuss the specifics of his workday, but he told Maureen many things that weren't classified. Some of them made her sad: they could no longer give the Afghani children pencils and candy and soccer balls because the kids had begun to throw rocks at the soldiers. Some of them made her laugh even though it wasn't really funny if you thought about it, which she would later, at much length: how Walter's unit had run out of water during their last mission and it had to be airdropped by a C-22. The crates landed on top of a mountain a klik and a half above where they'd broken camp. They had to pack everything up, march up the slope, wearing body armor and carrying hundreds of pounds of gear per person, to get the water, march back down again and remake camp. April was the wet season. By the time they got to the bottom, muddied, tendrils of steam rising off their shoulders, they'd already drunk it all. Water had to be dropped a second time where once again it landed on top of the same promontory.

"Things got a little out of hand there for a minute," Walter said.

"What happened?" she asked.

"Did you ever put up those curtains?" he said, changing the subject.

"Curtains?" Maureen racked her brain. Oh yes, she remembered that the last time she and Walter had spoken, she mentioned in a fit of unrealistic ambition that she was going to sew valances for the living room. The pretty fabric with a blue and rust paisley print she'd bought lay untouched next to the sewing machine in their bedroom.

"No," she said. "Haven't had time yet."

"Why not?"

Maureen ran through possible responses in her mind, each cleverer and more flippant than the last, but under the circumstances, she refused to fight with him.

"I'll do them this weekend." If her husband could endure war then she could spend one sleepless Saturday night sewing curtains. Maybe it comforted him to think of her in their house, sewing, instead of doing all of the other things she could be doing while he was away for a year at a time: going to the movies, playing tennis at the officers' club, snorting crystal meth, having an affair.

A few seconds went by before his next response. It was impossible to know whether the delay was due to the unreliability of their connection or because he was upset with her.

"Send me a picture," she heard him say. "Can't wait to see how they look in the new house."

"I'll get the kids," she said. "We have to leave soon for the pageant."

"That's today?"

Maureen rolled her eyes. "How did this happen to us? We're not pageant people."

He laughed. She had nearly forgotten what a good sound that was. His face would be tipped back, molars exposed.

"Love you," he said.

"Love you, too."

Maureen stood up from the computer, realizing only then that the kitchen had been dark for some time. She flipped on the light and ducked her head into the family room.

"Bethie, Tom—Dad's on."

Bethie sighed and dog-eared the page of the book she was reading before closing it. Her dour expression was incongruous with her heart-shaped nine-year-old face. As he got up from the couch, Tom's gaze lingered on the television, blaring some program about a surfing contest in Hawaii.

Upstairs, Maureen knocked on Christina's bedroom door.

"Come in," she said. Maureen found Christina in front of her vanity mirror, twirling a strand of her long blonde hair around a curling iron. The hair had been lightened with lemon juice behind Maureen's back when she had not allowed Christina to buy box dye at the drugstore.

"Mom, shut the door!"

"Sorry." She closed it behind her. "Come and talk to your dad."

Christina looked as though Maureen had asked her to drown a kitten.

"I have to get ready. I'm going to be late," she drawled in her recently acquired Southern accent. To hear a stranger's voice coming out of her daughter's mouth unsettled her. How readily Christina adapted to each new town: changing accents and hobbies and friends as easily as putting on a new outfit while the rest of them wandered through moves in a bewildered funk. Maureen was lucky to stay in one place long enough to finish unpacking all the boxes, let alone hang a picture or a curtain or make a friend she could really talk to. All these towns, nestled in soft green hills under flawless blue skies, had a vague, impersonal loveliness that couldn't be more different from the snowy city she'd grown up in.

"That's not a request, Christina. You're lucky you're going at all."

Now Christina was crying. She held a tissue under each black-rimmed eye trying to salvage her painstakingly applied makeup. To Maureen, she looked like a little girl about to rob a bank. For the umpteenth time that week, Maureen scrutinized her daughter and wondered if Christina was sexually active, but could not bring herself to say the words out loud. Had she and Walter really been that young, Maureen wondered, as she watched Christina blot her lipstick on a folded square of toilet paper and then study the bud-shaped imprint of her own lips.

"Can't I talk to him next time?"

"We don't know when that will be."

"It's not a big deal, Mom."

DURING THE CAR ride, Christina practiced her introduction.

"Hi, my name is Christina Weeks. I'm a sophomore, and I like cheerleading, soccer, and hanging out with my friends," she said as she videotaped herself on her smartphone and then played it back. "*Hey y'all,*" she corrected her facsimile, "my name is Christina. Hey y'all."

"Your normal voice is just fine," Maureen said, switching on the defogger. It had been one of those endless Southern springs where the sky stayed a damp smudge of gray but never rained.

At the high school, Maureen left Christina backstage with her friends and found seats in the auditorium. On one side of her, Tom had earbuds in and on the other, Bethie had her book open on her lap. She was going through a book a day and it looked as though she was almost done with this one. Maureen sighed, and relaxed into the seat. This was how it felt at the end of every day, as though a plug had been pulled from the root of her spine, and all her remaining energy suddenly leaked out.

"What are you reading, honey?" she asked, draping her arm over the shoulders of her youngest, whose diminutive body hardly took up half of the wooden seat.

"*Scandalous Sins,*" Bethie said, and showed her the cover featuring a woman with an aristocratic profile and low-cut period dress swooning into the arms of a towering, bare-chested ruffian.

It was the romance novel Maureen thought hidden safely underneath the pillow on her bed. Her one guilty pleasure and what hardly sufficed as a sex life during her husband's deployments. At home were bookshelves stocked with Melville, Austen, Twain, Poe. Of course this is what Bethie had chosen to read.

The nosy woman seated next to Bethie raised her eyebrows and smirked at Maureen.

Embarrassed, she took the paperback from her daughter, who protested loudly, and stuffed it into her bag.

The lights dimmed, and an endless stream of heavily made-up teenage girls in sparkling gowns sauntered down a confetti-strewn catwalk with what looked like football pads shoved into the shoulders of their dresses. Halfway through the pageant, Maureen was already yawning. She calculated how long it would take to gather her daughter away from her friends afterward. A half hour at best. Then there were still dishes waiting at home, and bills that could no longer be put off. Fine thing it would be for her husband to come home to a house that had been foreclosed on.

Ten more girls. Five more girls. Finally, Christina wobbled into the spotlight in Maureen's own high heels, a terrified smile drawn onto her face in shiny red lipstick. Maureen clapped and cheered, her lone voice reverberating against ceramic tile and asbestos. Tom put two fingers in his mouth and whistled deafeningly the way his dad had taught him to the previous summer at a Durham Bulls game.

Christina recited her speech, drawing out each vowel with just the right amount of twang. Then someone in the audience booed. Maureen looked around, in shock. The anonymous faces she saw only stared, unmoved, up at the stage. A few whispered to each other. She could only make out scattered words. *Trouble. Easy. Weren't going to let her in the pageant at all. Felt sorry for her.* Maureen didn't know any of these people. She had never been to a single PTA meeting—she'd always intended to go—and the few soccer games she made it to she spent buried in her planner or balancing her checkbook. A second person hissed. The utter lack of clapping finally penetrated Maureen's cluelessness, an excruciating, thudding silence that slammed into the auditorium like a meteor.

Several possible rescue scenarios entered her mind. She was half out of her seat. In one hand, she held Bethie's sleeve, in the other Tom's shirt collar. Her purse strap dangled awkwardly from her neck. She imagined racing onto the stage, shouting irate obscenities at the crowd. Dragging Christina away and whisking her home. Sending her to boarding school in France just as Christina had pleaded after Maureen read her *Madeline* at bedtime when she was in kindergarten.

"Poor girl," a woman who, unlike Maureen, had ample time to blow dry her hair, tsked to her husband, "Someone ought to get her off that stage quick."

Even from where she sat and through all the makeup, Maureen saw the blush springing up in large cartographic blots across Christina's chest and face. For a terrible instant, she stood frozen, the microphone still held to her mouth, then the stone-faced principal was guiding her off the stage. Some other frightened girl mumbled into the microphone to anemic applause, probably thanking her lucky stars that she was not as unfortunate as Maureen's own daughter.

"Excuse me," she said, turning to the helmet-haired woman next to her. "Do you know what's going on?"

"Are you Christina's mother?" Maureen thought she detected a hint of judgment. "I'm so sorry for your loss," the woman said, a perfect picture of sympathy. "I can't imagine what you must be going through."

"My loss?" Maureen blinked, the afterimage of Christina's humiliation burning behind her eyelids.

"I heard that your husband was just killed in Afghanistan. The IED?"

For a millisecond, Maureen actually believed her. It was enough to make her list backward.

Right then, what she should have said was, "You must be mistaken." Maybe because her elementary school–age daughter was reading smut, or because of the accusing, puffy, purple scar on her son's exposed knee, or because overnight her teenaged daughter had become someone she no longer knew, Maureen didn't set the woman straight. Instead, with as much haughtiness as she could muster, she said, "Thank you."

"But Dad isn't—"

Maureen cut Tom off with a shaky wave of her hand. "Take Bethie and go wait by the car," she said. "I'll be there in a minute with your sister."

Tom shuffled his feet, the rubber soles of his sneakers squeaking against the floor, but did as he was told, a first. Her children peeked over their shoulders at her on their way up the darkened aisle toward the exit, their small, trusting faces frowning in confusion.

On the way home from the pageant, Christina cried noiselessly in the passenger seat next to her. Right away, Tom stuffed his earbuds in, head bobbing in an invisible current, and Bethie, bookless, peered through the wavering membrane of her forlorn reflection at neon advertisements for fast food and adult videos glowing like alien architecture out of the black ruffle of treeline. Maureen rehearsed in her head, stern admonishments, pop psychobabble aimed at teens with low self-esteem, but by the time she pulled into the driveway and the garage door rumbled open, she hadn't spoken. Without a word, Christina streaked into the house and up to her room, slamming her bedroom door behind her.

Maureen put Bethie to bed, fully aware that she had hidden a flashlight and the forbidden book pilfered from Maureen's purse under her pillow. Tom was making a lot of racket in his own room, an incessant *pa-doom-pa-doom* from a tennis ball being thrown against the wall and ricocheting off the ceiling, peeved that he had not been allowed to rejoin his friends, who were still goofing off outside, even though it was after ten o'clock.

The crack beneath Christina's bedroom door was dark. Maureen knocked softly and went in without waiting for the response she knew wasn't coming. She could see from the square of light falling onto the bed that Christina had yanked her pillow over her head. Her dress lay in a puddle of fabric on the floor, the sequins glittering dully. Out of habit, Maureen picked it up and put it on a hanger in the closet, the smell of baby powder and hairspray slithering out of the folds. She resisted an urge to clamp it tight to her chest, and instead, sat down on the bed next to her daughter who was pretending to be asleep so hard that her body braced formless and rigid somewhere below the terrain of covers.

"You know," she said, rubbing Christina's back, "we could plan a fake memorial for Dad."

Christina shot up from the tangle of covers and stared at Maureen, horrified, her eyes large and black.

"I'll tell them tomorrow, Mom," Christina said.

"We'll announce it in the paper, have people over to the house and everything. Of course, you'll have to help with the picture slideshow because I can't figure that thing out."

"Stop it. I said I would tell people." Christina slumped down, her head resting on her mother's lap.

Maureen sighed and closed her eyes, charting the slow evening out of Christina's breaths into sleep, for real this time, as she stroked her hair.

When she opened her eyes, the tennis ball had stilled. The front door sucked open and clicked closed as covertly as a thirteen-year-old boy could manage. She just had time before she leaned back and fell asleep to notice, framed in the window, the tinfoil moon hung low from a brief opening in the cloud bank, as if from a length of yarn: remote, cold, beautiful.

Randi Ward

CATTAILS

Beth Adamour received her MFA in creative writing from the University of North Carolina at Greensboro. Her fiction has appeared in *West Branch, Nimrod* (finalist Katherine Ann Porter Prize), *Mid-American Review*, and various other literary magazines.

Jill Adams lives in Barcelona, Spain, where she teaches language and literature. She is the editor and publisher of *Barcelona Review*, founded in 1997.

Jeffrey C. Alfier's latest works are *Anthem for Pacific Avenue: California Poems; Bleak Music*, a photograph and poetry collaboration with Larry D. Thomas; and *Southbound Express to Bay Head: New Jersey Poems*. He is founder and co-editor of Blue Horse Press and *San Pedro River Review*.

Nancy Allen is a criminal defense attorney and yoga teacher/studio owner living in southwest Virginia. She has been published in *Tar River Review, Sow's Ear Review, JMWW, New Millennium Anthology*, and *Piedmont Virginian*.

Roberta Allen is a short story writer, novelist, and memoirist; author of eight books, soon to be nine: a story collection will be out this fall with Pelekinesis Press. Her latest book is the novel *The Dreaming Girl* (Ellipsis). She received the 2015 Honorable Mention for the Gertrude Stein Award. Over three hundred of her stories have been published, recently by *Conjunctions* and *Brooklyn Rail*. She is also a conceptual artist who has exhibited worldwide. www.robertaallen.com.

David Alpaugh's "Double-Title" poems have appeared in *Algebra of Owls* (UK), *Journal of American Poetry, California Quarterly, Exit 13, The HyperTexts, Lighten Up* Online (UK), *Marin Poetry Center Anthology, Mind Magazine, Mudlark, Spillway*, and *X-Peri*.

Cathy Alter's articles and essays have appeared in *O, the Oprah Magazine*, the *Washington Post, Washingtonian*, The Atlantic.com, and the *New York Times*. She is the author of *Virgin Territory: Stories From the Road to Womanhood*, the memoir *Up for Renewal: What Magazines Taught Me About Love, Sex, and Starting Over*, and *Crush: Writers Reflect on Love, Longing, and the Lasting Power of Their First Celebrity Crush*.

Emily Amodeo's stories have been published in *Phoebe, Pavan*, and elsewhere. She teaches writing and fiction at St. Peter's University, and holds an MFA from The New School and an MA from the University of North Texas, where she was a teaching fellow and recipient of the Jim Lee Award in fiction. Emily lives on Long Island and is at work on a novel.

Jacob Appel is the author of ten works of fiction including *The Mask of Sanity*. He practices medicine in New York City. More at www.jacobmappel.com.

Sara Backer is the author of two chapbooks: *Bicycle Lotus*, which won the 2015 Turtle Island Poetry Prize; and *Scavenger Hunt*, forthcoming from Dancing Girl Press. She's currently enrolled in the MFA program at Vermont College of Fine Arts.

Sarah Barlow-Ochshorn is a first-year student at Barnard College in New York City. She has received the Scholastic Gold Medal and several Scholastic Gold and Silver Keys, as well as an honorable mention in the City College of New York Poetry Contest for her poetry. She is an alumna of the Kenyon Review Young Writers Workshop as well as the Sewanee Young Writers' Conference.

Stacy Barton is the award-winning author of *Lily Harp* (IndieFab, 2015), *Like Summer Grass*, and *Surviving Nashville: Short Stories*. Her work has appeared in literary journals including *Gargoyle*, *Potomac Review*, *Ruminate*, and *Southern Women's Review*. She is also the author of several picture books, plays, and animated short films; dozens of her live shows have been produced by entertainment companies including Disney, SeaWorld, and Ringling Bros.

Delaware native **Nina Bennett** is the author of *Sound Effects* (Broadkill River Press Key Poetry Series, 2013). Her poetry has appeared in numerous journals and anthologies including *Napalm and Novocaine*, *Reunion: The Dallas Review*, *Houseboat*, *Yale Journal for Humanities in Medicine*, *Philadelphia Stories*, and *Broadkill Review*. Awards include the 2014 Northern Liberties Review Poetry Prize, second place in the poetry book category from the Delaware Press Association (2014), and a 2012 Best of the Net nomination.

Septuagenarian **Gary Blankenburg** is a retired English teacher whose doctoral dissertation treated the confessional poets: Berryman, Lowell, Snodgrass, Plath, and Sexton. He is the author of eight books of poetry and fiction. His most recent book, *Above All Things* was published in 2015 by Brick House Books. Blankenburg was also a founding editor of the now-defunct *Maryland Poetry Review*. Nowadays he reads Victorian novels, writes, and paints while gathering himself up for a meeting with The Great Perhaps.

CL Bledsoe is the assistant editor for *The Dead Mule* and author of fifteen books, most recently the poetry collections *Trashcans in Love* and *King of Loneliness* and the flash fiction collection *Ray's Sea World*. He lives in Northern Virginia with his daughter.

Diana Smith Bolton is the founding editor of *District Lit*. Her debut chapbook, *Just Universes*, was the winner of the 2016 Mid-Atlantic Chapbook Series and published by L+S Press. She lives in Northern Virginia.

Anthony Isaac Bradley is pursuing an MA in creative writing at Missouri State University. His stories and poems have appeared in *Slipstream*, *MacGuffin*, and other journals. He lives with his cat and the ghost of another.

John Bradley's most recent book is *And Thereby Everything* (Longhouse Books), poems on Billy the Kid conjuring Henry Ford. The recipient of a Pushcart Prize in poetry and two National Endowment of the Arts Fellowships in poetry, he teaches at Northern Illinois University.

April Michelle Bratten lives in North Dakota. Her work has appeared in *Southeast Review, Zone 3, Thrush Poetry Journal,* and *Boiler Journal,* among others. She is the editor-in-chief of *Up the Staircase Quarterly* and a contributing editor at Words Dance Publishing. April's latest chapbook, *Anne with an E,* was published by Dancing Girl Press.

Shirley J. Brewer graduated from careers in palm reading, bartending, and speech therapy. She serves as poet-in-residence at Carver Center for the Arts and Technology in Baltimore. Recent poems appear in *Barrow Street, Poetry East, Spillway, Slant,* and other journals. Her poetry chapbooks include *A Little Breast Music* (Passager Books, 2008) and *After Words* (Apprentice House, 2013). Shirley's new poetry collection, *Bistro in Another Realm,* is due out in 2017 from Main Street Rag.

Michael Brockley is a sixty-six-year-old school psychologist who is trying to reenter the poetry publication arena as he nears retirement in the next year or two.

Jamie Brown, author of *Sakura* (Best Book of Verse 2013, Delaware Press Association), *Constructing Fiction, Conventional Heresies,* and *Freeholder,* publishes books from Broadkill River Press. He is a poet, author (fiction and nonfiction), award-winning playwright, critic, and teacher (George Washington University, Georgetown University, the Smithsonian, University of Delaware), and former poetry critic for the *Washington Times.*

Kevin Brown has had fiction, nonfiction, and poetry published in over a hundred literary journals, magazines, and anthologies. He has won numerous writing competitions and fellowships, and was nominated for multiple prizes and awards, including three Pushcart Prizes. He cowrote the film *Living Dark: The Story of Ted the Caver,* which was recently sold to New Films International, and collaborated on a television pilot with Bloodworth-Thomason, creator of *Designing Women.*

Mary Ann Cain's recent publications include the *Denver Quarterly, North American Review, The Bitter Oleander,* among many others. A novel, *Down from Moonshine,* was published by 13th Moon Press in 2009. She is a professor of English and women's studies at Indiana University–Purdue University Fort Wayne.

Roger Camp lives in Seal Beach, California, where he tends a flower garden, walks his beloved Paris yearly, is apprenticed to a master mason, naps in a hammock, plays blues piano evenings, and kayak fishes. His work has appeared in *Atlanta Review, North American Review,* and *PANK,* and is forthcoming in *Tampa Review* and *Hopkins Review.*

Doritt Carroll is a native of Washington, D.C. Her poems have appeared in the journals *Coal City Review, Poet Lore, Nimrod,* and *Slipstream,* among others. Her collection *GLTTL STP* was published by Brickhouse Books in 2013. She has served as poet in residence at the Shakespeare Theatre Company and runs the Zed's reading series.

Grace Cavalieri is founder of *The Poet and the Poem*, for Public Radio, now from the Library of Congress. She celebrates forty years on air in 2017. The author of nineteen books and chapbooks of poetry, Cavalieri's awards include the CPB Silver Medal, AWP's George Garrett Award and the Columbia Award (both for service to literature) Bordighera and Paterson Awards, and two Allen Ginsberg Poetry Awards. She lives in Annapolis, Maryland.

Laura Cesarco Eglin was born in Montevideo, Uruguay, in 1976. She is the author of three collections of poetry, *Llamar al agua por su nombre* (Mouthfeel Press, 2010), *Sastrería* (Yaugurú, 2011), and *Los brazos del saguaro* (Yaugurú, 2015). Cesarco Eglin's poems also appear in *América invertida: An Anthology of Emerging Uruguayan Poets* (University of New Mexico Press, 2016). Cesarco Eglin holds an MFA in bilingual creative writing from the University of Texas at El Paso.

Patrick Chapman has published seven poetry collections and three books of fiction, including *Slow Clocks of Decay* (Salmon, 2016) and *So Long, Napoleon Solo* (BlazeVOX, 2017). He has written for film and television, as well as audio plays for *Doctor Who* and *Dan Dare*. In 2014, he produced B7's award-winning adaptation of *The Martian Chronicles* for BBC Radio 4, starring Derek Jacobi and Hayley Atwell. He lives in Ireland, where he co-edits *The Pickled Body*.

Juliet Cook is a grotesque glitter witch medusa hybrid brimming with black, gray, silver, purple, and dark red explosions. Her poetry has appeared in a peculiar multitude of literary publications, including *Arsenic Lobster*, *DIAGRAM*, *Diode*, *FLAPPERHOUSE*, *Hermeneutic Chaos*, *Menacing Hedge*, and *Reality Beach*. Her most recent full-length poetry book, *A Red Witch, Every Which Way*, is a collaboration with j/j hastain published by Hysterical Books in 2016. www.JulietCook.weebly.com

Robert Cooperman's latest collection is *Just Drive* (Brick Road Poetry Press). Forthcoming in 2017 are *Draft Board Blues* (FutureCycle Press) and *City Hat Frame Factory* (Aldrich Press).

Karen Craigo teaches English in Springfield, Missouri. A poet and essayist, she is the author of *No More Milk* (Sundress Publications, 2016), as well as three chapbooks, most recently *Escaped Housewife Tries Hard to Blend In* (Hermeneutic Chaos, 2016).

Rachel Dacus's poetry collections are *Gods of Water and Air, Earth Lessons*, and *Femme au Chapeau*. Her writing has appeared in *Atlanta Review, Boulevard, Drunken Boat, Prairie Schooner, Valparaiso Poetry Review*, and elsewhere. Her novel, *The Renaissance Club*, involving the great Baroque sculptor Gian Lorenzo Bernini, is forthcoming from Fiery Seas Publishing.

Michael Daley published *Of a Feather* last year. Since 1983, three collections of his poetry have appeared, several chapbooks, a book of essays, and a translation of Italian poems. His work has been published widely in journals and anthologies. He lives near Deception Pass in Washington state.

Mark Danowsky's poetry has appeared in *About Place, Cordite, Grey Sparrow, Shot Glass Journal, Third Wednesday*, and elsewhere. Originally from the Philadelphia area, Mark currently resides in north-central West Virginia. He is managing editor for the *Schuylkill Valley Journal* and founder of VRS CRFT, a poetry coaching and editing service.

Kristina Marie Darling is the author of twenty-seven books of poetry, most recently *Ghost/Landscape* (with John Gallaher; BlazeVox Books, 2016) and the forthcoming *Dark Horse* (C&R Press, 2017). She currently divides her time between the United States and Europe.

William Virgil Davis is an award-winning poet. His most recent book of poetry (his sixth) is *Dismantlements of Silence: Poems Selected and New* (2015). His first book of poetry, *One Way to Reconstruct the Scene*, won the Yale Series of Younger Poets Prize. His poems have been published worldwide.

Mary Stone Dockery is the author of the poetry collections *One Last Cigarette* and *Mythology of Touch*, and several chapbooks, including *Honey and Bandages*, written with Katie Longofono, and *The Dopamine Letters* (Hyacinth Girl Press). Her work has appeared or is forthcoming in *Word Riot, Arts & Letters, South Dakota Review, Stirring*, and other journals. She lives, writes, and teaches in St. Joseph, Missouri, where she coordinates the First Thursday open mic reading series.

Stephanie McCarley Dugger's chapbook *Sterling* is forthcoming from Paper Nautilus. Her work has appeared or is forthcoming in *Arts & Letters, Calyx, CUTTHROAT, Gulf Stream, Meridian, Naugatuck River Review, Southeast Review, Still: The Journal, Taos Journal of International Poetry and Art, Zone 3*, and other journals. She has an MFA from the University of Wyoming and is a PhD candidate at the University of Tennessee, where she serves as poetry editor for *Grist*.

Kristina England resides in Worcester, Massachusetts. Her writing has been published at *Gargoyle, Moon Pigeon Press, Yellow Mama*, and other magazines. She currently serves as the secretary on the Worcester County Poetry Association Board.

Joyce Maust Enzor has a degree in English and a minor in physics. As the daughter of a Conservative Mennonite bishop and the parent of a special-needs child, the many other aspects of her life have granted her an insight into unique worlds. Her poems have appeared in *Gargoyle* and *Broadkill Review*.

Kallie Falandays is the author of *Dovetail Down the House* (Burnside Review Books). You can read more of her work in *PANK, Black Warrior Review, Puerto del Sol*, the *Journal*, and elsewhere. She lives in Philadelphia, where she runs Tell Tell Poetry.

John Gallaher lives in rural Missouri and co-edits the *Laurel Review*.

Matthew P. Garcia's recent publication credits include poetry in *Cimarron Review, Skidrow Penthouse, Rock & Sling, Poetry Quarterly*, and a play forthcoming in *Clarion*.

Julia Geiser lives and works in Bern, Switzerland and has worked in the fields of theater, art management, marketing, and PR. At the Institute HyperWerk, Geiser is studying art and design, performance, nomadic arts management, and social-political activism. Her fields of research include the notion of the "Filter Bubble," according to which algorithms act as barriers to information that disagrees with users' viewpoints, progressively isolating users in bespoke cultural or ideological bubbles. http://julia-geiser.ch

Bernadette Geyer is the author of *The Scabbard of Her Throat* (The Word Works, 2013) and editor of *My Cruel Invention: A Contemporary Poetry Anthology* (Meerkat Press, 2015). She works as a writer, editor, and translator in Berlin, Germany. www.bernadettegeyer.com

Stephen Gibson's *Self-Portrait in a Door-Length Mirror* was selected by Billy Collins as the 2017 Miller Williams Prize winner from the University of Arkansas Press. Earlier collections include *The Garden of Earthly Delights Book of Ghazals* (Texas Review Press), *Rorschach Art Too* (2014 Donald Justice Prize, Story Line Press), *Paradise* (Miller Williams finalist, University of Arkansas Press), *Frescoes* (Idaho Book Prize, Lost Horse Press), *Masaccio's Expulsion* (MARGIE/Intuit House Book Prize), and *Rorschach Art* (Red Hen).

Born and raised in Washington, D.C., **Andrew Gifford** is the founder and director of the Santa Fe Writers Project (www.sfwp.com), an indie press dedicated to craft writing since 1998. You can find more details on *We All Scream* at www.andrewgifford.com.

Kate Gillespie had come to Baltimore to become a demented doctorate student. The synthesis of "stress proteins," a natural by-product expression of her thesis project, are to thank for her creative catalyst into a poetic PhD. Her offerings have appeared in *SilverBlade, Baltimore Ekphrastic project, Syzygy poetry journal, End of 83, Borfski Press*, and several local art collective poetry anthologies.

Sid Gold is a two-time recipient of the Maryland State Arts Council Individual Artist Award for Poetry and the author of three full-length collections. His poems have appeared in *Southern Poetry Review, Poet Lore*, and *Tar River Poetry*; and are forthcoming in *Free State Review, Backbone Mountain Review*, and *Innisfree Poetry Journal*. His fourth book, *Crooked Speech* (Pond Road Press), will appear in late 2017.

Jonathan Greenhause has won awards from Kind of a Hurricane Press, *Prism Review*, and *Willow Review*, plus he was a finalist in 2016 for the *Green Mountains Review* Book Prize, Soundings East's Claire Keyes Award in Poetry, the *Iowa Review* Poetry Award, the Aesthetica Creative Writing Award, *Oberon Poetry Magazine*'s Annual Contest, and New Millennium Writings' 41st and 42nd Poetry

Awards. His poems have appeared or are forthcoming in *The Believer*, *Rattle*, and *Subtropics*, among others.

Jay Griswold was born in New Orleans, Louisiana, and has traveled extensively throughout the world. He has an MA in creative writing from Colorado State University and currently resides in Ft. Myers, Florida. He is the author of three award-winning collections of poetry, *Meditations for the Year of the Horse*, *The Landscape of Exile*, and *Conquistador* (Main Street Rag Book Award, 2004).

Susan Gubernat has won the Prairie Schooner Prize; her new book of poems will be published by the University of Nebraska Press in September 2017. An opera librettist, she is a professor of creative writing at Cal State East Bay, where she cofounded and advises the *Arroyo Literary Review*.

Herb Guggenheim's writing has appeared in *Poetry Quarterly*, *Florida Review*, *Gargoyle*, *Main Street Rag*, and many other publications. He's the author of two books of poetry—*Sunset at the Hotel Mira Mar* and *Strange Encounter at the Shakespeare Motel* as well as a novel—*Violations of Causality*. He's been nominated for a Pushcart and a Best of the Net award and has received four honorable mentions in the *Writer's Digest* annual writing competition.

Maryanne Hannan has published poetry in *Rattle*, *WomensArt Quarterly*, *Minnesota Review*, previous issues of *Gargoyle*, and several anthologies. A former Latin teacher, she lives in upstate New York. www.mhannan.com

Until 2003, **David M. Harris** had never lived more than fifty miles from New York City. Since then he has moved to Tennessee, married, acquired a daughter and a classic MG, and gotten serious about poetry. All these projects seem to be working out pretty well. His first collection of poetry, *The Review Mirror*, was published by Unsolicited Press in 2013.

Johnny Hartner has a BA in English from Carnegie-Mellon University and a master's in the same from Duquesne. A full-time professor at the Community College of Allegheny, he has recently won an Honors Award for his poem "Deconstructing Football" from *Taproot Poetry Journal*. He owes his continued success to his muses Lorraine and Professor Princess Mom (Melissa).

j/j hastain has written many chapbooks, artist books, and full-length works. j/j is the inventor of The Mystical Sentence Projects and author of several cross-genre books, including the trans-genre *libertine monk* (Scrambler Press, 2012), *The Non-Novels* (Spuyten Duyvil, 2015), and *The Xyr Trilogy: a Metaphysical Romance of Experimental Realisms*. j/j's writing has recently appeared in *A Thing Like You and Me*, *FLAPPERHOUSE*, *Caketrain*, *Trickhouse*, *Housefire*, *Bombay Gin*, and *Tarpaulin Sky*.

In addition to publishing scholarship in academic venues and fiction in *Alaska Quarterly Review*, *Beloit Fiction Journal*, *34th Parallel Magazine*, *Defenestration*, and *Albuquerque Arts*, **Alice Hatcher** has placed poetry in *S/tick* and *The*

Storyteller. She is currently completing a novel and working as a freelance grant consultant in Tucson, Arizona.

Michael Hathaway was raised in central Kansas where he lives on the edge of a very small town with forty-one cats, all spayed/neutered and current on vaccinations. By day he is Keeper of History for Stafford County; by night he edits and publishes *Chiron Review* literary journal, which he founded in 1982. He also works part time for his veterinarian.

Gloria Heffernan's work has appeared or is forthcoming in forty publications including *Chautauqua Literary Journal, Columbia Review, Stone Canoe, The Healing Muse,* the *New York Times* "Metropolitan Diary," *Chronicle of Higher Education,* and *Talking Writing.* She teaches part time at LeMoyne College and holds an MA in Literature from NYU.

Arthur Heifetz teaches ESL to refugees in Richmond, Virginia. He has had over two hundred poems published in thirteen countries. In 2013, he won second place in the Reuben Rose international poetry competition in Israel. A sampling of his work may be found at polishedbrasspoems.com.

Robert Herschbach lives in Laurel, Maryland. He is the author of *Loose Weather* (Washington Writers' Publishing House, 2013) and *A Lost Empire* (Ion Books, 1994). Recent work has appeared in *Profane, Southern Poetry Review, Pittsburgh Poetry Review,* and *Watershed Review.*

Margaret Hickey lives beside the broad, majestic Shannon and is in the process of publishing her second book, *Ireland's Green Larder.* Go to this link for a quirky video about it: https://unbound.com/books/irelands-green-larder. Her first book, *Irish Days,* is a collection of oral histories, which Ronald Blythe found "an entrancing book."

Donald Illich has published work in *Iowa Review, Nimrod, Passages North,* and other journals. He lives in Maryland.

Wendy Elizabeth Ingersoll is a retired piano teacher. Publications include her book *Grace Only Follows;* two chapbooks; poems in *Poetry East, Naugatuck River Review, Connecticut River Review, Cahoodaloodaling, Passager, Main Street Rag, Mojave River Review, Worcester Review, Hartskill Review,* and *Broadkill Review.* Wendy moved back to her home state of Delaware fifteen years ago, made great new writing friends, and enjoys serving as reader for the *Delmarva Review.*

Alison Condie Jaenicke teaches writing at Penn State University, where she serves as assistant director of creative writing. Alison's poems, essays, and stories have appeared in such publications as *Storyscape Journal; Superstition Review; Brain, Child;* and *Literary Mama.* Her essay "I Slept Well If You Slept Well," published in *Isthmus Review,* was selected as a Notable Essay in *The Best American Essays 2016.* alisoncjaenicke.weebly.com

C a t h e r i n e   J a g o e is a writer and translator specializing in Spanish and Catalan. She has a PhD in Spanish literature from the University of Cambridge. Originally from the United Kingdom, she now lives in Madison, Wisconsin. Her translations include the Amnesty International award–winning Argentine novel *My Name is Light* by Elsa Osorio (Bloomsbury, 2003) and *That Bringas Woman* by the nineteenth-century Spanish novelist Benito Pérez Galdós (Everyman, 1996).

M i c h a e l   J o h n s o n's recent work has appeared in *Weber, Poetry East, Spillway, Cascadia Review, Event,* and *Shenandoah,* among others. His first book is *How to be Eaten by a Lion* from Nightwood Editions.

A b h a y   K . is the author of *The Seduction of Delhi* (Bloomsbury) and the editor of Capitals (Bloomsbury). His poems have appeared in over two dozen literary journals including *Poetry Salzburg Review* and *Asia Literary Review* and have been translated into Irish, Russian, Italian, Spanish, Slovenian, Portuguese, Mandarin and Nepali. He received the SAARC Literary Award in 2013. His "Earth Anthem" has been translated into twenty-eight languages. www.abhayk.com

G e o r g e   K a l a m a r a s, former Poet Laureate of Indiana (2014–16), is the author of fifteen books of poetry, eight of which are full length, including *Kingdom of Throat-Stuck Luck,* winner of the Elixir Press Poetry Prize (2011); and *The Mining Camps of the Mouth* (2012), winner of the New Michigan Press Prize. He is a professor of English at Indiana University–Purdue University Fort Wayne, where he has taught since 1990.

T o m   K e l l y received his MFA from Old Dominion University. His poems appear in *Southeast Review, Painted Bride Quarterly, Gulf Stream, decomP,* among others. Write to him at thomas.v.kelly@gmail.com.

J e s s e   L e e   K e r c h e v a l is the author of fourteen books of poetry and fiction, including the poetry collections *Cinema Muto and Dog Angel.* Her translations include *Invisible Bridge/El puente invisible: Selected Poems of Circe Maia* and *Fable of an Inconsolable Man* by Javier Etchevarren. She is also the editor of the anthologies *América invertida: An Anthology of Emerging Uruguayan Poets* and *Earth, Water and Sky: A Bilingual Anthology of Environmental Poetry.*

A n d r e w   K o c h lives in Texas where he is a doctoral student at the University of North Texas. He serves as managing editor for the long-running journal *Stirring: A Literary Collection* and is the author of the chapbook *Brick-Woman* (Hermeneutic Chaos). His work has recently appeared or is forthcoming in *Ninth Letter, Poetry Northwest, The Collagist, Zone 3, Whiskey Island,* and others.

S a n d r a   K o l a n k i e w i c z has recent poems in *Prairie Schooner, Per Contra, Australian Book Review, Blue Stocking,* and *Storm Cellar.*

L u i s a   K o l k e r is a shamanic-psychotherapist and writer based in Santa Fe, New Mexico. In 1985 she traveled to Tangier, Morocco, to say thank you to Paul Bowles for his books and ended up living on the Spanish island of Ibiza for five years.

B e t h   K o n k o s k i is a writer and high school English teacher living in Northern Virginia. She has published work in literary journals for many years, including past issues of *Gargoyle*, *Baltimore Review*, and *Mid-American Review*. Her chapbook of poems, *Noticing the Splash*, was published in 2010 by BoneWorld Press.

K a t h l e e n   K r a f t's chapbook, *Fairview Road*, was published in 2015 by Finishing Line Press. Her poems have been published in many journals, including *Five Points*, *Gargoyle*, and *The Satirist*, and she has been nominated for the Pushcart Prize three times. She lives in Jersey City, New Jersey. where she is a yoga teacher and freelance writer.

R o b e r t   K r a n t z graduated from the University of Akron, Ohio. His individual works have appeared in *Birch Gang Review*, *Pittsburgh Poetry Review*, and others. Bitterzoet Press recently published two chapbooks of his work *(Plus 4* and *Hansel)*. He makes his living as a sales engineer in the Midwest.

L e o n a r d   K r e s s has published fiction and poetry in *Massachusetts Review*, *Iowa Review*, *American Poetry Review*, *Harvard Review*, *The Writing Disorder*, etc. His recent collections are *The Orpheus Complex*, *Living in the Candy Store*, and *Walk Like Bo Diddley*. He teaches philosophy, religion, and creative writing at Owens College in Ohio.

W. F. L a n t r y's poetry collections are *The Terraced Mountain* (Little Red Tree 2015); *The Structure of Desire* (Little Red Tree 2012), winner of a 2013 Nautilus Award in Poetry; and a chapbook, *The Language of Birds*. Honors include National Hackney Literary Award in Poetry, CutBank Patricia Goedicke Prize, Crucible Editors' Poetry Prize, Lindberg Foundation International Poetry for Peace Prize (Israel), *Potomac Review* and Old Red Kimono Prizes. His work appears widely online and in print. He edits *Peacock Journal*.

M a r i e   L e c r i v a i n is the executive editor of *poeticdiversity: the litzine of Los Angeles*, a photographer, and a writer in residence at her apartment. Marie's newest poetry chapbook, *Philemon's Gambit* (International Word Bank Press, 2016), is available through Amazon.com.

K a t e e m a   L e e is a Washington, D.C., native. Her poetry has appeared or is forthcoming in print and online journals such as *PMS: Poemmemoirstory*, *African American Review*, *Gargoyle*, *Word Riot* and others, and she is the author of the chapbook, *Almost Invisible* (forthcoming). She is a Cave Canem Graduate Fellow and attended the Callaloo Workshop at Brown University. When she's not writing, she teaches English and women's studies.

L y n   L i f s h i n has published over 130 books and chapbooks including 3 from Black Sparrow Press: *Cold Comfort*, *Before It's Light*, and *Another Woman Who Looks Like Me.* The documentary *Lyn Lifshin: Not Made of Glass* is finally available on DVD. Forthcoming books include *Luminous Women: Eneduanna*, *Schererzade and Nefertiti: Femina Eterna*, and *Moving Through Stained Glass: The Maple Poems*.

Christopher Locke is the nonfiction editor of *Slice magazine* in Brooklyn. His poems have appeared in *Verse Daily, Southwest Review, Poetry East, North American Review, 32 Poems, Mudlark, West Branch, Rattle, Literary Review, The Sun,* and others. Locke has received a Dorothy Sargent Rosenberg Poetry Award and grants in poetry from the Massachusetts Cultural Council and the New Hampshire Council on the Arts. *Ordinary Gods* (Salmon Poetry) and his first book for children, *Heart-Flight* (Cedar Grove Books), were both recently released.

Rebecca Macijeski teaches at the University of Nebraska, where she serves as an assistant editor in poetry for *Hunger Mountain* and *Prairie Schooner.* She has attended artist residencies with the Ragdale Foundation and Art Farm Nebraska. Poems have appeared or are forthcoming in *Poet Lore,* the *Journal, Missouri Review, Nimrod, Sycamore Review, Tinderbox Poetry Journal, Whiskey Island, Border Crossing, Fourteen Hills,* and others.

Stephen Malin's journal publications include *Antioch Review, Beloit Poetry Journal, Green Mountains Review, Sewanee Review,* and many more. Appearing on *Verse Daily* and other electronic outlets, his poems have also been anthologized in *Poetry Southeast* and in the *Southwest Review*'s half-century collection; more of his work, translated into Russian, was reprinted abroad in *Amerika Illustrated.* His collection, *Underlight,* came out in 2014.

Allie Marini (Batts) rarely sleeps, and her mother has hypothesized that she is actually a robot fueled by Diet Coke and Sriracha. Forthcoming titles include *Southern Cryptozoology: A Field Guide to Beasts of the Southern Wild* (Hyacinth Girl Press), and *Heart Radicals,* a collaborative collection with Les Kay, Janeen Pergrin Rastall, and Sandra Marchetti (ELJ Publications). https://www.facebook.com/AllieMariniBatts or @kiddeternity.

Judith McCombs's work appears in *Beltway, Calyx, Delmarva, Innisfree, Nimrod* (Neruda Award), *Poetry, Potomac Review* (Poetry Prize), *Shenandoah* (2012 Graybeal-Gowen Prize); her fifth book is *The Habit of Fire:* Selected & New. Winner of the Maryland State Arts Council's highest 2009 Individual Poet Award, McCombs is active in Word Works, Federal Poets, and George Washington University's Splendid Wake; and arranges the Kensington Row Bookshop poetry readings.

David Memmott has published four books of poetry. His Vietnam-era antiwar novel, *Canned Tuna,* is forthcoming from Redbat Books in 2017. He is editor and publisher of *Wordcraft* of Oregon and founding editor of *Phantom Drift: A Journal of New Fabulism.* He lives in La Grande, Oregon.

Stephen C. Middleton is a writer working in London, England. He has had five books published, including *A Brave Light* (Stride) and *Worlds of Pain/Shades of Grace* (Poetry Salzburg). He has been in several anthologies, including *Paging Doctor Jazz* (Shoestring), and *From Hepworth's Garden Out* (Shearsman, 2010). For several years, he was editor of *Ostinato,* a magazine of jazz and jazz-related poetry, and the Tenormen Press. He has been in magazines worldwide.

Devon Miller-Duggan has published poems. She's won prizes, grants, a fellowship, been both a nominee and a finalist. She teaches for the Department of English at the University of Delaware. Her books are *Pinning the Bird to the Wall* (2008), (Neither Prayer, *Nor Bird* (2013), and *Alphabet Year* (2017).

Miles David Moore is founder and host of the IOTA Poetry Reading Series in Arlington, Virginia, and the author of three books of poetry. In April 2016, he received an award from the Arlington Arts Council for his services to poetry.

Maria Nazos's poetry, translations, and lyrical essays are published in the *New Yorker, Tampa Review, Mid-American Review, North American Review, Florida Review, Southern Humanities Review, Drunken Boat,* and elsewhere. A Great Plains Fellow attending the University of Nebraska–Lincoln's PhD program, she studies and teaches creative writing. www.marianazos.com

With five hundred and fifty to six hundred pieces published between 1992 and 2015 (without the Internet), **normal** remains "one of the last American primitives" in the underground press. His most recent book, *I See Hunger's Children, Selected Poems 1962–2012,* was published by Lummox Press in 2012.

Valeria Numinosa is a manifestation of neoliberalism living in upstate New York with her partner, her partner's partner, her PTSD, and their cats. Her poetry appeared sporadically throughout 2015 and early 2016 at the surrealist blog *Uut Poetry,* and has been remixed twice by Texas Fontanella.

Born in Sydney, Australia, the son of an American sailor and an Australian school teacher, **John O'Dell** was raised and educated in the United States. He was a French and English teacher in Prince George's County. In 1984, he was part of the Jenny McKean Moore Poetry Workshop at George Washington University taught by Julia Alvarez. His books are *Painting at Night* and *At Beauty's Pawnshop.*

Susan Okie is a doctor, a former *Washington Post* reporter, and a 2014 graduate of the Warren Wilson MFA Program in poetry.

Frances Park is the author of ten books including the novel *When My Sister Was Cleopatra Moon* (Hyperion), the memoir *Chocolate Chocolate: The True Story of Two Sisters, Tons of Treats and the Little Shop That Could* (St. Martin's Press), and *Good-bye, 382 Shin Dang Dong* (National Geographic Books). She's currently at work on a novel and a collection of personal essays.

Simon Perchik is an attorney whose poems have appeared in *Partisan Review, Forge, Poetry, Osiris,* the *New Yorker,* and elsewhere. His most recent collection is *The B Poems* published by Poets Wear Prada (2016). For more information, including free e-books and his essay titled "Magic, Illusion and Other Realities," please visit his website at www.simonperchik.com.

Ginger Peters is a freelance writer living in Santa Fe, New Mexico. A variety of magazines and journals have published her fiction, nonfiction, and poetry over the last twenty years. Recent work appears in *Seek Magazine, Purpose Magazine, Lookout Magazine, Dialogue Magazine*, Ginosko *Literary Journal, The Write Place at The Write Time*, and *The Secret Place*.

Kathleen M. Quinlan's full-length collection, *Moorings* (2016), and pamphlet, *From We to I* (2015), are published by Cinnamon Press. She edited *How Higher Education Feels: Commentaries on Poems That Illuminate Emotions in Learning and Teaching* (Sense Publishers, 2016). Her poetry has appeared on both sides of the Atlantic. Originally from rural Maine, she now lives in England. www.kathleenmquinlan.net/Kathleen M Quinlan

Jessy Randall is the author of the poetry collections *Suicide Hotline Hold Music* (Red Hen Press, 2016); *There Was an Old Woman* (Unicorn, 2015); *Injecting Dreams into Cows* (Red Hen Press, 2012); and *A Day in Boyland* (Ghost Road Press, 2007), which was a finalist for the Colorado Book Award. Her poems, poetry comics, and diagram poems have appeared in *Poetry, Rattle, McSweeney's*, and *Asimov's*, and she occasionally guest-edits the online magazine *Snakeskin*. She is curator of special collections at Colorado College.

W. M. Rivera grew up in the Irish Channel of New Orleans. He wrote poetry early on and published in 1960 a book of poems titled *At the End of Legend's String*. A career in international agricultural development took him to thirty countries worldwide. Since retirement from the University of Maryland (1981–2009), he has published four collections of poems.

David Romanda lives in Kawasaki City, Japan. His work has appeared in *Ambit, Gargoyle*, and *Poetry Ireland Review*.

John Roth is a poet from Ohio who strives to find the hidden beauty in words. His work has appeared in various places online including *Dead Snakes, Bone Parade*, and *Aberration Labyrinth* among a few others. He wishes he was more interesting than this.

Daniel Saalfeld's poems have appeared in many journals, including *Hopkins Review, Southeast Review, Seattle Review, Cimarron Review, Tampa Review, Tar River Poetry, South Carolina Review, Gargoyle, Poet Lore*, and *The Pinch*. A Fulbright Scholar, he lectured on modern and contemporary American poetry and creative writing in Russia. He teaches creative writing at George Washington University.

Taylor Sacco lives and writes in Vermont. His work has appeared previously in *HOOT Review*.

Bruce Sager's work has won publication through contests judged by Billy Collins, Dick Allen, and William Stafford. His newest book, *The Indulgence of Icarus*, was recently released by Echo Point. Four new volumes—one of short stories, three of poetry—are forthcoming by mid-2017 via Hyperborea Publishing and BrickHouse Books.

On sunny days, Dr. **Kate Sampsell-Willmann** teaches in the shadow of Mt. Rainier. She wonders often whether Pompeiians were similarly awed by the startling proximity of their volcano.

Gerard Sarnat, MD, has been nominated for a 2016 Pushcart Prize. He's authored *Homeless Chronicles* (2010), *Disputes* (2012), *17s* (2014), and *Melting the Ice King* (2016). Mount Analogue selected "Kaddish for the Country" for distribution as a pamphlet on Inauguration Day 2017 as well as at Washington/nationwide women's marches. Gerry's built/staffed clinics for the marginalized and been a CEO of health care organizations and a Stanford professor. GerardSarnat.com.

M. A. Schaffner has had poems published in *Shenandoah, Prairie Schooner, Agni, Poetry Ireland, Poetry Wales,* and elsewhere. Other writings include the poetry collection *The Good Opinion of Squirrels* and the novel *War Boys*. Schaffner spends most days in Arlington, Virginia, or the nineteenth century.

Lorraine Schein is a New York writer. Her work has appeared recently in *Hotel Amerika, Mad Scientist Journal, Gigantic Worlds,* and recently in the anthologies *Phantom Drift, Wreckage of Reason,* and *Drawn to Marvel*. Her poetry book, *The Futurist's Mistress,* is available from mayapplepress.com.

Claire Scott is an award-winning poet who has been nominated twice for the Pushcart Prize (2013 and 2014). She was also a semifinalist for both the 2014 Pangaea Prize and the 2014 Atlantis Award. Claire was the grand prizewinner of the Maine Review's 2015 White Pine Writing Contest. Her first book of poetry, *Waiting to Be Called,* was recently published by IF SF Publishing.

With her English degree, subsequent studies, and stubbornness, **Cathryn Shea** has earned a living from writing most of her life. Her second chapbook, *It's Raining Lullabies,* is forthcoming from Dancing Girl Press in 2017. Find her recent poetry in *Permafrost, Rust + Moth, Tinderbox,* and elsewhere, and in 2016 anthologies by Into The Void and *The New English Verse* by Cyberwit.net. Cathryn serves on the editorial staff for *Marin Poetry Center Anthology.* www.cathrynshea.com

Max Sheridan lives and writes in Nicosia, Cyprus. His short fiction, about sex, death, and midgets, is available online and in print from select, degenerate publishers. Find him at maxsheridanlit.com.

David Sheskin employs a distinctive format he refers to as Artxt, which involves the creative integration of art and text, which in the case of his piece in this issue utilizes the format of a Scrabble board to provide a unique perspective on fictional themes, fairy tales, and a variety topical subjects—or alternatively, one or more people at a museum viewing one of his Artxt commentaries.

Kristina Webster Shue is an eccentric secular agnostic earth-based spiritualist, writer, and all-around creative type currently living in Ohio where she is trying to figure out what adulthood means for someone whose regrets have left them as of yet degree-less. She will eventually finish her bachelor's in writing (maybe).

Noel Sloboda is the author of the poetry collections *Shell Games* (sunnyoutside, 2008) and *Our Rarer Monsters* (sunnyoutside, 2013), as well as several chapbooks, most recently *Risk Management Studies* (Kattywompus Press, 2015). Sloboda has also published a book about Edith Wharton and Gertrude Stein.

J. D. Smith's fourth poetry collection, *The Killing Tree*, was published in 2016. He is currently circulating a fifth poetry collection and a first collection of short stories, as well as working on projects in several genres. www.jdsmithwriter.com

Lana Spendl's chapbook of flash fiction, *We Cradled Each Other in the Air*, is available from Blue Lyra Press. Her work has appeared in *Cortland Review*, *Hobart*, *Greensboro Review*, *Quarter After Eight*, *Lunch Ticket*, *Fiction Southeast*, *storySouth*, *Monkeybicycle*, *Watershed Review*, *Bayou Magazine*, and other outlets. She is currently working on her first novel.

Kurt Steinwand has been published in *Cincinnati Review*, *Poet Lore*, *New Millennium Writings*, and *Arroyo Literary Review*. He holds an MFA in creative writing from the University of Tampa, and is a teacher of students with special needs at a middle school in Brandon, Florida, where he lives.

M.G. Stephens is the author of eighteen books, including the novel *The Brooklyn Book of the Dead* and the essay collection *Green Dreams*. Recent poems, stories, and essays have appeared in *Missouri Review*, *Notre Dame Review*, *The Hollins Critic*, *London Magazine* (UK), *Wordlegs* (Ireland), *Gargoyle*, *Brooklyn Rail*, *Exquisite Corpse*, *Solstice*, *Poetic Matrix*, *South Boston Literary Gazette*, *Insolent Aardvark*, and *Penny Ante Feud*, among others.

Belinda Subraman has been around a long time. Edited *Gypsy* and Vergin' Press for ten years, mostly from Germany. Published in hundreds of places. Had a few years off from publishing. Started submitting again this year. Just published in *Red Fez*, *Tribe Magazine*, and *Outlaw Poetry*, among others. These poems are fresh and unpublished (and pretty darn good, she thinks). She also makes organic and vegan products like soap and body balm under the name Mystical House.

Tim Suermondt is the author of three full-length collections of poems: *Trying to Help the Elephant Man Dance* (Backwaters Press, 2007), *Just Beautiful* (New York Quarterly Books, 2010), and *Election Night and the Five Satins* (Glass Lyre Press, 2016). He has poems published in *Poetry*, *Georgia Review*, *Ploughshares*, *Prairie Schooner*, *Blackbird*, *Bellevue Literary Review*, *North Dakota Quarterly*, *december magazine*, *Plume Poetry Journal*, and *Stand Magazine* (England). He lives in Cambridge, Massachusetts.

Sharon Suzuki-Martinez is the author of *The Way of All Flux* (2012), winner of the New Rivers Press MVP Poetry Prize. Her recent work appears in or is forthcoming in *Clockhouse*, *Duende*, *Dusie*, *Quarterday Review*, *The Lake*, and *Algebra of Owls*. She is the editor of *The Poet's Playlist*, a music and poetry blog. sharonsuzukimartinez.tumblr.com/

Marc Swan's poems have recently been published in *Scrivener Creative Review*, *Passager*, *Crannóg*, *Mudfish*, *Sheila-na-gig*, *Turbine*, and *Coal City Review*, among others. Current project is a collection of poems about growing up in Binghamton, New York. He lives with his wife Dd in Portland, Maine.

Kelly Talbot has edited books and digital content for twenty years, previously as an in-house editor for John Wiley and Sons Publishing, Macmillan Publishing, and Pearson Education, and now as the head of Kelly Talbot Editing Services. His writing has appeared in dozens of magazines.

Jenniey Tallman lives in the Twin Cities with her husband and their three sons. Recent writing can be found in *DIAGRAM*, the *Austin Review*, *Nashville Review*, *Slice Magazine*, and Electric Lit's *Recommended Reading*, among others. She works as a teacher, editor, and social media consultant.

Devin Taylor studies English and creative writing at Washington College. His work can be found in *Five 2 One*, *Maudlin House*, and *BLYNKT*, among others. He has forthcoming publications in *Infinity Ink*, the *Yellow Chair Review*, and elsewhere. He reads at open mics in the D.C. area under the alias of Chuck E. Cheese, and aspires to be a golden retriever. He plays bass and electric kazoo in the band Knuckleberry Finn.

Ed Taylor is the author of the novel *Theo* and the poetry collection *Idiogest*. His fiction and poetry have most recently appeared in *Southern Poetry Review*, the *Literary Review*, *St. Petersburg Review*, *New American Writing*, *Slipstream*, *Clackamas Literary Review*, *The Moth*, and an anthology on the theme of drought.

Terrell Jamal Terry is the author of *Aroma Truce*, forthcoming from Black Lawrence Press in 2017. His poems have appeared (or will soon appear) in *Denver Quarterly*, *Poetry Northwest*, the *Literary Review*, *West Branch*, the *Journal*, *Green Mountains Review*, *Crab Orchard Review*, and elsewhere. He resides in Pittsburgh, Pennsylvania.

Parker Tettleton is a Leo, a vegan, and a resident of Portland, Oregon. He is also the author of *Ours Mine Yours* (Pity Milk Press 2014), *Greens* (Thunderclap Press 2012), and *Same Opposite* (Thunderclap Press 2010).

Teniola Tonade teaches philosophy at the University of Lagos. His work has appeared in *Word Riot*, *Tinderbox*, and *Vinyl*, and is forthcoming in *The New Republic*.

Sally Toner is a high school English teacher who has lived in the Washington, D.C., area for over twenty years. Her work has appeared in *Gargoyle*, the *Delmarva Review*, and *Clementine Poetry Journal*, and is forthcoming in *Postcard Poems and Prose*.

Idea Vilariño (1920–2009) was an Uruguayan poet, essayist, and literary critic and a well-known member of the Generation of '45 literary group which included

Juan Carlos Onetti, Mario Benedetti, Amanda Berenguer, and Jorge Luis Borges. A professor of literature at the Universidad de la República in Montevideo, she wrote twelve books of poetry, including *Nocturnos* (1955) and *Poemas de amor* (1957), and five books of essays and literary criticism.

Randi Ward is a writer, translator, lyricist, and photographer from West Virginia, and a recipient of the American-Scandinavian Foundation's Nadia Christensen Prize. She is a Pushcart Prize and Best of the Net nominee whose work has appeared in the *Anthology of Appalachian Writers, Asymptote, Beloit Poetry Journal, Cimarron Review, Cortland Review, Thrush Poetry Journal, Vencil: Anthology of Contemporary Faroese Literature, World Literature Today*, and other publications. www.randiward.com/about

Originally from Louisiana, **Anna Lowe Weber** currently lives in Huntsville, Alabama, where she teaches creative writing at the University of Alabama in Huntsville. Her work has appeared or is forthcoming in *Rattle, Ninth Letter, Salamander,* and the *Florida Review*, among other journals.

Katherine West is the bemused possessor of a lit degree and a scuffed-up hard hat. Following a career welding and inspecting railroad cars, she's working on adult literacy materials and marketing a retelling of "Rumpelstiltskin."

J. T. Whitehead's work has appeared in *Left Curve, The Iconoclast,* and *Gargoyle*. He is a Pushcart Prize–nominated short story author and a Pushcart Prize–nominated poet, and he received the 2015 Margaret Randall Poetry Prize. Whitehead is editor-in-chief of *So It Goes: The Literary Journal of the Kurt Vonnegut Memorial Library*. His poetry collection *The Table of the Elements* (Broadkill River Press, 2015) was nominated for the National Book Award.

Gregg Wilhelm graduated from the MFA in creative writing program at the University of Tampa in 2014. He founded the nonprofit CityLit Project in Baltimore in 2004 and is publisher of its CityLit Press imprint. He is a recent recipient of a Rubys Artists Project Grant from the Greater Baltimore Cultural Alliance and an Individual Artist Award from the Maryland State Arts Council. Gregg's poetry might be found along D.C.'s new Purple Line in the future. www.GreggWilhelm.com.

Sarah Louise Williams's nonfiction has been published in *Grand Street* and *Vogue*. Her short fiction has appeared in *StoryQuarterly, Enhanced Gravity: More Fiction by Washington Area Women,* and *Gargoyle*. She has an MFA from Sarah Lawrence College and is currently at work on a collection of linked stories. Sarah lives in Chevy Chase, Maryland, with her husband and three sons.

A. D. Winans is a San Francisco award-winning poet and writer. He has been published internationally. He edited and published *Second Coming* from 1972 to 1989. In 2002, a song poem of his was performed at Alice Tully Hall, NYC. In 2006, he won a PEN Josephine Miles award for excellence in literature. In 2009, he was presented with a PEN Oakland Lifetime Achievement Award. In 2014 he received a Kathy Acker award in poetry and publishing.

Pamela Murray Winters lives and works in Maryland. Her poems have appeared in many issues of *Gargoyle* and also in the *Northern Virginia Review*, the *Gettysburg Review*, *Beltway Poetry*, the anthologies *Takoma Park Writers 1981*, *Gathered: Contemporary Quaker Poets*, and *Unrequited: An Anthology of Love Poems about Inanimate Objects*, and other publications. She helps run two poetry series in Annapolis, Maryland, and is currently seeking a publisher for her first full-length collection of poems.

Shannon Connor Winward is the author of the Elgin Award–winning chapbook, *Undoing Winter*. Her work has appeared in (or is forthcoming from) *Fantasy & Science Fiction*, *Analog*, *Persistent Visions*, *The Pedestal Magazine*, *Literary Mama*, and the *Monarch Review*, among others. In between writing, parenting, and other madness, Shannon is an officer for the Science Fiction Poetry Association, poetry editor for *Devilfish Review* and founding editor of *Riddled with Arrows Literary Journal*.

To support his writing habit, **Nick Winewriter** worked as a bartender in Washington, D.C., for thirty-seven years. Published in the *Washington Post*, *Washington Times*, *Antietam Review*, *DC City Magazine*, *Best of Photography Annual*. Looking for a publisher for his photo essay on D.C. bartenders. Lives in Ocala, Florida, where he's a part-time freelance correspondent for the *Ocala Star Banner*. If possible, Nick would read twenty-four hours a day.

Born in Hong Kong, **Pui Ying Wong** is the author of two full-length books of poetry—*An Emigrant's Winter* (Glass Lyre Press, 2016) and *Yellow Plum Season* (New York Quarterly Books, 2010)—and two chapbooks. She has poems published and forthcoming in *Prairie Schooner*, *Ploughshares*, *Atlanta Review*, *Plume Poetry Journal*, and the *New York Times*, among others. She is a book reviewer for *Cervena Barva*. She lives in Cambridge, Massachusetts, with her husband, poet Tim Suermondt.

Andrea Wyatt is the author of three poetry collections and co-editor of *Selected Poems* by Larry Eigner and *Collected Poems* by Max Douglas. Her work appears in *Pea River Journal*, *Rust & Moth*, and *Clakamas Literary Review*. She is associate editor for *By&By* and works for the National Park Service.

Katherine E. Young is the author of *Day of the Border Guards*, 2014 Miller Williams Arkansas Poetry Prize finalist; her poems appear in *Prairie Schooner*, the *Iowa Review*, *Subtropics*, and many others. Young translated *Two Poems* by Inna Kabysh; her translations of Russophone authors have won international awards and been published widely. She is a 2017 National Endowment for the Arts translation fellow and serves as the inaugural Poet Laureate of Arlington, Virginia. http://katherine-young-poet.com/.

Peacock Journal: Beauty First

A daily online Literary & Arts journal

Fiction, Non-Fiction, Poetry, Translation, Music, Visual Art and Photography

Send us your most beautiful work

PeacockJournal.com